IT Manager's Handbook
Getting Your New Job Done

About the Authors

Bill Holtsnider is an experienced writer, educator, and software professional, with more than sixteen years of experience working in the computer industry. His IT expertise includes working in such areas as biotechnology, interactive television, risk management, and software development. He is the author of several books and a wide range of technical and marketing documentation.

Brian D. Jaffe is a seasoned veteran in the IT community, with more than eighteen years of related experience. Throughout his tenure as an IT professional, he has worked for several Fortune 500 companies, including Bristol-Myers Squibb, Philip Morris, and Random House. Currently, he is vice president of information technology for McCann-Erickson in New York City, one of the country's leading advertising agencies, and is a contributing editor for *eWeek* (formerly *PC Week*). His articles have appeared in *Computerworld*, *InfoWorld*, and *The New York Times*.

IT Manager's Handbook
Getting Your New Job Done

Bill Holtsnider
Brian D. Jaffe

MORGAN KAUFMANN PUBLISHERS

AN IMPRINT OF ACADEMIC PRESS
A Harcourt Science and Technology Company
SAN FRANCISCO   SAN DIEGO   NEW YORK   BOSTON
LONDON   SYDNEY   TOKYO

Acquisitions Editor: Jennifer Mann
Publishing Services Manager: Scott Norton
Production Editor: Howard Severson
Production Assistant: Mei Levenson
Assistant Acquisitions Editor: Karyn Johnson
Cover Design: Ross Carron Design
Cover Image: © Ken Tannenbaum/Imagebank
Text Design and Composition: Rebecca Evans & Associates
Copyeditor: Ken DellaPenta
Proofreader: Jennifer McClain
Indexer: Steve Rath
Printer: Courier Corporation

Designations used by companies to distinguish their products are often claimed as trademarks or registered trademarks. In all instances where Morgan Kaufmann Publishers is aware of a claim, the product names appear in initial capital or all capital letters. Readers, however, should contact the appropriate companies for more complete information regarding trademarks and registration.

ACADEMIC PRESS
A Harcourt Science and Technology Company
525 B Street, Suite 1900, San Diego, CA 92101-4495, USA
http://www.academicpress.com

Academic Press
Harcourt Place, 32 Jamestown Road, London, NW1 7BY, United Kingtom
http://www.academicpress.com

Morgan Kaufmann Publishers
340 Pine Street, Sixth Floor, San Francisco, CA 94104-3205, USA
http://www.mkp.com

05 04 03 02   5 4 3 2

Library of Congress Cataloging-in-Publication Data

Holtsnider, Bill, date.
    IT manager's handbook: getting your new job done / Bill Holtsnider, Brian D. Jaffe.
        p. cm.
    Includes bibliographical references and index.
    ISBN 1-55860-646-7
      1. Industrial management—Data processing. 2. Management information systems.
    I. Jaffe, Brian D.   II. Title.

    HD20.2 .H657 2001
    658'.05—dc21

                                                            00-063397

This book is printed on acid-free paper.

For M&D
—B.H.

For my mother and father
—B.D.J.

Brief Contents

Contents

Chapter Three

Managing Your IT Team   49

Chapter Four

User Support Services   69

Chapter Five

Managing Projects   81

Chapter Six

Chapter Seven

IT Infrastructure Fundamentals   **113**

Chapter Eight

Hardware   133

Chapter Nine

Chapter Eleven

Internets/Extranets/Intranets   223

Chapter Twelve

Enterprise Applications 257

Chapter Thirteen

Security   273

Chapter Fourteen

Preface

What This Book Is About

This book introduces you to the key concepts you will face as a *new* information technology (IT) manager. It also provides you with suggested methods for dealing with many of the large issues that arise, including specific recommendations for actions as well as places to look for further help.

Why Did We Write This Book?

Many technical professionals are eager to join the ranks of management. But as the saying goes, be careful what you wish for. We have seen a lot of technical professionals—developers, programmers, installers, hardware techs—suddenly thrust into positions of management in their IT departments. Not only were they given no formal training or clear idea of what the position entailed, they were also expected to know a great deal about a lot of different things.

As senior IT professionals ourselves, we have seen this situation repeated many times. We wanted to write a book that would help new IT managers navigate the choppy seas of management.

This book aims to help you with any responsibilities that you are suddenly given, that you suddenly acquire, or that you suddenly realize need to be addressed. We don't spend much time talking about the theory of IT management. We spend most of the book describing what you need to worry about if you need to know how to deal with a particular situation like creating a budget or writing an ad for a recruitment program.

Who Is This Book Written For?

We wrote the book for *new* IT managers and *future* IT managers. Much of the material in this book will be familiar to experienced IT managers—those people who have managing IT departments since the space program in the 1960s. But for many individuals, the late 1990s and early 2000s have brought a radical change in responsibilities with little or no help along with it. This book is written to help you identify, deal with, and (if necessary) look for further help on many of the key issues that are suddenly facing you as a new IT manager.

We also recognize that one of the more difficult career steps in the field of Information Technology is moving up from technician to manager. For those hoping to make this leap, this book can be useful to let you know what awaits you on the other side. By learning more about an IT manager's job, it will help you know what skills sets to focus on, so that you can demonstrate to your company that you are prepared and ready to be a manager.

How Technical Is This Book?

This book discusses the basic principles of such "nontechnical" issues as staffing, managing your IT team, managing projects, and budgeting. It also discusses in some detail the more difficult topics of hardware, software, networks, the Net, and so on. Finally, it covers topics that might be considered somewhat "in between" the technical and nontechnical: security, disaster recovery, and enterprise applications. It is for technical professionals, but it is not crammed with code.

How Timely Is This Book? Isn't It Out of Date Already?

In today's rapidly changing technical environment, we know that printed books cannot provide the only source of information you need; the Net will give you much more up-to-the-minute facts. But what an IT manager, and any worker in today's quickly changing corporate world, needs more than quick data is *perspective:* We try to tell you what the big issues are and what to look out for, what to address first, and how to make quick decisions about complex stuff in the 1.7 minutes you have to deal with them before the meeting starts.

How Is This Book Structured?

We worked hard to write a book that we, as busy technical professionals, would use ourselves.

We have structured the material in easy-to-read, easy-to-grab chunks. We don't have any free time and we assume you don't either. The book is designed to be scanned for critical information.

We have put in as many cross-references as we could, knowing that one topic often leads to another and that you want to make the jump right away, not after looking in the index.

Key topics for each chapter are identified right at the start. In the technical world, it is often as hard to identify *what you don't even know* as it is to get specific data about what you do know. You may know that you have to put together a budget, for example, but you may not even realize that there are some important things to think about when running a project. We try to quickly identify the things you absolutely need to know.

Just Exactly What Is in This Book?

In this book, we will be discussing various aspects of an IT manager's role. Through extensive research and a lot of experience (combined, the authors have over 25 years in the computer industry), we have identified the following key elements of an IT manager's job as the new century starts: staffing, managing, infrastructure, hardware, software, data networks, internet/intranet/extranet, managing projects, security, enterprise applications, budgeting, disaster recovery, support services, and remote access.

Chapter-by-Chapter Summaries

Let's take each chapter and examine what we are going to talk about:

Chapter	Why You Should Care about This	Page
1. What Is an IT Manager?	Read what the point of your job is, why it is so important, and how this book can help you do it better.	1
2. Staffing Your IT Team	Hiring and all its aspects are some of the classic managerial responsibilities. This chapter talks about the problems you'll face and offers some concrete suggestions for solving them.	7
3. Managing Your IT Team	While it is tempting to think of hardware and software as your most critical IT resources, it is actually people who run, support, and manage the technologies that are the most critical.	49

A Note on URLs and Web Resources

State-of-the-art information is critical to IT managers and IT professionals of all kinds. Many of the sources for this book are sites on the Web. And, as any Web user, experienced or new, understands, Web content changes quickly. We have included Web addresses whenever we can, knowing full well that sites get changed, material gets deleted or added, and pointers that worked when we wrote the book may not necessarily work when you read it.

Regardless, we thought it best to give you a reference where we found worthwhile information. You can use that information as a starting point for your search for useful data.

Acknowledgments

Trying to condense the topic of IT management into one book isn't an easy task. It required a delicate touch to both properly balance technical and nontechnical issues as well as to determine which topics in each area to focus on.

It is not possible to mention each and every person that contributed to developing the book that you now hold in your hand. Still, we have to be sure to thank Bruce Caldwell, *Information Week;* Tom Conarty, Bethlehem Steel Corporation; Dan Deakin, Zentropy Partners; Rob Hawkins, Hofs-Hut, Inc.; Robert Rubin, Elf Atochem NA Inc.; Matt Tavis, Sapient Corporation; Philip Tolley, Matrix Rehabilitation Inc.; and Janet Wilson, Mutual Insurance Company of Arizona, for helping us to fine-tune the initial proposal by adding and eliminating various chapters and sections.

We are especially grateful to Curtis Johnsey, O'Connor Kenny Partners; Brian McMann, Tanning Technology Corp.; Curt Wennekamp, Medshares, Inc.; Mark Jones, Boeing; and Janet Wilson, Mutual Insurance Company of Arizona, for reviewing the manuscript and their invaluable suggestions and comments. They helped us keep the book focused on its goals and made certain that important topics, as well as differing perspectives, were not overlooked or given short shrift. We would also like to thank our editors, Jennifer Mann, who agreed to publish the book, and Karyn Johnson, who kept us on course throughout the long adventure that writing this book became.

A large portion of the ideas presented here represent what we've learned from others. Accordingly, we must give credit to those who taught us (often unknowingly) throughout the course of our careers in corporate IT—colleagues, co-workers, those we have reported to, and those who have reported to us. We are indebted to, and grateful for, these 'accidental mentors.'

Finally, we are eternally indebted to friends and family for their support and understanding while this book was being written. It is motivating to know that as the final edits are being made and this period of self-imposed seclusion ends, they are anxious and eager to forget about those declined invitations, missed dinners, and nonexistent weekends.

Bill Holtsnider
Denver, CO
bholtsnider@earthlink.net

Brian D. Jaffe
New York, NY
brian@red55.com

What *Is* an IT Manager?

CHAPTER ONE

What You Will Learn

- The specific good—and bad—aspects of being an IT manager
- Why IT managers *and their IT departments* have a much more critical role to play in the future of corporations

Introduction

An information technology (IT) manager needs to wear a lot of hats. Different parts of the organization will have different expectations of this position, and you'll have to address them all. Finance expects you to manage costs, Sales and Marketing will want to see IT generate revenue, and the administrative assistant down the hall just wants her printer to stop smudging. In this chapter, we'll delve into the roles and responsibilities of an IT manager.

1.1 Just What Does an IT Manager Do?

Congratulations! You're now an IT manager. You may be thinking, "What exactly have I gotten myself into? I've been angling to get promoted into this position for the last two years, and now I realize I'm not even sure I know what the job is."

IT managers now have many, many responsibilities (data centers, support staff, telecommunications, servers, workstations, Web sites) and connect with almost all the departments (Accounting, Marketing, Sales, Distribution) within a company.

This is both the good and the bad news. At some companies, an IT manager can have direct influence on the strategic direction of the company, suggesting and helping implement e-commerce initiatives, for example. In other companies, an IT manager is really a technician, a phone or network installer. And, to complicate things even further, those definitions change quickly over time. Yesterday's network installer becomes today's e-commerce consultant.

By the way, "IT" (Information Technology) and "IS" (Information Systems) have now become synonymous terms. While they are often used interchangeably, "IT" is becoming much more widely used. Some people may use "IS" to refer to activity related to business software applications, but this use has waned considerably.

Why All That Change/Flexibility Is Good

The position of IT manager can be very challenging, is extremely varied in scope, allows you to come in contact with a large portion of the company, provides you with opportunities to directly affect the overall direction of your company, and is excellent professional experience to acquire as we turn the corner of this century.

As important as all that is, there is an added bonus: IT has taken on a critical strategic value in the roles companies play in the new economy. Not only is your job interesting and rewarding, it is also important, too. What more could you ask for?

Why All That Change/Flexibility Is Bad

On the other hand, being an IT manager is a difficult, often thankless task. Like many service jobs, if you do it superbly, most people don't notice. In addition, the definition of the responsibilities differs radically from company to company. Some companies actually have many IT managers and several layers of management. At others (and this number is shrinking), an IT manager is a part-time role someone fills while doing their "real" job.

And, to complicate things, the role of an IT manager can often vary within an organization, depending on who is making the decisions at that time. While the techniques might vary, a "Western Sales Manager" pretty much knows what his or her role is—get more sales as soon as possible—and that is not going to vary much from company to company. An IT manager, on the other hand, can mean many things to many people. Addressing all these needs and people can mean that time for "extras" like sleep and meals has to be sacrificed.

1.2 What Is All This about the New Strategic Value of IT?

IT management has become one of the most critical positions in the new economy. As corporations have embraced the efficiencies and excitement of the new digital economy, IT—and IT professionals—have grown dramatically in value.

IT is no longer "just" a department, no longer an isolated island like the MIS departments of old corporations where requests for data would flow in and emerge, weeks later, in some kind of long, unreadable report. Many companies now make IT an integral part of their company, of their mission statements, and of their spending.

Your role is more critical than ever before.

The CEO's Role in IT

"First, the CEO must be sure to regard information technology as a strategic resource to help the business get more out of its people. Second, the CEO must learn enough about technology to be able to ask good, hard questions of the CIO and be able to tell whether good answers are coming back. Third, the CEO needs to bring the CIO into management's deliberations and strategizing. It's impossible to align IT strategy with business strategy if the CIO is out of the business loop."

—Bill Gates
Business @ the Speed of Thought, p. 318

Development vs. Operations

Most IT organizations have two key functional areas: development and operations.

Development

Companies often see the real value of IT as only the applications that serve the company's core business. The applications are what allows one business to become innovative, more efficient, and more productive and set itself apart from its competitors. Careers within application development include analysts, programmers, and testers. Many people within IT like working in applications development because it allows them to really learn how the business operates. As a result, it may often provide opportunities for increased involvement with people in other departments outside of IT.

However, many programmers find the job is too isolating because their daily interactions may only be with the program logic displayed on their screen and the keyboard.

Operations

The technical support function is the oft-forgotten area of IT. The operations organization is responsible for making sure that the computers are up and running, and operating as they should. Their jobs go well beyond the computer hardware and often include the network (routers, hubs, telecommunication facilities, etc.), database administration, operations, backups, operating systems, and so on. Like most important and underappreciated jobs, when operations is doing their job well, you don't even know they exist.

However, those in operations may find the time demands stressful. Some system maintenance can only be done during weekends and evenings when users won't be affected. Similarly, it will be the operations staff that is roused by a mid-REM-sleep phone call when the system crashes in the middle of the night. Some people can wear pagers and have a life, but some refuse to even try.

Your Department's Goals

Your goal as an active manager and caring employee and employer is to make sure that your department's aims are in line with those of your organization. It does not matter if you are an IT manager for a nonprofit citizen's group or midlevel manager for General Motors; you need to discover what the organization's goals are and make them your own.

Your IT goals should be measured in the same terms as the business units that you support—reduce per-unit costs of the division's products and increase the capacity and throughput of the business and manufacturing processes. Your tactics must clearly satisfy these goals.

Your boss should be clear about communicating those to you. But they should not be a secret anyway. If your company makes widgets, make sure the company's strategy includes an appropriate use of IT throughout the company. Is the widgets factory truly automated? Can the Accounting department talk to the Human Resources department?

1.3 Why Are IT Managers So Critical Now?

IT is a brave new world to many of today's corporations. Many executives now know Word, Excel, and e-mail, but they have little or no understanding of the deeper, more complex issues involved in IT. They imagine IT to be a powerful but complex world where rewards can be magically great or frighteningly terrible. These executives, and their corporations, need professionals to both explain and execute in this new world. This is where you come in.

You can leverage your technical knowledge, experience, and interests with your company's direct profit and loss requirements. *Together*, you and your company can provide a powerful business combination. *Alone*, your individual skills and passions can wither into arcane interests, and their business expertise can build models relevant to an economic world decades in the past.

Will your technical expertise and recommendations occasionally clash with their corporate needs and vision? Absolutely. Will your ideas about technical directions sometimes be in direct opposition to their perceptions of "market forces"? Absolutely. Will you "win some and lose some"? Absolutely.

The purpose of this book, however, is to help you win—and your company win. We want to help you accomplish the famous "win/win." If you know what the goals, responsibilities, and land mines of your job are, and you have an understanding of how your job fits into the overall corporate mission, you will both succeed.

1.4 Further References

Books

- Bysinger, Bill, and Ken Knight (Contributor), *Investing in Information Technology: A Decision-Making Guide for Business and Technology Managers,* John Wiley and Sons, 1996.

- Cortada, James W., *Best Practices in Information Technology: How Corporations Get the Most Value from Exploiting Their Digital Investments,* Prentice Hall, 1997.

- Evans, Philip, and Thomas S. Wurster, *Blown to Bits: How the New Economics of Information Transforms Strategy,* Harvard Business School Press, 1999.

- Galliers, Robert D., et al. (Editors), *Information Technology and Organizational Transformation: Innovation for the 21st Century Organization (John Wiley Series in Information Systems),* John Wiley and Sons, 1998.

- Gates, Bill, *Business @ the Speed of Thought*, Warner Books, 1999.

- Laudon, Kenneth C., and Jane Price Laudon, *Management Information Systems: Organization and Technology in the Networked Enterprise,* Prentice Hall, 1999.

- Lewis, Bob, *Bob Lewis's IS Survival Guide,* Sams, 1999.

- Lucas, Henry C., Jr., *Information Technology and the Productivity Paradox: The Search for Value,* Oxford University Press, 1999.

- Plotnick, Neil, *The IT Professional's Guide to Managing Systems, Vendors & End Users*, Aviation Archives, 1999.

- Remenyi, Dan, Michael Sherwood-Smith, and Terry White, *Achieving Maximum Value From Information Systems: A Process Approach,* John Wiley and Sons, 1997.

- Strassmann, Paul A.,*The Squandered Computer: Evaluating the Business Alignment of Information Technologies,* Information Economic Press, 1997.

- Thorp, John, *The Information Paradox: Realizing the Business Benefits of Information Technology,* DMR Consulting Group, McGraw-Hill, 1999.

Staffing Your IT Team

CHAPTER TWO

What You Will Learn

- How IT managers *must* be directly involved in the hiring process
- How to write a position description
- How to advertise for IT candidates
- Whether or not you should use a recruiter
- How to interview candidates
- How to make a good offer to a prospective employee for an IT position
- Which career paths are available for yourself and your employees

Introduction

Your success and failure as a manager is based almost entirely on the people that work for you. Every time you hire, it is an opportunity to add value to your team, as well as to adjust the balance of skill sets and personality of the team. As such, each hire should have your full attention and not be dismissed as another administrative chore. This chapter discusses the important details associated with the various elements involved in recruiting for your team.

2.1 Hiring: Why Do I Need to Do This?

Hiring means dealing with agencies, your Human Resources department, reviewing resumes, conducting interviews, and negotiating an offer. If you secretly wish that the first candidate you meet is "the one" and you are grateful your job isn't in personnel, don't worry, you're not alone. That means you feel the same way as every other IT manager.

It is precisely this urge to "hire first, ask questions later" though, that can get you and your company into real trouble. This chapter deals in detail with some of the issues to watch out for, the questions to ask (both yourself and interviewees), and other things you should be concerned about when you are considering bringing someone new onto your team.

Justifying a Hire

Of course, before you hire someone, you may need to get approvals. Whether it is simply replacing someone who recently left or adding to staff, you may need to convince others that this hire is necessary.

If it is a new position, you'll have explain why this role is needed and what benefit it will deliver. Sometimes the position description, which is discussed later in this chapter, has enough information; other times you may need to go into more detail. Some ideas to consider include the following:

- The department's work load has grown by x percent in the past year, and additional staff is needed to keep up.
- We've brought in new technologies and need to hire people who are already skilled and experienced in order to use the product effectively.
- The company can save time and money if certain processes are automated, but we need staff to do this.
- We'll be able to respond to our users/customers x percent faster if we expand our staff.

2.2 Hiring: How Do I Write a Position Description?

Most likely, you're going to have to prepare some type of "position description" or "job description." A position description is a relatively detailed description of a specific job.

Value of Position Descriptions

Your Human Resources department may ask you to write a position description so that they can post it internally within the company, or they may use it to relay the pertinent details to agencies and recruiters. They may also use the information in position descriptions to help prepare an ad for the newspaper or for a job-posting site on the Internet.

Even if you aren't required by your company's procedures to prepare a job description for the hiring process, however, it is a good idea to do so. Every member of your staff should have a job description of their own job. This way, there is little doubt as to what their responsibilities are. It will also be likely to be used for performance evaluations, salary considerations, and staffing justification.

Along these lines, it is important to remember that the position description is just that—a description. *It is not a contract.* There are several reasons this distinction is important, but the most important two are the following:

1. Many companies have formal contracts with their employees, and a position description is not designed for that purpose. Some companies—depending on the company, the region, and the position—have formal, legal contracts that they require employees to sign upon joining the organization. These contracts are generally strong legal instruments with very specific terms. They are not good methods of determining what a person *should* do; they are often a list of things a person should *not* do. A position description does not serve this legal function.

2. Things change. While your staff may or may not appreciate the pace of change or your responsibilities, it is still incumbent on you to maintain your flexibility. Your boss will demand a wide variety of things from you, often adding or subtracting duties the same week. You will need to adapt quickly to those new challenges and be able to turn your staff in the new direction. A position description that carefully defines what an IT professional can do severely limits that individual's flexibility and radically constrains the manager and the department.

The format of the position description can vary. Your Human Resources department may have a standard format that it likes to use. It is often very much like an outline, and is usually kept to one or two pages. The position description should start with the simple facts. See Figure 2.1 on the next page for a sample "PD."

Job title: Senior Java Developer

Position summary: Writes application code for company's new e-commerce site

Immediate supervisor: Robert Smith, Manager of E-commerce Development

Number of direct reports: None

Travel: None

Specific requirements: Minimum 3 years Java development, 10 + years development in another language (C, C++, Perl, SQL)

Salary: $75,000–$95,000

Figure 2.1   Sample Position Description

General Requirements

The following are the general requirements for a position description.

- **Job title:** Hopefully, the title will be something descriptive about the job and will be one that a prospective employee will be proud to have on his business card. Something along the lines of "IT Associates II" is of little meaning. Use titles and descriptions that are industry standard, so that both you and the potential employees can readily do comparisons of qualifications versus salary and benefits.

- **Position summary:** A quick two- or three-sentence description of what the job entails.

- **Immediate supervisor:** Identify the title of the individual the person will be reporting to. This will help give some perspective to where the position is in relationship to the entire IT organization.

- **Number of direct reports:** Indicate the size of the staff that reports to this position. It might even help if you provide some simple description of the staff (operators, programmers, other managers, etc.).

- **Minimum vs. specific requirements:** For all critical issues, list the minimum requirements (and name them as such) as well as any specific requirements. If you must have a coder with *at least* 3 years of development experience, say so clearly. If you need someone with SAP in the background somewhere, be clear about that.

- **Education, training, and certification requirements:** If this is a requirement for this job, say so.

- **Experience necessary:** If formal training is not required, companies often ask for a minimum number of years of "real-world" experience in a given field.

- **Travel:** If there is travel required in the position, it is important that it be identified. Traditionally, it is identified as a percentage of time. It is important to be as honest here as possible. Since most candidates look negatively on travel requirements, you might want to be overly careful and overestimate the amount of travel. You may also want to describe the travel in more detail (local/domestic/international, or short trips of two or three days versus weeks or months at a time).

- **Salary:** When a salary is included on a position description, it is generally given as a range. If there is a bonus, you can indicate a range for the bonus, or simply say "bonus eligible."

Further Details

With this information out of the way, you can now get into more detail. This will include specific responsibilities, accountabilities, and preferred requirements. See Figure 2.2 on the next page for a sample detailed position description.

The responsibilities section of the position description will probably be the largest. In this section, you can document what the expectations of the job are. The types of items you might include are

- Estimated size of the budget (if any) the position is responsible for

- Regular reports and/or presentations the individual is expected to provide

- Any metrics that will be used to measure degrees of success (uptime, resolution time, response time, transactions per hour)

- Operational responsibilities (backup, data maintenance, system start-ups and shutdowns, regularly checking resources and services to ensure they are operating as they should, etc.)

- Interpersonal skills

- Requirements to document work and/or procedures

- Specific security responsibilities (physical, application, etc.)

- Significant upcoming and ongoing projects

- Any system resources (applications, hardware, operating systems, communication facilities) that the position is responsible for maintaining, implementing, and so on

- Coordinating activities with other departments within the company, or other teams within IT

Size of the budget: N/A

Regular reports and/or presentations: Weekly status report to manager, weekly staff code review presentation (informal but important).

Success metrics: No formal metrics, but will work closely with development team to meet tight deadlines. Progress of all code is carefully monitored to identify and correct potential logjams and stumbling blocks.

Operational responsibilities: No system responsibilities, but must follow both standard and company-defined development procedures, including backup procedures, system integration methods, etc.

Interpersonal skills: Must be able to work successfully on an intense, deadline-driven team.

Requirements to document work and/or procedures: See above. Follow company standards for commenting on and documenting all code.

Specific security responsibilities: Signing a nondisclosure agreement (NDA) is required. Breaching confidentiality of projects in development or company secrets is grounds for dismissal.

Significant upcoming and ongoing projects: Responsibility for ongoing maintenance of e-commerce applications once they are put into production.

System resources that the position is responsible for maintaining: N/A

Coordinating activities with other departments within the company: Must work closely with both sales engineers and senior IT staff to complete projects on time.

Responsibilities for quality assurance, testing, disaster recovery, etc.: Systematic testing procedures are followed throughout the development cycle.

Requirements for being on call: N/A. The position requires a significant amount of overtime.

Figure 2.2   Sample Detailed Position Description

- Responsibilities for quality assurance, testing, disaster recovery, and so on
- Requirements for being on call (e.g., 24 × 7, beeper, remote access, cell phone, etc.); early, late, or rotating shifts

Accountabilities Section

An accountabilities section can serve two purposes:

1. It can further refine the responsibilities section and help indicate the success criteria for the position.

2. More importantly, even though the position may have one identified boss, it probably serves multiple masters. For example, a programmer responsible for the order processing applications is probably accountable in various degrees to the Order Entry, Customer Service, Sales and Distribution departments. These dotted lines should be identified in the position description.

Lastly, you may want to include a preferred requirements section. In fact, they may not even be "preferred," they might be *prerequisites.* Regardless, this section allows you to expand on the type of skills and experience you are seeking.

Items Not to Overlook When Writing a Job Description

Certain aspects of a job, such as the amount of travel required or your environment, can have significant impacts on your staffing decisions. It is important that these aspects be included in the job description.

- **Project experience:** For example if you're shopping for a database administrator (DBA), and you know that she will spend the next 12–18 months implementing a data warehouse, you should specify previous data warehousing experience.

- **Environment size:** You may want to seek someone with experience in an environment of a similar size to yours, particularly if you have an especially large or small environment.

- **Number of locations:** If your environment consists of many remote sites, you might want to specify that the candidate have experience in a similarly dispersed environment.

- **Industry experience:** Since IT environments can vary drastically depending on the company's industry, you could specify a preference for specific industry experience (e.g., finance, manufacturing, law, publishing, advertising, consumer products, health care, etc.).

- **Multiplatform experience:** If your environment has mixed technologies (perhaps as a result of a merger or acquisition, or because of upcoming migration), you could seek someone with experience in an environment where these technologies coexisted.

- **Type of work:** If the job revolves around implementations rather than maintenance, or is more strategic than operational, it should be indicated.

- **Solitary vs. team assignments:** If the position is responsible for doing a lot of team-oriented work, or is very solitary in nature, say so. Are the teams static and long-lived, or are they very dynamic with short-term project assignments?

It is easy, and sometimes tempting, to get too carried away with your job description. Avoid the temptation: the position description should provide a simple and accurate description of what the job is about and its expectations.

2.3 Advertising: How Do I Write an Ad for an IT Job Posting?

At some point you may need to write a formal advertisment.

Objectives

When you write an ad for a job posting, you have several objectives:

- Accurately describe the requirements and the position so that both under-qualified and overqualified candidates don't apply, thereby saving both your time and theirs.
- Make the job sound exciting and interesting enough to attract the right kind of candidates.
- Be careful to tell the truth—do not oversell the position. This mistake can cost both you and the candidates valuable time and effort.

Other Considerations

Of course, when you are writing a want ad, either for your newspaper, company bulletin board, a trade journal, or a job-posting site, you are generally very limited in space. You're challenged to make it descriptive, accurate, and inviting, without overselling or underselling the position. A newspaper gives you less space, but your entire ad is there at a glance.

On a Web site, you may have more space available, but you have other challenges: job seekers generally scan through lists of job postings, and the parameters of the job have to entice them to click on your posting among all the others (see Figure 2.3 on the next page).

Specific Items You Should Mention

There are some things you should try to mention in your ad:

- If the official *title* of the job is somewhat nondescriptive or unappealing, try using a more common title understood by everyone in IT. For example, if

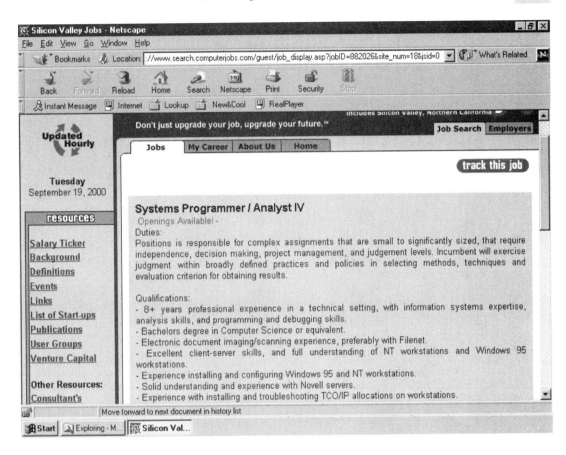

Figure 2.3   Sample Job Posting on the Web

your opening is called "Network Resource Coordinator," you might want to use "LAN Administrator" instead.

- While some people don't like to include one, it is generally a good idea to mention a *salary range*. A figure will eliminate people who are already being paid more. And the salary range indicates whether the job is closer in status to entry level or senior. If there is a bonus with the position, simply state "+ Bonus."

- If you do not or cannot mention your company, you should at least mention your *industry,* and give some indication of the size of the IT environment.

- Give a brief summary of the *requirements*—specific technologies, work experience, personality type (e.g., self-starter, team player), and so on. Include those items that are "must haves." If there are other items you'd like to mention that aren't absolute requirements, list them with "a plus."

- Mention anything that puts the position in perspective or adds some *excitement*. This might include specific large projects or migration efforts. Adjectives like "high-tech," "progressive," or "e-commerce" might be very meaningful to candidates.

- It can be helpful to ask for a *cover letter* to help gauge the candidates' verbal skills as you scan the resumes. You can ask for a "salary history" or "salary requirements," but don't be surprised if most candidates don't provide them. If a candidate's resume looks good to you, but there's no salary history and you're concerned you can't afford them, give them a call or send them an e-mail. If you don't get an answer to the direct question, it might be in your best interest to move on.

- If your company has anything *special* to offer (benefits, flextime, telecommuting), you may want to mention it.

- Lastly, include the *method* you prefer for them to submit resumes: mail, fax, e-mail.

If you're posting your ad on a Web site, you can include all the details of the position description discussed above. However, you may want to take some of the "corporate-ese" out of it so that the environment doesn't sound too stuffy.

You may be able to get your Human Resources department to take care of writing your job posting. Or, you should at least be able to get their general input for company procedures regarding what can be stated in ads. If you are placing your ad in a newspaper or trade journal, the individual who takes your ad may be able to offer some suggestions and pointers.

Key General Considerations

Keep in mind the following guidelines:

1. Be very specific.

2. List *all* your requirements.

3. Sell your company. Most (if not all) of your best prospects already have a job—you must convince them to join *your* company.

4. Sell the job—with few adjectives. "Exciting, fulfilling, rewarding"—what job does not claim to be these things?

5. Work out with HR the response mechanism(s) you will use: do you want only e-mail, only letters, no phone calls? How do you want to deal with the responses? Be specific.

You will get a *lot* of responses, most of them unwanted. (Despite your best efforts, you will be flooded with unqualified candidates. Be ready.)

2.4 Advertising: Where Should I Advertise?

Once you know *what* you want to say to effectively attract the best candidates, then you have to figure out *where* to say it. You may have something great to say, but if you don't relay your message where the right people will hear it, you may as well keep it a secret.

Traditional advertising venues include

- TV
- Billboards
- Radio
- Print (newspapers, trade journals)
- Internet
- Agencies/recruiters/headhunters
- Networking
- Job/recruiting fairs

In general, IT has relied on the last five from the above list for getting the word out about a job opening, although, in tight labor markets, the use of radio and billboards is not unheard of. Traditionally, print advertisements have always taken the lion's share. Like many other information-related activities, however, advertising is being radically affected by the advent of the Internet. Web-based classified advertising is changing the way jobs and job seekers are matched up, and nowhere is that more true than in the high-tech industry.

The Value of Print Advertising

Nonetheless, don't overlook print options. Your city's Sunday classified ads at least target people in your geographic area, and trade journals reach the people who probably show the most interest in their field (although that fact does not necessarily give you an indication of the quality of their skills). The Web has become a favorite for more technically oriented jobs. If your job opening is for a senior-level spot and is geared more towards management than hands-on technical skills, you may still be better off using print; this is still where most upper-level candidates look, although the trend is starting to shift.

Advantages of Print over Web Advertising

Another advantage to print is that all the ads are there for job seekers to scan as quickly as they'd like, with all the relevant information in one place. On the

Web, while potential candidates can put in specific search parameters and generally find more detailed position descriptions, there are some disadvantages:

- The job seeker is slowed by response time issues. Print ads are ready to read.

- Job search results on the Web usually yield screens of titles and companies, with little information about the job itself. Often, the user has to further click on those jobs that seem interesting. While that extra click may not sound overburdensome, combined with the slow response times mentioned above, it can be more of a deterrent than you might imagine.

Advantages of Web over Print Advertising

Of course, the Internet has seen explosive growth as a tool to match job hunters with job openings. And nowhere has this tool been used more than in the IT industry. The Web offers several advantages over print:

- It is much, much cheaper to post an ad. There are many Web sites that offer low- or no-cost job listings, whereas print ads can cost thousands of dollars for a single-issue run.

- Ads can be changed/updated at any time. Print ads, of course, are much harder to change.

- By using search parameters, job seekers can easily find your posting, instead of having to scan column after column and page after page in the paper.

- Job sites generally allow job seekers to respond immediately by filling out a form, or e-mailing their resumes as soon as they find a job that they are interested in. This quick response time far outpaces print ads that run telephone numbers to call in their ads, and not every company is willing (or should) do that. On the Web, you can get fast results.

- There are many, many job sites available on the Internet. In addition to sites focused exclusively for posting jobs, many businesses will use their own Web site to list job openings. Also, in the move from print format to the digital format, traditional newspapers now have Web-based versions of their classified ads.

- Automated agents on Web sites can benefit you and job seekers. Many Web sites now have automated search agents that will notify you (via e-mail) when it finds a candidate that matches your requirements. Similarly, job seekers can use agents to be notified when a job is posted that matches what they're looking for.

- You can ask for—and reply directly and quickly to—a candidate's e-mail address.

Popular Web Sites

Although there are numerous job sites for posting your opening, some of the more popular ones include *computerjobs.com, headhunter.net, monster.com, careermosaic.com, hotjobs.com, dice.com, techjobbank.com, vault.com, incpad.com, 1-jobs.com, careercast.com, skillsvillage.com,* and *techies.com.*

Web Posting Issues to Think About

If you post your job opening on the Web, there are some things you will want to consider:

- How well known is the site? Will it attract enough job seekers?
- How good is the search engine used by job seekers when trying to locate jobs that match their career goals?
- Does the site ensure anonymity—for both you and the job seekers? You may or may not want this anonymity. However, some job seekers may respond to a specific Web-based ad, but will not post their resume on a job site unless they're certain that certain identifying information is not included. These job seekers are concerned that their current employer might find out about their job search.
- Does the site allow you to post the information you want to about the job?
- How does the job posting look when viewed by a job seeker? Web sites usually have very limited means for formatting this type of information. Be sure to browse your own job posting so that you will see how it appears to job seekers.
- How long will your job stay posted? Will it be deleted automatically after a certain period of time?
- Are jobs openings displayed in a certain order when a job seeker does a search? Or can you pay a premium to have your job stand out (at the top of the list, with colors, or icons)?

Job/Recruiting Fairs

While the value of job fairs is often viewed with less than total admiration, a *Computerworld* survey (*Computerworld*, 1/10/00, "So, When Do I Start?") found that "10% of all IT workers are hired at recruiting events. That's way behind the leading tool—employee referrals, at 25%—but it is fourth on the list, ahead of search agencies (8%) and paid Internet recruiting services (also 8%)." The article goes on to note: "People use these fairs."

And you should, too, given that information. Will all of your needs be filled at the first event you attend? No. But IT professionals attend these events, and you should do the same. You can spend a lot of money and waste a lot of time just going endlessly to events like these (they seem to be offered almost every week these days), but a targeted effort, with specific presenters and detailed planning, can reap rewards.

On the plus side of job fairs, it is the best opportunity for seeing the greatest number of candidates in the least amount of time. You can glance at a resume and chat with a candidate for a few seconds or a few minutes. Candidates are also looking to meet with as many employers as possible. Candidates' feelings aren't hurt if you move on to someone else after exchanging just a few words.

On the other hand, job fairs are not generally charming places with a warm ambience. This atmosphere may deter many candidates from attending. And, since a typical lunch hour may not provide enough time for a candidate, most people assume that a significant percentage of job seekers at job fairs are out of work and have been unable to find a position through other means.

2.5 Advertising: Can I Fill a Job without It?

Certainly. A significant percentage of jobs openings are never advertised. So how do you fill a job you don't advertise? With good old-fashioned, manual, low-tech *word of mouth*. In today's culture, even the simplest of ideas need an impressive-sounding title. IT people use "legacy" to refer to outdated technologies and products; in this case, the term "networking" is used to refer to making contacts with other people.

Networking

Filling a job via networking can be a very rewarding process. You simply start by talking to your professional contacts (peers, subordinates, human resources representatives, coworkers from former jobs, sales representatives). You don't have to go into great detail, just briefly mention the type of job you have open, along with a brief description of what you're looking for.

But your "network" of contacts extends far beyond the people you currently work with, as well as those you used to work with.

Your professional contacts include the following people:

- The Human Resources department may have recently interviewed someone who was rejected for a position in another department, but perhaps fits your requirements.
- Members of your, or other, departments may know of people at their former jobs.

- Your vendor representatives, who are probably already familiar with your environment, may know individuals at their other customer sites who would be a good match.

- Perhaps someone who was a close second for a previous open position can be called back in for this position.

Your personal contacts include the following people:

- People on your staff may have friends and colleagues who they can vouch for and know are looking for jobs. (This connection brings a double bonus: what higher compliment is there for you as a manager than for one of your subordinates to recommend a friend to work for you?)

- Your community can provide you with a rich source of potential job leads. Let the word get out to your friends, to fellow church members, to neighbors, to fellow squash players, that you are looking to hire someone.

- For all you know, the next person you meet at a Fourth of July barbecue softball game could know the ideal candidate for you.

Does networking work? It sure does. Does it work every time? No. It's a matter of luck and timing, the people you contact, and the way you talk about the job, as well as other factors that you can't always identify. You never know the chain of connections that will lead you to the right contact. In fact, one of the authors found his current job via someone he went to Sunday school with and hadn't spoken to in over 15 years.

One of the nice things about networking is that it can be the cheapest way to find candidates, but it may not be the fastest or most effective. However, you can always use networking in conjunction with other recruiting methods.

2.6 Recruiters: Should I Use One?

Whether you call them recruiters, agents, or headhunters, they are a fact of life. Headhunters do not generally have a great reputation. Sometimes that poor reputation is deserved; many other times, however, a recruiter can mean the difference between success or failure of a project that is relying heavily on certain personnel. Using a recruiter has both advantages and disadvantages. Weigh them carefully before deciding. The costs for making the wrong choice can be high.

If their less-than-stellar reputation is deserved, the way they are compensated may be one of the reasons. Agents generally receive between 20% and 30% of the starting salary of a person they place. With high commissions, coupled with weeks or months between successfully placing a candidate, a headhunter has high incentives to do his best to succeed at every opportunity.

Positives

The primary reason for using headhunters is that they take the lion's share of the recruiting burden off the IT manager. You can articulate precise technical requirements to an agent, whereas your in-house HR representative might roll their eyes with every acronym and buzzword. Your HR department may do nothing more than use one or two of the recruiting media mentioned above. The recruiter, on the other hand, will place the ads and work the phones. In addition, he'll do the initial screening of candidates and resumes. He will make sure that the candidates he sends you are in the right salary and skill range. Many recruiters will also meet candidates before sending them to you to be sure that they have the appropriate "presentation" for you.

The last four sentences above state what the recruiter "will" do. More appropriately, they ought to say "should." It is the "wills" and "shoulds" that separate good recruiters from bad ones. In large metropolitan areas where there is a large pool of talent, agents can help you separate the wheat from the chaff. In areas where the pool of talent isn't quite so deep, a recruiter may be able to help you find the shade in a desert.

Reasons to Use a Recruiter

There are a number of reasons why you may want to use a recruiter.

1. If your marketplace is a difficult one to recruit in. For example, many downtown metropolitan areas have an intensely competitive hiring IT environment. Qualified IT professionals know they can easily find a job and are generally very savvy about doing so. Are you prepared to find the right avenues, investigate the common sources for this position, and so on?
2. If the job you are hiring for is a complex one.
3. If the job you are hiring for is a popular one.
4. Do you want the hassle of finding the needle in the haystack? Determining the top 10 candidates for a job can be a chore, especially if you have to look through 50–100 resumes.

Things to Watch Out For

In general, working with agents is a mix of personalities—yours and theirs. And since you're the one paying, you can, and should, choose not to work with those who don't seem to work well with you.

Keep an eye out for recruiters who

- Don't appear to be listening to you and your requirements. If they continually send you candidates and/or resumes that clearly aren't suitable matches, change to another recruiter. This is a *very* common problem. Recruiters have bodies they want to place, but that is not your problem. Demand what you are paying for.
- Try to convince you to ignore your own instincts. If you reject an agent's candidate, the recruiter should ask why, so he can learn what you don't like and increase the odds of sending you people you will like. But if your agent tries to argue with you, or convince you that you should consider someone you didn't like, it's time to move on. There are plenty of fish in this sea.
- Try to increase the odds of success by overwhelming you with resumes. One of their primary functions (as described above) is to separate the wheat from the chaff; if you are not saving time using a particular recruiter, switch.

Reasons Not to Use a Recruiter

Don't use a recruiter if

1. You don't have the additional budget. Recruiters charge a fee. *How* they charge can vary; typically, the fee is a percentage of the hiree's first-year salary. With consultants, it is usually a cut of the hourly fee.
2. You know exactly *what* you are looking for and *where* to look for candidates, the criteria for the job are well-defined, and you have the time and experience for reading resumes.

Recommendation

Evaluate your own skills, time, and money before deciding whether to "outsource" this task. If you haven't done much hiring before, if you have the budget and can afford the fees, and/or you don't have time to do it yourself, consider getting a recruiting agency to do it.

2.7 Recruiters: How Do I Find the Right One?

Finding good recruiters is more of an art than a science, but probably not terribly different from how you found your accountant. You probably took a friend's or relative's recommendation the first time you needed an accountant. Later, you may have changed, perhaps based on another recommendation, because you weren't 100% comfortable with the first one. You may have gone through a few options before finding one you're comfortable with. In essence, you networked.

Finding a good agent, whether to help you find a job or to help fill an open position, is the same process. You can start by asking people you know which headhunters they've used. Ask who they liked, disliked, and why. Your company's Human Resources department can probably offer you some references of agents they've worked with in the past, as well as those they've had bad experiences with. You can also ask others in your department about agents they've used. If you really don't know where to turn, you can always look in your local newspapers' help-wanted sections and see which agents have ads there.

You need to find agents you like working with. You may prefer agents who are fast paced, or those who are more laid back. It is entirely possible that you may never meet some, or even all, of the agents you work with. As such, you'll have to rely on your instincts to judge them as you work with them and speak to them on the phone.

As complicated as the world gets, and as competitive as recruiters are, it's somewhat surprising to know that many agreements with recruiters are done verbally. And, if you don't meet them in person, you won't even have the proverbial "handshake."

Things to Keep in Mind

Some important things to remember when dealing with recruiters:

- Fees generally run 20–30% of the annual salary that is offered and are usually negotiable. Some recruiters may not accept less than 25%. Agree on the fee up front, and preferably in writing. Include terms about when the fee is paid, and what happens if the employee is fired or quits soon after being hired.

- Oftentimes, a recruiter will ask what your company normally pays as a *finder's fee*. If they do, this is a great time to offer up a low number. Recruiters know that if you use them once, you may use them again. So they're not willing to give up a potentially lucrative relationship for a few percentage points.

- The headhunters' fees are usually paid *after a certain period of time.* This is to ensure that the candidate doesn't quit, or isn't discovered to be a disaster, immediately after being hired. Agents often request to collect their fees after 30 days. You can usually push that out to 60 or 90 days. Do not pay the fee early on the promise that you'll be credited with a refund if the new hire bails out before the agreed-upon period. Before using a headhunter, agree on the payment and guarantee terms, preferably in writing.

Reading Resumes

There are several important things to remember about reading resumes.

- Most don't tell the whole story. Assume that the resume you are reading is a reflection—but only a partial reflection—of the person you are interviewing.

- Writing a resume is difficult. The best resumes reflect the person's skills very well; poor one's omit, inflate, or misrepresent the individual. People do lie on resumes, of course, but more often, they simply do not portray accurately what they are trying to convey.

- One of your key roles as an interviewer is to carefully match the person's skills with their resume. If a series of questions from you reveals that the person is lying outright about certain skills or experience (many people lie some, but some people lie a lot), it is your duty to address this issue directly: do not hire this individual. If they can lie right at the beginning of your relationship and get away with it, they will certainly feel comfortable doing so going forward into the relationship.

- The skills on paper could be miles away from the real experience of the person. If they list "Perl" as a skill set, for example, and you really need a Perl developer to write hundreds of key scripts for you, probe their Perl experience in detail. Maybe all they did was write a couple of scripts for a friend during a lunch hour. Or were they the department's key Perl source for two years? Define your needs, then be prepared to ask about them.

- Well-written resumes have both an advantage and a disadvantage. They are easier to read and are more likely to contain action words and clearer distinctions between jobs. But these kinds of resumes will also be glossier, full of excitement and marketing material ("Was single-handedly responsible for all Y2K operations for $6 billion company") that makes it harder for you to figure out what is really true, and what is only approximately true. (It turns out the candidate was responsible for the Y2K operations of his company's cafeteria.) Be ready with your specific questions.

- When you find a candidate you like, some agents will offer to do the *reference checks* for you. While this may be a tempting way to save time, it is important to remember that since the agent has a vested interest, he may not be completely objective.

- If time permits, *meet with the recruiter in your environment* to discuss the job openings. This will help to establish a more personal relationship and give the recruiter a better feel for your environment, which in turn may enable him to find candidates who are better matched.

Using Multiple Recruiters

It is quite common, and not considered unethical, to give an assignment to multiple recruiters. As long as you can deal with working with several agents, it will increase your odds of finding the exactly right person. On the off chance that two recruiters send you the same candidate, the professional thing to do is to work with the recruiter who sent you the candidate first. (If there are two identical resumes on the fax machine, or in your e-mail in-box, use the time stamp to tell you who sent it first.)

2.8 Interviewing Candidates: How Can I Do This Well?

Interviewing and hiring are key components of your job as an IT manager. Some managers enjoy the process; they like the ability to have direct responsibility and control over who joins their team, and to have direct input into the process itself. Other managers are intimidated by the prospect and look for chances to avoid the situation. Hiring your own team is a great opportunity and a key component of managing any team, IT or otherwise.

A good interview consists of the following parts:

- **Brief introduction to the company and the job:** You should talk first and give a brief overview of the position and the company. Talk only a little: just try to set the tone for the conversation.
- **General questions:** "How did you hear about the job? Where do you work now? What type of role are you looking for?"
- **Key questions:** "Why are you leaving your current job? What is the environment like and what are your responsibilities? Why do you think you are qualified for this particular job?"
- **The technical aspects of the job:** This includes describing the job, the environment, and asking questions to ensure the candidate has the skills and expertise to meet your needs.

Telephone Screening

After screening resumes, but prior to face-to-face interviews, some managers like to do telephone interviews to narrow down the list of candidates. A quick 5- to 10-minute telephone conversation can reveal quite a bit.

For the more hands-on and technical positions, you can use a few technical questions to gauge their level of expertise. Telephone screening is ideally suited for customer service representatives (like Help Desk analysts), since it gives you some insight into their telephone manner and how they'd be interacting with customers and users.

For the less technical and more supervisory positions, you still might be able to use a brief telephone interview as a gauge to their interpersonal skills—especially if these skills are a critical part of the job requirement.

At What Level Should I Interview?

If the position reports to one of your managers, consider having that manager do the first round of interviewing, so that you only meet candidates who have passed the first stage of interviewing. This saves your time and empowers your manager. If you have several levels of staff reporting to you, you may not feel the need to be involved in the interviewing for every position in your organization. However, you should be involved in interviewing for

- Positions that report directly to you
- Positions that report to your direct reports
- Positions in your organization that are highly visible or very critical

Even if you feel you don't need to be involved in interviewing for a typical position, you may want to at least briefly meet with finalists before offers are extended.

General Interview Guidelines

Some guidelines for conducting interviews include the following:

- The candidate may be nervous or tired (especially if he's met with several others before meeting with you). Try to make him feel comfortable with a few light comments (for example: "I hate interviews, don't you?") or by asking a few easy questions (e.g., "How are you? Did you have any difficulty finding the office?").

- After you get started, see if you can get the interview away from the Q&A format, into more of a conversation or discussion. Both you and the candidate will benefit from a more relaxed exchange of information. Not every person can relax in an interview, however, and there are other factors (such as the chemistry between the two of you) that may influence the tone of the meeting. Do not overemphasize this aspect of the interview, especially for individuals whose interpersonal skills are not as critical to their success on the job as, say, their technical skills.

- Don't tell the candidate too much about what you're looking for. If you do, the smart interviewee will simply regurgitate what you told her back to you.

- More importantly, don't do all the talking! Many interviewers spend a great deal of the first interview talking. It is the candidates who should do all the talking, but they can't do so unless they are given a chance. You are there to evaluate them first; all your other responsibilities (like presenting the position, representing the company, and so on) come second.

- Avoid asking yes/no or other short-answer questions. Use questions that force the candidate to give descriptive answers. Questions that start with "how" or "why" are great for this. Make them think on their feet.

- Towards the end of the interview, always give the recruit a chance to ask her own questions. Most candidates are usually armed with a couple of standard questions for this opportunity. The smart candidate might ask you a question about something discussed in the interview to demonstrate that she was listening or is interested.

Preparing a List of Questions

Always prepare a list of questions that you can refer to during the conversation. You can, and should, ask both technical and nontechnical questions (performing a technical interview is discussed later in this chapter). The balance of questions will depend on the position you are recruiting for. For example, if you are recruiting for a project manager, you might be more concerned about the candidate's leadership and management skills than you would if you were interviewing a programmer. However, if you are involved in interviewing a programmer who reports to one of your project managers, you may not have the expertise to ask meaningful technical questions. Still, your interview in this situation can be just to evaluate the individual's background, professionalism, maturity, and personality.

Once prepared, ask the candidate what they think the key issues in their field are and how well they know them. Also ask them if they can provide a specific example that can confirm what they just said about themselves.

Nontechnical Questions

Some nontechnical questions that you can ask include:

- How was this position described to you? (This is a great way to find out if the hiring manager and you—not to mention the candidate—have the same understanding.)

- What were your responsibilities at your last job?

- What did you like/dislike at your last job?

- Tell me about the relationship you have with your current manager. Do you work well together? What would she say about you? Is she a good manager? Why do you say that?

- How would you describe your own style of working?
- Which industry trade journals do you read?
- What do you like to do when you're not at work?

What Not to Ask

Court decisions and legislative statutes have placed some areas off limits in interveiws, like race, gender, age, handicap, sexual orientation, and religion, among others. Not only should these items never be discussed in an interview, or any other job-related discussion, you cannot use them as factors in making decisions. For example, if a petite woman applies to be a PC technician, you may doubt her ability to do the lifting of equipment that the job requires. However, you cannot dismiss her out of hand. What you *may* be able to do is say to her that "the job requires you to unpack, move, and lift PC equipment that weighs up to 50 pounds; are you able to perform these tasks?"

Similarly, if the same small woman applies for an operations position in the computer room, you may be concerned about her being able to reach the tape cartridges stored on the top shelves. If she is otherwise qualified, the courts would probably tell you to hire her and invest in a step stool.

These are all very sensitive areas. Before asking any list of questions, consult with your HR or Legal department. You may be putting your company at risk of litigation.

Other Interviewers

Allow others to interview the candidate, whether it's for technical reasons or to compare personalities and demeanor. You can have your own peers interview the candidate, as well as individuals who are at peer level to the open position. You may want to have your boss meet the recruit. The Human Resources department, if they have not done the initial screening, will also be able to provide an alternative view. And if you're interviewing someone who will have management or supervisory responsibility, it is not unheard of for them to interview with some of the people who will be their direct reports.

Key Concepts for a Good Technical Interview

Technical interviews are needed to help judge if a candidate has the appropriate skill level for the job. However, it is quite common for IT managers to lack the knowledge base for conducting in-depth technical interviews. This is most frustrating if you are interviewing for a position that reports directly to you. In some cases, you can have others within the IT organization conduct technical interviews. And it is not uncommon to hire a consultant to conduct technical interviews with candidates you are interested in.

Don't be ashamed that you don't have detailed technical expertise. You are *never* going to have all the expertise that your employees do—the IT world is changing too fast. And, since you're a manager, you may no longer be spending your days doing the hands-on work you did just a few months or years ago. Find out what the key issues are for the technical area that you are interviewing for. Talk to some of your other employees—they may know some of the key topics.

Do Some Preliminary Reading

Do research on the Web or in print materials on the particular topics of concern. If it is really hot, the Web is the best source of information besides other workers in the field. Even if you don't ask specific technical questions, you can ask a candidate about important issues associated with his area of expertise. (What does he think of a particular vendor's support, or quality assurance? What does she think of competing products? What does he think of the government's antitrust action against Microsoft? What is her prediction of the future of Linux?)

Let Them Explain Technologies to You

A clever way to hide your ignorance, as well as get an education, is to ask candidates to *explain certain technologies to you.* "What is a subnet mask? What is meant by object-oriented programming? What does RAID mean? What are the pros and cons of Java versus C++?" Of course, you may not know if the candidate's answers are correct, but you'll probably be able to judge if he's just "winging it" or really has an understanding of the matter at hand. And you'll also be able to determine what type of interpersonal skills she has: can she articulate complex thoughts clearly? Does she come across as condescending?

Testing an Interviewee

You may also consider giving the employee a formal test. This could be one you develop yourself, or done with the assistance of testing software. Of course, many candidates many not like taking a test: they realize that it may show particular skill deficiencies, or they may be poor at taking tests (especially since they'll have reference material at the ready when they're actually doing their assigned work). But more importantly, the testing may create an impersonal atmosphere that places more value on specific knowledge than on the individual person and their ability to contribute, accomplish, and succeed on a team.

Also, testing only evaluates the mechanics of a skill. It doesn't evaluate the employee's aptitude with it. Nor does it evaluate the employee's other qualities—dedication, ability to juggle multiple priorities, interpersonal skills.

Nonetheless, testing can be an effective technique for some positions. Jobs that have very specific and easily quantified requirements (specific software application experience, for example, or words-per-minute typing skills) are good candidates for screening tests.

You should have a standard test with an answer key. If you have a very small department or company and you cannot develop your own test, call in a consultant to help you craft one. Having the test results readily available can also give your technical staff something concrete to discuss with the candidate—it forges an instant bond if the chemistry is there.

One final note of caution: some companies have strict guidelines *against* testing candidates. The legal implications of testing is unclear; be sure to verify with your HR department regarding what your company allows you to do.

How Do I Know When a Candidate Has the Right Skill Set for the Job?

Have a well-defined list of criteria before you start. Use this list to weed out resumes, and then use a fine-tuned version of that list to interview candidates. Bring the list to the interview itself—you are running the show, so worry more about being thorough and complete and less about appearances.

Keep in mind there are two skill sets that you are interviewing for. One is *technical skills*, and the other is *everything else*: their attitude towards work, ability to juggle multiple priorities, ability to work with others, general intelligence, resourcefulness, potential for growth, dedication and commitment, professionalism, maturity. You may also be looking for project management skills, supervisory skills, interpersonal skills, as well as the ability to write reports or give presentations.

How Do I Know When to Accept "Similar" Experience?

We always hope for the perfect candidate to be the first resume we look at and the first interview we conduct. Of course, that is rarely the case. In fact, the perfect candidate rarely comes along. You need to accept the fact that you'll probably have to compromise on some of your requirements—or you will never finish the recruiting process.

Rank Criteria

With a well-defined list of criteria for a job established *before* you go into the interview, you have a plan. As part of the definition process, you can rank each criterion in terms of importance. These rankings will vary from department to department and company to company. Some organizations rank teamwork way ahead of technical skills; others place a much higher value on technical competence than they do on the ability to work well with others.

You may find that an interviewee is a bit weaker in one area than you would've liked, but significantly stronger in another area. And, more than likely, you'll see resumes and candidates who have "similar" experience to what you're looking for. You may find that a candidate's technical expertise is weaker than you would like, but they strike you as you someone who is very bright, picks up new skills quickly on their own, and is a very hard worker. In the end, as you weigh all of these issues to make your choice, don't be surprised if you feel you're making a judgment call—you are.

Skills and Needs

Should you accept similar experience? It all depends on how similar the experience is to what you're looking for. It also depends on your needs. If you need to put someone to work on the first day, to be productive on a critical project, your definition of "similar" might be quite narrow. However, if you can afford to invest time to bring an individual up to speed, then your definition of "similar" may be more forgiving.

With your responsibility as an IT manager revolving around technology, it is easy to get caught up in specific technology experience when recruiting—hardware model numbers or software version numbers. Of course, these are important, but the technical skill set is only a portion of the qualifications.

Other Requirements That You Might Be Flexible About

- **Years of experience:** What's more important than the number of years is *what the candidate did* in those years.

- **College degree:** Perhaps this is more important for a manager, but it is less so for a technologist. And the more years *since* that college degree, the less it adds value as opposed to experience.

- **Training:** Pertinent training? Fundamentals or advanced? How long since the classes were taken? Have the skills been used out in the real world?

- **Specific hardware and software technology:** Is a dot version or two behind in software truly a disqualifier? These days, *everything* gets outdated quickly.

- **Environment size:** Whether measured in Mips, users, or number of locations.

- **Certification:** It may not show more than that they can cram and memorize to pass an exam. See later in this chapter for a separate discussion of this issue.

- **Industry experience:** Frequently, IT workers don't see enough of their company's business environment to really have a legitimate feel for the industry they're in. While similar industry experience is nice, you may want to broaden it to a more macro level: manufacturing or services, for example.

Ability to Learn

When considering prerequisite technical skills, remember that virtually everyone in IT must be at least smart enough to master new skills and adapt to changes in technologies and products on a regular basis. If you have faith that a person is smart enough to learn new skills, you may want to consider trusting that faith with someone who might have to take some time to come up to speed on the specific technology set in your environment.

Example

For example, if you're looking for an HP-UX administrator, you might consider someone with skills in IBM's AIX to be quite close enough. You may figure that if they mastered the IBM product, they could certainly master the HP product in short order. On the flip side, if the ideal candidate does not have any Unix skills, but is a genius with IBM's mainframe MVS software, you might be concerned about investing the time and training to bring this individual up to speed in mastering Unix. Then again, there's no reason to suspect that an MVS genius couldn't become a Unix genius. It all depends on your tolerance and ability to allow those skills to develop.

　If you like a candidate, but have concerns that his experience isn't similar enough, share your thoughts with him directly. "I like your background, Pat, you have excellent experience, you'd be perfect for the job, but I'm concerned that you don't have enough experience with X technology." At the very least, by doing this, you're being honest with the candidate and letting them know why there is a chance they won't get the job. More importantly, you're giving the candidate an opportunity to respond. For all you know, Pat may have something in his background that wasn't mentioned on his resume that will make you feel a lot more comfortable about his experience or about his ability to compensate for the gap.

Certification: How Do I Know Its Worth?

The IT world is going a little crazy with certification. Chances are that if you've heard of a particular hardware or software product, the vendor is offering some type of certification for it. Certification really hit the front pages with Novell's Certified Netware Engineer (CNE). In the late 1980s and early 1990s, everyone wanted to be a CNE. To many it seemed like the passkey to dream jobs. However, by the mid and late 1990s, a new term was coined: "paper CNE." This term referred to people who took crash courses, studied intensively, and passed the CNE exams, but had virtually no experience to go with their new accreditation on their resume. Novell's restructuring of their certification program helped to deal with this.

　Vendors must monitor their certification programs like the Federal Reserve monitors interest rates to balance between too much and too little growth. Vendors don't want their certification program to be so easy that it has no value or cachet, but at the same time, they don't want the programs to be so hard and elitist that too few people are able to pass the tests.

Test-Taking Skills

Whether it was in high school, technical school, or the department of motor vehicles, we all learned that a passed exam only represents knowledge at that particular moment—which may only in itself represent the ability to study prior to the exam. The same can be said of technical certification.

If someone is certified, you know what their knowledge set was at the moment they were tested, which could mean they have the ability to study very hard, or a steel-trap memory, or they actually have information that was ingrained during years of experience. While many IT managers recognize this, many also look for certifications on resumes. Similarly, many managers looking for programmers prefer individuals with four-year college degrees even though a college degree may add no value to a programmer's skill set.

Value of Commitment

One aspect of accreditation that is often overlooked is its representation of commitment and persistence. Getting certified usually means passing a series of exams. For many, it also means taking a series of classes. Doing this takes time, energy, and motivation. When you see someone who has been certified, perhaps the first thought you should have is "here's someone who can stick with something, and see it through to the end." Not a bad trait for someone who will be managing projects.

When you see a candidate with certification, be sure to consider *how long it's been since that accreditation was obtained* and *to what degree those skills have been used since.* If required, ask them if they have kept their certification current with continuing classes and exams.

Checking the Value of a Certification

There are a number of steps you can take ot check the value of a certification:

- Speak with your own network of contacts.
- Contact the technical area's association—if there is one. They will talk about the value of certification, and they might be also able to point you to a source that can either verify or deny their claims.
- Contact the product manufacturer. Companies like Lotus and Microsoft have extensive certification programs and local contacts. Again, they will tout its

benefits, but might also be able to point you to specific individuals who benefited from or are looking for those skills.

- Scan the classifieds and the Web. Are other employers asking for this in their ads? If the certification appears often, that is a good sign.

Education: What Should I Look For?

Education is one of those things we always look for—because that's the way we've always done it. However, when you see someone like Bill Gates, who dropped out of college, you think: "Hmm, maybe I should re-evaluate this criteria . . ."

When looking at education, consider three things:

- Type of education
- Direct value to the job
- Indirect value to the job

Type of Education

As a rule, the more hands-on and technical a position, the less *direct* value a typical four-year degree has. This is even truer for a graduate degree. Is a Java programmer with an MBA *a better programmer* than a Java programmer who only finished high school? Some might argue that the programmer with only a high-school degree might be better since all those years went towards actual experience, rather than the more theoretical academic experience.

Indirect Value to the Job

A college-educated employee can provide several important *indirect* benefits to a position. Pursuing a four-year degree can be a difficult and complex task; it can show the individual's willingness to make a commitment and follow through. It can be a financial challenge; many people have to earn a portion of their college education themselves. It can be intellectually challenging; a person may be pursuing a programming career now, but 10 years ago chose biochemistry as a major in college.

At the minimum, you should seek a high-school degree for virtually all positions. This should at least give you an indication (although no guarantee) that the individual has the fundamental skills to operate in a job (reading, writing, basic math, etc.). As you move up the education ladder (two- and four-year degrees, graduate degrees, etc.), look to it as an indication not necessarily of a higher degree of technical skill, but of more skilled analysis, comprehension, and verbal skills.

Direct Value to the Job

On the other hand, a college education is of more value to a position that involves supervisory or management responsibilities. As a general rule, actual experience and skill should always carry more weight than any educational requirements. And even for someone who has significant educational credentials, the value of that education generally decreases with time.

The most important point here is: how frequently does the candidate learn new things? The world and the marketplace we work in change quickly and significantly. Has this candidate shown the ability and interest to learn new tools and skills as they become the new standards? Lifelong learners are often the most productive employees in an organization.

Business-Related Degrees

If their degree is in a business-related discipline, it may indicate that they've been exposed to many ideas and concepts that they will encounter to various extents within IT. This exposure may be valuable for someone who does systems analysis or is involved with management.

Hard Sciences–Related Degrees

If their degree is in one of the hard sciences, it *may* show that they have a stronger ability for logical and analytical thinking.

Soft Sciences–Related Degrees

If the person has a degree in one of the social sciences (e.g., psychology), they *may* have greater skills in user-oriented activities (support, training, designing interfaces, etc.).

Famous Schools

A well-recognized and prestigious school is nice, but don't let the reputation overwhelm you. Pay careful attention to the questions you brought to the interview and focus on the candidate's answers. If a candidate seems to be name-dropping his well-known school frequently, it may indicate that reputation is important to him, and he has high status expectations of the job and the company—issues that may be at odds with your environment. He may also be relying more on reputation than actual experience in his background: ask pointed questions to see if it is all show, or real meat, that he is bringing to the table.

Certification Issues

Many candidates now list on their resume individual technical courses they have taken—even if they haven't received any certification. Depending on the content of the courses and how recently they were taken, this type of education may be more important than a traditional degreed program. Periodic classes may indicate that they've been able to keep up with technology.

Other Education Issues

Here are other issues related to education that you may need to consider:

- Education requirements vary widely from company to company. Find out if your company has a minimum education requirement.

- In days of low employment and high demand for skilled workers—especially high-tech workers—standards are often lowered. But be careful: those standards were often created for very legitimate reasons. If you are considering getting a standard lowered or waived for a candidate, start building your case during the interview itself. Have the candidate (directly or indirectly) help you explain why he should be hired in spite of his lacking a specific requirement.

- If the degree is from a foreign country, get the candidate to evaluate the school for you—and then verify her evaluation.

Team Interviewing

Some companies require that candidates be interviewed by a certain number of the members of a team. Others have a more informal policy, but strongly encourage various members of a team to engage in the personnel selection process.

There is less to lose in team interviewing than it may appear, and much more to gain. It appears to cost a lot—it is expensive to have multiple employees in one room, performing what is not (yet) a revenue-generating activity. Time and money are being chewed up.

In fact, the costs of getting the right people on your team are worth every penny. It is difficult to quantify, but every manager who has ever had serious personnel clashes to deal with knows well that any methods of avoiding a problem of this magnitude are worth a lot of time and money. The right people—not only the right skill sets—could determine whether your team thrives or crashes. There are two key positives to team interviews:

1. Multiple people interviewing a candidate will provide a glimpse of how this person relates to the other members of the team. If there is an instant clash of personalities, you have discovered an issue before all the papers are signed. It does not mean this person should definitely not be hired, but it does mean you have a significant issue to deal with. On the other hand, the chemistry may be very good right away for one candidate and not for the others. This is a plus. Not the only criterion, remember, but an important one.

2. Other people can ask questions you did not think of and see things you cannot see. In addition, candidates have less time to prepare their answers when they are faced with multiple interviewers, which generally leads to more truthful answers.

Candidates are nervous on interviews to begin with, and if they feel they are being double-teamed (or more), they could really start to sweat. Unless it is your intent to see the candidate squirm, you should make efforts to try to put the candidate at ease. The best way to soften the sense of intimidation and tension is to have your staff adopt as relaxed a posture (figuratively) as possible. A few light-hearted comments to start can help put the candidate at ease.

2.9 Making an Offer: How Do I Know How Much to Offer for an IT Position?

When you start to recruit for an opening, you should have a salary range in mind. This range can come from several key sources of salary data:

- The HR department of your company
- Recruiters
- Classified ads
- Web and computer magazine salary surveys
- Other individuals in your company doing similar work
- Salary of the previous individual in that job
- Salaries of the staff members, if any, that report to this position

Before Making the Offer

Make sure that HR and whatever other upper management individual(s) need to approve the final offer are in agreement on the specified range. You'll know if your range is too low based on the response you get to your recruiting efforts. If only a handful of people apply, you're probably offering too little. Although it is not uncommon for someone to change jobs for the same salary, most people expect at least a 10% increase. This increase compensates them for the risk that is inherent whenever someone changes a job, but also entices them to take your job. Nonetheless, you can't offer more than you, or your company, can afford to pay. And you are probably not the only person who decides that figure.

If the last individual in the position was a poor performer, that might be justification to convince yourself, HR, and the powers-that-be that you need to offer more money to attract better talent. An extended search that doesn't find any reasonable candidates can also be a justification for reviewing the salary range.

Using Agencies

Be careful when you share the salary range with any agencies you use. Since their commission is based on the annual salary, they have a vested interest in placing someone at the highest possible salary. Also, it makes their job easier if there is as much money as possible. If the recruiter winces when you tell her the approved salary range, don't take it too personally—she's just doing her job.

Other Ideas Besides More Money

Invariably, the candidate you like the most will be the one that stretches the envelope of your salary range. If you don't think you'll be able to attract this person with your salary offer, there are a few things you can try:

- Consider promising a salary review (not a guaranteed *increase,* but a *review*) six months after the person starts. Don't commit to a specific increase amount (after all, the candidate may not work out, or the company may change its salary ceiling). But the chance of an increase in six months may be just what you need to attract the person. (Make sure to get approval from HR/management before you promise anything.)

- Make the position and environment sound as exciting and attractive as possible. (Naturally, remain truthful about it. Making something exciting does not mean lying about it.) You want the person to be as motivated to take the job as you are in offering it to him; that will make finding a middle ground much easier.

- Get the candidate to look at the entire package. Today's competitive IT environment has spawned a wide range of noncash incentives that can be far more lucrative than "mere money." Emphasize those to the candidate. Does the position have *bonus potential?* Make sure the candidate includes that figure in her consideration. Does your company offer a *stock purchase plan? A profit-sharing plan? A matching 401(k) plan?* Also make sure that the candidate is fully aware of your company's *benefits programs*; health and insurance benefits can have very important positive tax benefits. *Stock options* should also be clearly specified if you are making them part of your offer. Originally a benefit only for the upper reaches of a corporation, stock options have now become a part of many workers' pay plans throughout the ranks of an organization. Companies are offering employees a more direct participation in the profits of the organization as a whole. Is it a *good working environment,* with little demands for overtime and beepers? If so, it could be a key selling point. What about *flextime?* Or *telecommuting?* Or the *on-site gym?*

2.10 The Human Resources Department: What Is Their Role in the Process?

Because recruiting for an IT position usually involves a lot of technical skills and resumes with acronyms and buzzwords, many Human Resources departments that normally lead recruiting efforts for all other departments will take a back seat and let you drive. But this is not always the case. Talk to HR and discuss the following:

- Is there an approved list of recruiters to use? What is the policy on their finder's fees?
- Can I locate/use my own recruiters?
- Who is responsible for placing ads in newspapers and on Web sites? Who pays for the ads?
- Will HR do the initial screening of applicants' resumes?
- Who should be the point of contact for agencies and applicants?
- Who does background and reference checks?

As indicated, many HR departments recognize that IT recruiting is a special skill. Accordingly, they may ask you to take as large a role as possible. If this is the case in your company (and do not assume it is), HR may only want to get involved as part of the very final round of interviews, and to discuss benefits and make the formal offer.

"In-House" Recruiters

Alternatively, some large companies that rely heavily on technology may have an individual assigned specifically for recruiting for IT positions. Ideally, this person looks at resumes for certain types of technical skills and experiences, and can explain to recruiters, in sufficient detail, the requirements of the positions. This person, for example, understands that Novell and Netware are essentially synonymous terms, and that Windows 9x is not a distinct and separate product from Windows 95 and Windows 98. An in-house HR recruiter like this can save you an enormous amount of time and effort. On the other hand, if he is busy recruiting candidates for several IT managers, as well as you, you might feel that things would be more effective if you did the recruiting yourself. Be careful not to run afoul of HR. The best way to do this is to have your role and

Are "Profile" or "Personality" Tests Useful?

"I have found these tests—which we call 'Profile tests,' by the way, because 'personality tests' is *not* what they are—to be an extremely useful hiring and management tool. Here's some things to consider if you are going to try them:

- The "softer" aspects of a person can be difficult to evaluate in a two-hour interview process. These tests often reveal information that we would not have figured out until later, after the person was hired.

- While these tests are very accurate about some items, *the final decision is still up to you* on how to use the information they provide. They measure raw intelligence power well, for example. However, not every job needs to be performed by a very intelligent person; at the same time, some jobs are complex, analysis-driven positions that require high IQ power just to understand. These tests can help you make that determination.

- When we decided to use these tests, we tried them on *everyone* in the company first. We found them to be very good predictors of corporate behavior.

- We use them on the *second interview*; the first interview is a general one, where we try to keep our commitment level and the candidates' to a reasonable level. Sometimes, despite all the paper, it only takes a few minutes for a person and a company to figure out they are not a good match. Profile tests (which take about 45 minutes and are administered by an outside firm) are done once the first hurdle has been passed."

—Cathy Thompson
Cofounder and Principal, Thompson, Doyle, Hennessey & Everest,
commercial real estate firm, Boston, Massachusetts

---

theirs defined up front, before ads are written and candidates brought in. If you're going to expand or decrease your role in the process, make sure they are OK with it.

Company Differences

The HR department's role varies radically from company to company. Some companies have active Human Resources departments that are involved in every stage of the hiring and firing process. Other companies (especially small companies, or companies that are just getting started) do not even have a formal HR department. The function is performed by one or more individuals, along with their other responsibilities.

Even companies with HR departments, however, do not act the same when it comes to hiring people. Some departments run the whole process and call you in when your expertise and decision making are required; in other companies, you have to do most of the work yourself and get what help you can from your HR department. Figure out where your HR department is on the above scale, and plan your hiring procedures accordingly.

The methods HR departments use to evaluate potential employees also varies widely. Screening employees is a difficult task; getting the right individual with the correct technical skills in the very tight labor market of the last several years is a daunting task.

Partially to save time, and partially to increase the long-term value of their hiring procedures, HR departments have begun using a range of different tools. Personality tests (see sidebar), competency exams, job shadowing—these techniques all are designed to make the match between the employer and the potential employee a happier one.

2.11 Career Paths: What Are Current Career Paths for Myself and My Employees?

The nice thing about IT as a career choice is that it allows you to choose a variety of professional paths. Sometimes, of course, having too many choices makes things more complicated than having too few.

Within the IT industry, you'll have to make various selections as your career progresses: consultant versus permanent employee, operations versus development (see page 4), management versus hands on. Before trying to figure out the appropriate career path, let's examine each of these choices in more detail.

Consultant vs. Permanent Employee

Consultants, also called "contractors," are becoming increasingly popular within information technology. The reason to choose one working style over another can be summarized as follows: which is more important to you, *security* or *freedom?* By that, we mean: do you prefer the security of a full-time job, with its attendant benefits, salary, and defined work, or do you prefer the freedom of choosing your own projects, potentially higher income, and a wider range of projects? Not every full-time person is chained to one project, and not every consultant is free to pick and choose her own projects. And each style has its serious negative sides. Let's examine the two options more closely.

Why Companies Even Hire Consultants

There are a variety of reasons why companies hire consultants to perform tasks full-time employees could also do:

- IT is a very project-centric function. Companies often bring in consultants to supplement existing staff only for specific projects. Consultants can be brought in, used for the length of the project, and then let go. Permanent employees are not so expendable.

- In this regard, consultants can often be a cheaper alternative to using a permanent employee. While the short-term cost of a consultant often exceeds that of a full-time person, when all the costs are factored in (salary, benefits, equipment costs, costs of not having that employee on another project), the consultant can be a less expensive option.

- Consultants often have specialized skill sets that full-timers do not have (and may not want to acquire). Often consultants are experts in very esoteric areas, fields that few professionals venture into because the demand is not there. (Of course, consultants can also be people with skill sets that are in very high demand; this volume guarantees them work and provides them with the personal freedom they often want.)

Different Types of Consultants

Consultants come in many working styles. There are consultants who work on the same project, at the same site, for such long periods that they run afoul of the IRS, who has a list of 20 criteria you must fulfill in order to define yourself as a consultant for tax reasons. Most consultants, however, move around a lot. They may not travel across the country or internationally (although many do), but they often move from project to project and company to company.

The Consultant Lifestyle

As a result, consultants have to get used to a somewhat nomadic lifestyle. Their assignments frequently last only a short time and may end with little or no notice. On the other hand, it is not unheard of for an assignment, which was initially defined as "3–6 months," to last several years, and eventually lead to a permanent position as a hired employee.

Many contractors enjoy the opportunities that consulting brings: consulting allows them to experience many different types of environments and work assignments, and their status as a consultant allows them to ignore most of the petty annoyances of office politics. On the downside, many companies often treat consultants as second-class citizens in terms of the meetings they are invited to and office and cubicle space. Consultants are rarely ever given training and usually have to pick up new skills on their own. The possibility of getting laid off at any time puts significant uncertainty into a consultant's income stream, but that worry can be offset by a pay schedule that offers more money, and a work schedule that offers greater control over their own destiny.

Management vs. Hands On: Do You Have to Be a Manager to Advance or Make Good Money?

In the old days, those of *Father Knows Best* and *Leave It to Beaver,* the only way to advance within a company (or make better money) was to work your way up the corporate ladder into a management function. That is no longer the case in IT. It is now very possible to have a successful and lucrative career in IT without being a supervisor or manager, without having to worry about budgets, and without having to wear a suit and tie. By continuing to master new skill sets, IT staffers are finding the market and their companies will continue to reward them—even if their office space never grows beyond a cubicle.

Some companies are instituting a formal "dual-ladder" system that allows individuals throughout the company to advance their careers without following a management track. "Senior Technical Leader" might be a title for an individual with important technical skills and long years of experience who has no interest in managing others.

Alternatively, just like any other department, IT does need management. Whether it is a staff of programmers or PC technicians, someone has to set priorities, resolve conflicts, conduct performance reviews, and ensure that the assignments are being completed. Obviously, managing requires a certain set of skills. For whatever reason, many who have excelled at the hands-on technical roles within IT have trouble making the transition to a supervisory role (probably because they have not read this book yet).

As a result, many companies look for a "hands-on manager." Frequently, a hands-on manager's day-to-day activities and assignments will be very similar to those she is managing. But, additionally, she will also be responsible for serving as a leader.

Many More Choices

The categories and choices described above are the traditional ones in many corporate IT departments. However, there are many other possibilities outside these boundaries. For example, instead of working for a corporate IT department, you may consider working for an IT hardware and software vendor. You may also consider working for a small start-up organization where a lack of resources requires that everyone be able and willing to do everything. Some people thrive in environments that are relative free-for-alls, with everyone responsible for everything. When the chaos settles down and the product is shipped and the marketing plan is defined, those people move on, and those who enjoy more definition and organization move in.

Choosing a Path

Careers last a long time. It's silly to assume that the choices that are right for you today will be the right choices for you 20, 30, and 40 years from now. Fortunately, IT is such a dynamic and growing field that it allows you to re-evaluate your choices and change directions over and over again.

Things to Consider

There are many things to think about when you consider your future within IT. You should give thought to

- Where you think your skills lie
- What types of work activities you enjoy doing
- What your personal goals are

It is not uncommon for some of these things to be at odds with each other. A top-notch programmer may have his eye on the VP's corner office. However, his programming skills are not going to be enough to take him there. He'll need to have project management skills, communication skills, maturity, and professionalism. Similarly, someone who enjoys doing reports and presentations, and determining how to juggle priorities, may not enjoy a position as a database security administrator.

Typical Lengths of Service

Think about the job(s) you've had and the people you have known during that time. Two to three years is a common length of time to be in one IT position. It is not a *rule*, of course, and it should not be an *expectation*, but change happens so quickly in the corporate world these days that typical lengths of stay in one position are shorter than they used to be.

How Can an IT Manager Affect the Career Paths of Employees?

As an IT manager, it is an important part of your job to coach and counsel your staff with their career path. It is important that you consider your staff's career path interests when making assignments. This will allow you to make more effective assignments, and you'll be considered a better manager for nurturing their aspirations. Of course, you're likely to be faced with someone who has unattainable goals. You may have a staffer with weak technical skills who has hopes of being a network engineer. Or you may have someone with horrendous interpersonal skills who aspires to be a supervisor.

It is important to remember that, ultimately, everyone is responsible for their own career path. However, as a manager, you have the opportunity to work with your employees and give them constructive feedback and assessment of their skills and potential, and help them formulate their goals. With your assignments, you can give them exposure to various functions and disciplines, challenge them in different areas, and watch them either rise to your expectations or lose interest. It is in this role that you have the opportunity to set yourself apart as a manager, to help people make decisions that will affect them for many years into the future.

For Yourself

IT management is an exploding field—you have chosen (or found yourself in) one of the hottest careers out there. Your career options include CIO, Director, VP of IT, and CTO. Your employees have your job, of course, as an option. But many companies are also installing a formal technical track to parallel the management track. Consider your career, and those of your employees, carefully. But don't stress out about it. There are many more employment options available for technical professionals, and all the projections only point to their options increasing over time.

2.12 Further References

Web Sites

- *www.salary.com* (salary survey data)
- *www.tekcheck.com* (candidate skills testing)
- *www.wageweb.com* (salary survey data)

Articles and Books

- Bultinck, Christina, *The Recruiter's Bible*, Infokey, 1998.
- Dawson, Charlie K., *The Complete Guide to Technical Recruiting*, Management Advantage, 1999.
- Fein, Richard, *101 Hiring Mistakes Employers Make . . . and How to Avoid Them*, Impact Publishers, 2000.

- Jaffe, Brian D., "Checking Up," *Computerworld*, June 9, 1997.

- Jaffe, Brian D., "Be a Signpost for Employee Career Paths," *PC Week*, June 21, 1999.

- Schreyer, Ray, and John Lewis McCarter, Jr., *The Employer's Guide to Recruiting on the Internet*, Impact Publishers, 1998.

- Ulfelder, Steve, "So, When Do I Start?" *Computerworld*, January 10, 2000.

- Vaas, Lisa, Anne Chen, and Matt Hicks, "Web Recruiting Takes Off," *PC Week*, January 17, 2000.

Managing Your IT Team

CHAPTER THREE

What You Will Learn

- How to keep your employees focused on the right tasks
- Ways to help your employees avoid burnout
- How to know when your employees need training
- How to conduct meaningful and effective performance reviews
- How to develop an effective IT strategy
- How to keep your IT department central to the company's operations

Introduction

Even with the advanced functionality available in today's hardware and software, it still comes down to the human factor that is the biggest influence on how effectively technology is put to use in your environment. These people are your staff. They are the ones who will select, implement, configure, monitor, and manage the technology. The technology products in your environment behave in a fairly predictable manner, but people don't. Managing a staff is an art, not a science. Become good at it, and it becomes your most valuable skill, and your staff becomes the most valued part of IT in your organization. Fail to master it, and you'll see every one of your department's goals and objectives become an uphill battle.

3.1 Tasks: How Do I Keep My Employees Focused on the Right Ones?

IT Managers must clearly set priorities, explain the company mission, and communicate often with their team.

Priorities

One of the most important, but often unnoticed, functions of a manager is to set priorities, such as allocating staffing and funding to various projects. Employees who spend months at a time working on a project often wonder what exactly it is that their manager does. In truth, the manager is doing one of the most important parts of his job by deciding which projects get worked on, when they need to start and finish, and what resources are assigned to them. A manager's real worth is in his ability to set goals and objectives and to set priorities and make decisions to achieve them.

Doing this means managing your staff and your team so that their work echoes your priorities. A manager's merit is often found in his staff's work. Of course, your decisions and priorities may be totally off base. Or they may be 100% on target. But if you fail to manage your staff well, your goals and objectives will never be realized.

Company Mission

A second method of keeping your employees focused is to clearly outline the company's mission, vision, and values. These should not be your responsibility as an IT manager to define and articulate: someone else should do that for you (and the rest of the company). But once your company has agreed upon a mission statement, communicate it with your staff. Make it clear how this mission, and the vision statement that details *how* you are going to achieve that mission, directly affects the actions of every employee.

Company values are the final means you should use to keep your employees on the right track. If your company has not made its values clear, ask your management to do so. Again, defining and communicating values are not your job; you can participate if a companywide committee is formed, but you should not have to come up with these on your own. "Company values" are defined by the entire company and can be very useful guides in determining employee behavior.

In addition to communicating the company's mission, goals, and values to your team, it is also vital that you share with them the goals and values of the IT department, which should reflect your own goals and values.

Communicate with Your Team

First and foremost, you need to communicate your vision to your staff. They should understand where you want to go and the plan you have for getting there. Both are important. You don't want to be the manager who makes the trains run on time, but doesn't know what to put in the boxcars. Similarly, you don't want to be known as being a blue sky visionary who doesn't know how to turn vision into reality.

The communication of your goals and priorities to your team is vital. The way you communicate them will vary with the project's scope. A two-year project to implement an enterprise resource planning (ERP) application will require different communication than managing a weekend effort to relocate your computer room.

Here are some guidelines when talking to your team:

- Make sure they understand the overall objective and goal. Explain it in practical terms: For example, implementing a new accounts payable system might include eliminating all manual processes, reducing turnaround time to 24 hours, and ensuring that no unauthorized payments are made.

- Explain how you envision achieving the goal. You don't have to offer too much detail, especially on a large project, but you should have some thoughts, visions, and ideas you can articulate as a kind of road map.

- Encourage questions and input. There are two reasons why you should do this: Asking for your staff's input (and taking it seriously) will make your team feel like a part of the decision-making process; they will work better and harder on a process they feel a part of. And secondly, they are a lot closer to the work than you are—they'll be the first to recognize a dead end.

- If the goal or plan is especially challenging, or perhaps it deviates somewhat from the norm, you'll have to be that much more motivational and excited when you communicate with the team.

- Ask questions of the team to ensure that they have an appropriate understanding of the project. For example: "How do you think we should start? Where do you see danger zones? What are the key milestones? What kinds of resources do you think we will need?"

- Listen carefully. Notice the staff's comments, tone, and body language. Use these as clues to determine if your team is behind you. Make sure everyone feels free to air any doubts or concerns. One technique is to go around the table at the end of each meeting and to ask each member to express any concerns they have, and then address them accordingly.

- Meet regularly to review. Meeting frequencies might vary depending on the project work at hand. Weekly and monthly meetings are common. During critical times, it is not uncommon to have daily meetings. You can have too many meetings, or too few—it depends on the project. Try to establish a rhythm that people can work around; if you establish a meeting time of every Friday morning, the team will work throughout the week with that event in mind. If it is daily, people will work towards that event.

Project management meetings (which are discussed in more detail in Chapter 5) should have three functions:

1. Clarifying the purpose and priorities of the project
2. Determining the status of the project
3. Addressing any concerns, problems, or delays that come up

However, as a manager, you want to get more out of the meeting. You want to use it to gauge the team's enthusiasm and to remotivate them as needed. You may need to adjust resource allocations, deadlines, and so on as needs warrant.

Be Prepared for Radical Changes

The first law of project management is that *projects do not go as planned*. Almost everything will change, from the scope, to the time lines, to the staff size and makeup. You should take these changes in stride and, if possible, learn to anticipate and welcome changes. Naturally, this is easier said than done, but today's rapidly evolving marketplace makes the ability to integrate change a critical skill for both managers and nonmanagers alike.

Optimism and pessimism are both very contagious. If your team sees that you're confident, they will become more confident, too. If you appear intimidated and discouraged by setbacks and problems, so will your staff.

Be as Clear as Possible about Your Real Priorities

Remember that it takes more than just *saying* something is a priority for everyone to realize that it *is* a priority. If coding a specific interface is a critical task for a larger project, you have to say so. But also remember that your actions can dilute your words. If the status of the interface barely gets mentioned during staff meetings, even though you say it is a priority, you'll be sending mixed signals. You can demonstrate the task's importance by focusing on it during meetings, reallocating additional resources to it, sacrificing lesser priorities for it, and so on.

3.2 Burnout: How Do I Help My Employees Avoid It?

With IT being so critical to today's organizations, the demands on the staff can be enormous. Glassy-eyed programmers, cases of Jolt soda, sleeping bags under desks, and 3 AM pizza deliveries are becoming all too routine. This is a major issue in IT. Reasons that it is such a big deal now include the following:

- The tasks are hard, complicated, and intense. And the solutions to the problems are often hard, complicated, and intense.

- In this coming digital world the workplace is often 24/7, and the demands are nonstop. The technology allows people to work 24 hours a day, squeezing in time for sleep only when the body refuses to stay awake.

- Also, the lure of a complex technical challenge often excites people to work 20 hours a day. (In the early days of developing the Macintosh, Steve Jobs handed out T-shirts that read: "Working 90 hours a week and loving it.")

- Unlike in the days of piece-part labor, the work of IT today is not measured in units produced per unit of time. So there are no clear external indicators of when the work is "complete." ("The IT job is one where you get an 'F' if you fail but only a 'C' if you succeed—this stuff is *supposed* to work, right?" Bill Gates, *Business @ the Speed of Thought*, p. 322.)

Highly energized and motivated employees may not even realize the condition they are getting themselves into. While it may be tempting to push your staff, or allow them to push themselves, to the limit, it is important to remember that you won't get much work out of them once they've hit that wall. There are a number of steps you can take to avoid employee burnout.

Make Your Employees Aware of the Problem

Often people most susceptible to burnout are the ones not aware of the problem. They work like dogs for two years and then crash. Bring it up in your weekly team meeting. (You *do* have a weekly team meeting, right? If you don't, you definitely need to start.)

Outline the Prices Employees Can Pay

When making them aware of the problem, outline the prices that burnout brings:

- Deterioration of health
- Problems at home
- Loss of job

The short-term gains for working weekends for two years in a row do not outweigh the long-term losses of any of the above.

Deal with the Situation

As their manager, you need to be more aware of the problem and to take steps to monitor and avoid the situation:

1. Be very clear about your performance and productivity expectations regarding your employees. Define clear measures and metrics and communicate them clearly and often. Get real commitments from your employees regarding time lines and deliverables. And make sure they feel safe in telling you when your expectations are unrealistic.

2. Be very conscious of the levels of effort all of your team members are putting out. And do not think in abstract, "absolute value" numbers, either. A 10-hour day may not seem like a big deal to you, but it can be an enormous commitment for a single parent or a person just coming off working two demanding projects.

3. Spread the effort around. The amount of IT work is endless—as a manager, you have a responsibility to your company and your employees to carefully allocate work across the board. Certainly people have different work outputs, just as they have different working and communication styles. But your job is to consider the team as a whole, each person as an important part of that whole, and get the jobs done within that context.

4. Make changes in personnel to reflect the needs of the jobs your team must perform. Need more people? Ask for them—and do so with concrete, numerical evidence of why you need them. Is one person verging on burning out because the company has overworked her? Shift that person's responsibilities. Is one person over his head in this job? Look for other places within the company that this person can contribute. In general, the IT world in the early 2000s is not for the faint of heart.

5. Be aware of how much different people can give. Some employees can only deliver 40 hours' worth of work in a week, even if they are at their desk 60 hours. Others can easily double their efforts—for short times—in response to simple requests.

Often, running at top speed is not the fastest way to get there. Be sensitive to what motivates your employees, as well as their needs and limitations. Recognize that people can only be pushed (or even push themselves) so far. Recognize when they can be pushed further, and when you have to insist they take a break. Do this well, and you'll be rewarded with a far more productive and motivated team.

3.3 Training: How Do I Know When My Employees Need It?

Training is always an issue for managers. While they know that it's a perk that employees like, and it improves their skills, they are also concerned about its cost, the employee being away from his full-time responsibilities, and the fear that the employee will use the newly acquired skill to seek another job elsewhere. On the other hand, a few days or a week at a training class can serve as a respite, to avoid burnout for a hard-working employee, as well as increase his skill set.

However, since learning new skills is an inherent part of working in IT, providing training is an important part of managing an IT staff. There are so many IT classes being offered on some topics that it wouldn't be difficult to have someone spend more time at training classes than they do at work. Of course, that's not really practical. So as a manager you have to balance a few items when doling out training:

- Cost
- Need
- Employee morale
- Scheduling demands

Cost

There are two issues involved here: the cost of the training itself, and the cost of having the employee away from her full-time responsibilities. Often, the second item far outweighs the first. The expenses for an employee to attend a training class vary greatly, of course; some classes are offered locally or are on-line, and may be three hours in length. But many training options now include cross-country travel, which requires hotel, rental car, and travel expenses that can inflate the cost of the class by a factor of two or more.

Despite those variances, the real cost issue is often the expense of having an employee be away from work for a period of time. Can you spare this individual for an entire week? Sometimes people can be replaced with contractors, in which case the costs are fairly easily measured. But other times, some of your other employees or people from other departments need to fill in; the "cost" of these solutions, while not always visible, is often much higher than a week in a hotel.

Need

What is the short- and long-term value of this kind of training for an employee? Often the needs are well defined: Joe needs an NT administrator class because he will back up Maria while she is on vacation. But other times, the issue gets cloudy: Mark wants to take an advanced Java programming class, but that is not his exact responsibility right now and it is not clear that the company is going to be using Java anyway.

"Need" may appear to be the clear deciding factor, but often the value of taking a training class is not clear. If that is the case, you need to use some of the other criteria listed in this section to help you decide whether or not to agree to have an employee take a training class.

Employee Morale

Many employees view training as a reward. It provides them with concrete resume-enhancing skills, sometimes lets them "get out of the house" by traveling to a warm spot in midwinter, and often allows them to interact with professionals with the same interests and questions that they have. Granting someone a training course—or even suggesting it yourself—can be an excellent way to motivate employees. Both you and your employee need to monitor skill sets to make sure they are current and useful; some kind of training in today's IT world is really necessary.

Scheduling Demands of Having Staff Out of the Office

This is probably the most difficult issue to deal with. Many of your own staff will find the issue difficult, rightly recognizing that a week away from the office means a week of catching up when they get back. Who will cover for them? If they are overburdened right now (as many IT people are), how are they ever going to make up for a lost week's worth of work?

The answer is pretty simple: evaluate the short-term costs versus the long-term gains. See the above three items; if the direct costs are not overwhelming, if the employee (and your department) needs the training, and if their morale will be improved, go for it—and have them go for it.

How Do You Know When Your Employees Need Training?

There are three principal ways:

- They tell you. IT people are deluged by training class offers, and by situations where they are aware of their technical shortcomings in one area or another. Asking the boss for a class or two is a common request. (Asking for a week-long class on a cruise ship in the Bahamas is less common, but not unheard of.) You should consider an employee's request for training as a positive indication that they are interested in learning and doing more for the company. (It could also be an indication that they like being out of the office. Methods for dealing with this issue are discussed in the section above.)

- Your customers tell you. The IT department's customers can be a variety of groups: they can certainly be outside customers, but they can also be (and only are, for some companies) internal people. In either case, if you have been proactive about soliciting feedback from your customers about what their IT needs are, you will hear about specific technical needs that your department cannot provide without either (1) getting more training for current employees or (2) hiring someone else to do the job. You *will* face this situation—the IT world is too demanding and too changeable.

- You find out on your own because you are a proactive manager. You like to address issues before they become problems. If you do this, you will save yourself tremendous time, money, and effort over the long term. You will anticipate your department's needs for Java programmers and start running the ads months in advance, knowing that talent is hard to find. You'll budget for a new Help Desk support rep early in the cycle, before the seasonal sales cycle kicks in and all the calls come in. And you will send your people for training in Windows 2000 network administration, for example, months before the project to upgrade is even approved.

What about Certification?

Most IT managers don't have the luxury of sending people to training just for the sake of training. As such, few IT departments are willing to sponsor their employees for training that leads to vendor or technology certification. This is simply because managers know that some of the classes in a certification program these days are fillers—they are of little or no use to a specific employee's job responsibilities. Of course, there are exceptions. Some managers may use certification as a way of rewarding highly valued employees, or for those employees whose responsibilities are very specialized. Of course, sending an employee to the requisite classes doesn't guarantee certification; the employee still has to pass the exam.

What If the Employee Takes a Training Class, and Then Uses His New-Found Skills to Find Another Job?

This is a common concern. Many companies have a policy that says an employee has to sign an agreement to reimburse the cost of training if she resigns within *X* months of taking a class. Of course, many employers and employees are hesitant about even making such an agreement because it creates somewhat of a nontrusting, nonsupportive relationship. Before asking your employees to agree to something like this, make sure you discuss the issue with your Personnel department.

Be Honest about This Problem

One effective technique is simply to address the issue with the employee beforehand, while you are still making a decision about whether they should go to training or not. As is often the case in business situations, bringing the topic out in the open can go a long way towards easing everyone's fears. Just discussing the issue does not create any legal arrangement, of course, but it should let both sides know where the other stands. As a manager, you should openly express your concern about the possibility of the employee "taking the training and running." You hope the employee will reply that the job is much bigger than one skill set, they like the environment, they would work here for free they like it so much, and so on. But if they don't, if they hedge or are evasive, or blurt out a series of negative statements, you've got a problem that a training class is not going to solve.

What about Nontechnical Training?

When we think about IT training, we generally think about technical training. It is important to remember that some of your staff may also benefit from nontechnical training:

- Time management (for those who have trouble staying organized)
- Business writing (for those who have to prepare memos and reports)
- Presentation skills (for those who have to give presentations to groups)
- Interpersonal skills (communications, conflict management)
- Supervisory skills (for those who have a staff to manage)
- Project management (for those responsible for keeping projects on track)
- Leadership skills (for those who have to manage others)

Nontechnical training can have tremendous value. Employees may not appreciate it as much as technical training, but you will value it. You can say to an employee that you're sending them to a nontechnical training because you have plans to move them up in the organization, or you might tell them that their deficiencies in these areas are holding them back.

Your HR department—if you have one—can be the best source for nontechnical training information. Training options are now more flexible and more accessible than ever before; in addition to the explosion of night and part-time schools, companies that provide on-site training, on-line courses, and the myriad of different media-based educational options make getting educated a lot more convenient.

How Do I Know If the Employee Is Learning from the Training?

If you send an employee for training, it is because you see the need. It is then up to you as their manager to make sure that they are putting these skills to use. You should review the course curriculum, and perhaps even speak to the instructor to get a feel for what the employee should be able to do after completing the class. If an employee is not using the skills learned in a class, it could be because the selection of that particular class was a poor one, or that you haven't challenged them to use their newly acquired skills. There are some ways of testing technical skills. See Section 2.8 for tips on conducting technical interviews.

3.4 Performance Reviews: How Do I Conduct Useful and Meaningful Reviews?

Performance reviews are probably the single most important discussions you'll have with members of your staff. Although performance reviews are traditionally a once-a-year event, some companies are now doing them twice a year. Regardless of the frequency, a professionally done review should be done just like you should do your taxes: the end result should be the formalization of 12 months of discussion, feedback, analysis, and evaluation. Do the work in small bits all year, and you will be ready when the Big Moment arrives. Neither you nor the employee should be shocked at the contents.

The annual review process gives you a chance to document the employee's accomplishments, dedication, commitment, challenges, and opportunities for improvement. Many companies have official evaluation forms that have been developed by the Human Resources department. Other companies have no form and leave it up to each manager, or simply rely on a memo-style format. However, a form generally won't help you since a useful evaluation should really consist of descriptive narratives, and not merely checked boxes.

Two Key Thoughts to Keep in Mind

Performance reviews are often used to resolve two other important company issues: terminating underperforming employees and rewarding overperforming employees. Poorly written evaluations make both of these tasks even more difficult, and the costs of failing at this are high: mishandled terminations can (and often do, these days) end in lawsuits, and mishandled reviews of star performers often lead to the key employee using a job switch to get what they should've received from you.

Key Areas of Evaluation

Areas that you want to consider when reviewing an employee's performance include

- Quality of work
- Ability to complete assignments in a timely manner
- Ability to pick up new skills on their own
- Interest in staying aware of current events in their area of expertise
- Ability to manage staff
- Ability to manage short- and long-term projects

Specific Evaluation Statements

Almost Useless

- "Mark is a fine worker with a good attitude; he works hard and has done a good job for the company."

  While it may be true, this statement tells Mark nothing concrete about his past performance and gives him nothing to improve on in the future. Nor is the company served by this kind of statement. How valuable an employee is Mark, and how can it help Mark grow?

Positive

- "Martha was exemplary in her efforts to complete her major project on time. In addition to working over several weekends, she also enlisted the help of two departments to meet her deadline."

  This is a very useful comment for Martha; she knows her efforts were noticed and the company knows they have a committed employee.

Negative

- "Mary Jane showed no interest in expanding her professional skill set; she turned down several offers for training classes in new languages and refused to move to a new project that would have required her to learn new procedures."

  Mary Jane knows exactly what she did wrong and, if she chooses, how she can change her behavior to act differently in the future.

- Proactive versus reactive thinking
- Interpersonal skills, including communication and intrateam interaction skills
- Documentation

If the individual being reviewed has a position that is hands on in nature, you can include quantitative metrics in the review:

- Network uptime
- Systems response time
- Call resolution/response time
- Number of incidents/calls addressed per hour/day
- System reliability

Guidelines for Reviews

Don't forget: both you and the members of your IT staff are salaried profession-als. Act as such, and treat them that way. Your respect will be rewarded.

No Surprises

As mentioned above, preparing for a review is a year-long process that ends with the written evaluation and the meeting with the employee. As such, a perfor-mance review shouldn't contain any surprises for the employee, especially bad surprises. Any negative comments that you include in the review should be items that you've discussed with the employee multiple times in the course of the year.

Be Objective

It is important to remember that a performance review is the company's formal assessment of the employee's performance. Be as objective as possible. Remem-ber reviews that you were given—often the most contentious items are the sub-jective ones. With this in mind, your performance review should be full of exam-ples and specifics to back up your assessment.

   Also, remember that other people will read this review in the future. Other people in the company, for example, may read this review when thinking about transferring the employee into their department. Or the person may leave and may later reapply at your company.

Carefully Record Details

The more specifics you can provide, the more useful your review will be. The more specifics you can provide *now*, the more understandable it will be in the *future*. It's hard to recall the incidents you need when you're looking back on the past 12 months. Review your own status reports for ideas. And, during the year, jot quick notes to yourself on scraps of paper that you toss into the employee's file. (While this sounds like great theory, it is in fact something many good managers do on a regular basis. Details matter, and details fade. Record them as they hap-pen and both you and the recipient of your work—for this is real work that man-agers have to do—will be better for it.)

   As you prepare the review, you can even ask the employee for her own list of accomplishments over the past 12 months. This can help jog your own memory and help you understand what the employee considers her greatest achieve-ment. Additionally, it helps you see what the employee thinks were her most important contributions. Getting her input can help you avoid being embar-rassed by failing to mention something that was important to her.

Negative Reviews

Performance reviews that are mostly or entirely negative are difficult for both the reviewer and the reviewee. There are two important points to keep in mind if you are in this situation: be as specific as possible and keep HR informed. Not only will the session(s) probably be very emotional, but the end result can be more positive when you are very specific about what happened. This detail includes not only past performance but current events; be clear and detailed in your notes about what conversations took place and what each party said.

Also make sure to keep your HR department informed. If your company does not have an HR department, find an appropriate third party to keep informed of the situation. (Perhaps your boss is a logical choice.) If you keep someone else involved and aware of the situation, you will always have a third party to check with (if required) later in the process.

Be Professional

Take extra care to make sure that what you write comes off in a highly professional manner. Resist the urge to list failures. Instead, cite circumstances where the employee "fell short of expectations" to identify areas where the employee needs to focus his development efforts. In some situations, an employee may not be aware of his own weakness. (For example, his staff meetings are more like speeches, instead of discussions.) If this is the case, consider it a *coaching opportunity* for you and a *development area* for him.

Have Employees Review Themselves

Many companies have adopted the formal policy of having employees—in addition to their managers—review themselves. The employee uses the same form as the manager and evaluates her performance over the specified period of time. Naturally, self-reviews (like resumes) contain some elements of—how shall we put it?—"skill inflation"? Nonetheless, the exercise is a very valuable one for both the employee and the manager. The employee gets a chance to express her concerns and talk about what she thought her strengths and weaknesses were. While obviously not taking the material at face value, the manager can take the information from the self-review and use it when making his own evaluation.

What to Do during the Actual Review

When it's time to meet with the employee to go over the performance review, remember it is a *discussion*—make this an interactive time, not a linear one. Do not simply read the review to him. In fact, you may want to consider giving the employee time to read the review in advance of your meeting, so that he has time to digest it and can then discuss it intelligently. Remember though, as a manager, to discuss it with conviction. This is your "assessment" of his performance. You'll appear weak as a manager if you consistently point a finger to "HR," "upstairs," or your boss as an explanation for your decisions. You don't have all the leeway in the world, but you are the decision maker and you need to clearly explain your actions and be prepared to defend them.

Tone of the Discussion

You need to be clear in your discussion with the employee. Depending on the employee's performance, your tone may need to include hints of motivation, hard-heartedness, and optimism. At the end of the review, there should be no doubt in the employee's mind as to what you think of their performance, where they need to improve, and steps they need to take to do so.

In certain cases, you might want to have specific follow-up meetings with an employee at regular intervals after the formal performance reviews. If necessary, you may want to consider additional interim informal reviews at certain, prespecified times. In cases such as these, you can provide the employee with an interim report of their performance, but it is for your and their eyes only—no copy goes to Personnel.

3.5 Strategy: How Do I Develop an IT Strategy?

The cosmic question "Why are we here?" applies to corporate departments as well. It is entirely possible that many, if not all, of your staff don't have the full understanding of how the IT department serves the organization. When it comes to their job, they may understand what's critical for today. But, while today is important, it is also vital to know about tomorrow and beyond. If they're looking at the trees, you have to be the one to let them know about the forest. The strategy should include feedback from your employees and should be cleared by your boss, but you should drive it.

Without an IT strategy, you won't be able to align your long-term goals with your short-term responsibilities. You need to have these things decided and written down, so that when your boss tells you to do *X,* and your employee needs *Y,* and the other manager down the hall that helped you last week needs *Z,* you have a clear map of how to make that decision.

Some companies have huge IT departments, with layers and layers of managers. Organizations of this size have formal IT strategies and substrategies. But many smaller companies are just now getting formal IT departments, with managers, budgets, and expectations.

Wherever you are on the size and formal structure spectrum, you should have a strategy. And you should write it down. It should include items like the following elements:

- Who are your team members?
- Why/how is technology important to your organization?
- What are your assets?
- Who are your customers?
- What are your customers' needs?
- How do you plan to satisfy these needs?

While this all sounds simple, it is definitely not. However, the very act of getting this all down on one or two sheets of paper—remember, you are not trying to make this superformal, you are just trying to get it right—can be of great value.

Who Are Your Team Members?

This seems like a simple task—just list the people in your department. In fact, your team members may or may not be all the people on your staff. You may have someone on your staff who has part-time responsibilities to another department. This person is on your team, but you cannot count on them 100% of the time.

Or somebody from another department, who is not on your payroll and reports to some other remote branch of the organizational chart, is in fact a very useful person to your department. They might call you when they hear about certain problems on the system, for example, or help you when someone in your department is out sick. These people are not on your payroll, and they are not in your department, but they are on your team.

Why/How Is Technology Important to Your Organization?

Virtually every organization today has some technology, just as they all have telephones. However, how the technology is used can vary tremendously. In a law firm, it might be used simply for word processing. Or it might be used to accurately track billings. Additionally, it could be used to scan and archive documents, so that every single piece of paper related to a case is on-line where it can be indexed, cross-referenced, and immediately retrieved.

In a retail organization, technology can be used for all the traditional back office activities (billing, purchasing, etc.) but probably serves its most vital function by helping the store managers to know what products are the most profitable, and which should be dropped from inventory. The store might also use it for space planning so that the shelves are stocked in a way that maximizes space usage, as well as profitability.

What Are Your Assets?

This topic is discussed in detail in Section 7.1. In general, though, you can be sure of two things: you are responsible for more things than you think you are, and you are liable for more than you think you are. Read that section to figure out how to better manage your assets.

Who Are Your Customers? What Are Their Needs?

Whether your customers are other employees, suppliers, consumers, or other businesses, they are the ones you need to serve. Find out who your customers are. Figure out what their needs are. Then spend your time addressing those needs.

1. Your customers are probably not retail customers, although they could be. More likely, your customers are other internal departments in the company and your boss. Different jobs have different customers, and there are departments (like Sales and Marketing) who should spend all day figuring out what their external customers need. IT, on the other hand, commonly serves other departments in the company—like Sales, Marketing, Accounting, and Management.

2. Figure out what your customers' needs are. Are they products or services? Data and information? Reduced costs? Improved efficiency or productivity?

3. Ask them directly. Set up meetings with representatives from their department, ask questions, record the answers, and change the way you are doing business to reflect their needs and concerns.

4. Look up from the end of your nose—and see the whole picture. That is how you drive your car—now drive your department the same way.

You will look like a hero for *just asking*.

3.6 Tactics: How Do I Keep My Department Central to the Company's Operations?

Make sure the strategy mentioned in the above section is carefully aligned with the goals of the entire organization. *This is critical.* If your immediate boss's needs are out of alignment with what the entire company is doing, you have a serious problem.

Let the rest of the organization know what you're doing in IT. To many of the other department managers, IT may not mean much more than "the people at the Help Desk that can reset passwords." Periodically, have a meeting with the other department heads. Let them know what you're doing in IT, what you've accomplished, and what you plan to do. With a little luck, light bulbs will start going off. They may see uses for the technology that you hadn't thought of. Get some good discussion going and you may learn a way to deliver a lot more value by slightly modifying your plans.

The reality is that in today's corporate world, IT departments are, for the most part, automatically in the middle of action. Everyone is becoming aware of the values that computerization can bring to an enterprise. Wineries, toy shops, bookstores, and sandwich places—supposed havens for the nontechnical—now have sophisticated computerized inventory systems, customer service mechanisms, on-line ordering counterparts, and—gasp—even fax machines to take preorders. Information technology is pretty much everywhere.

3.7 Further References

Articles and Books

- Broadwell, Martin M., and Carol Broadwell Dietrich, *The New Supervisor: How to Thrive in Your First Year as a Manager,* Perseus, 1998.

- Fournies, Ferdinand F., *Why Employees Don't Do What They're Supposed to Do and What to Do about It,* McGraw-Hill, 1999.

- Jaffe, Brian D., "Following a Few Simple Rules Can Ease the Pain of Employee Reviews," *InfoWorld,* January 26, 1998.

- Lewis, Bob, *Bob Lewis's IS Survival Guide,* Sams, 1999.

- Maslach, Christina, and Michael P. Leiter (Contributor), *The Truth about Burnout: How Organizations Cause Personal Stress and What to Do about It, Jossey-Bass Publishers, 1997.*

- Potter, Beverly, et al., *Overcoming Job Burnout: How to Renew Enthusiasm for Work,* Ronin Publishing, 1998.

- Straub, Joseph T., *The Rookie Manager: A Guide to Surviving Your First Year in Management,* Amacom, 1999.

User Support Services

CHAPTER FOUR

What You Will Learn

- How to set up and staff a Help Desk
- What service level agreements (SLAs) are and how to define them
- How to arrange for user training
- How to select a call tracking package

Introduction

Whether it goes by the name of "Help Desk," "Support Center," "User Services," or any of a variety of other similar sounding monikers, your IT department needs some kind of organization to provide assistance to your user population—be it employees, clients, customers, or business partners. In general, IT Help Desks are designed to be one-stop shopping for all computer-related requests. For the majority, your support organization is the only interaction they will have with IT. For these users, IT is only as good as their last call to the Help Desk. As such, your support organization has an incredible opportunity to add value and improve the perception of your entire department.

4.1 Help Desk: How Do I Set One Up?

A Help Desk's responsibilities can include

- Ordering new equipment
- Password resets
- Requesting new IDs
- Computer supplies (diskettes, toner, CDs)
- Installation and move requests
- Scheduling training
- Routing and coordinating requests with other IT groups (application development, operations, networking, etc.)
- Providing application support
- Reporting and resolving hardware problems
- Helping remote users with dial-in connectivity

Two Critical Help Desk Issues

In setting up a Help Desk, you need at least two essential items:

1. *A centralized way for users to reach you*—usually a phone extension and/or e-mail address
2. *Sufficient staffing* to answer and deal with the phone calls and e-mail messages

Centralized Method of User Contact

The Help Desk is more of a set of resources than a physical place. In a small environment, staffing the Help Desk may be something done in addition to an individual's regular assignments. In a large environment, it may consist of an entire department staffed round-the-clock dedicated to the function.

When you think of the functions of a Help Desk, one of the common assumptions is that it provides support for applications like Word and Excel. In truth, questions like these generally represent a small portion of the calls that go to the Help Desk. More typical are calls about network issues, program crashes, hardware problems, and security requests.

Ideally, the goal of the Help Desk should be to resolve 100% of the requests that come in during that first phone call. More likely, when a user calls the Help Desk they are having a problem in trying to accomplish something. If they have to wait for a call back, or for a technician to be dispatched, the user is likely to be frustrated because they will be further delayed in getting their problem resolved and their work done.

Of course, it is unlikely that your Help Desk will be able to resolve every request and problem during that first call, but there are several ways of increasing the rate and minimizing user frustration.

Staffing

Staffing the Help Desk with the right individuals is vital to its success. Not only must they have appropriate technical expertise, but they also must have excellent interpersonal and telephone skills. They have to be adept at diagnosing problems based on a telephone conversation, and walking users through resolution procedures. They must possess a high degree of professionalism to deal with users at all levels of the organization. Lastly, they must convey a certain degree of calm and confidence to the users to prevent an irate user from trying to escalate the problem up the IT organizational chart. Help Desk staffing is discussed in detail later in the chapter.

Telephone System

The majority of requests to the Help Desk will probably come via telephone. You should take care that a user never gets a busy signal. Ideally, if the call can't be answered immediately, it should give the caller an option of waiting on hold or going to voice-mail. Voice-mail messages should be acknowledged (with a call back to the user) as soon as possible to avoid the user assuming that their request fell into a black hole. You may want to consider an ACD (Automatic Call Distribution) system. ACDs can route calls to technicians based on menu prompts and can provide you with detailed reports about activity.

Procedures

Analysts at the Help Desk should have documented procedures for handling different types of calls—particularly those that they cannot resolve themselves. They should know how to route different types of calls, how to escalate, when to follow up, and so on. Procedures should include the names, phone numbers, beeper numbers, and so on of various resources—internal and external. Call tracking software, intranets, and so on can aid in ensuring that procedures are followed.

Access

The more a Help Desk analyst can do, the more effective she'll be, and the more likely she'll be able to resolve a problem on that initial call. Consider giving your analysts various degrees of administrative access so that they can reset passwords, change access levels, see users' files/data, and so on. Of course, this type of access has to be carefully considered first before it is granted. Analysts should be made aware of the capabilities they have, and warned about the potential they have, and that it must not be abused. They also need to be aware that special access means they can *cause* problems as easily as they resolve problems.

Tools

In addition to the access privileges mentioned above, a Help Desk can benefit from a variety of tools.

Knowledge Base

Since no Help Desk analyst can be expected to know everything, a knowledge base of information can be a valuable resource. This might be something developed internally, or part of a call tracking system or an external resource.

Remote Control

Very often a call may go unresolved during the initial phone call because the user was unable to accurately describe the problem or couldn't follow directions provided by the Help Desk analyst. Using a remote control package (e.g., PC Anywhere from Symantec, SMS from Microsoft, etc.), a Help Desk analyst can see exactly what the user sees on their PC, and even take control of the user's PC, all without ever leaving the Help Desk chair. This saves times, increases user satisfaction, and tremendously improves the effectiveness of the Help Desk.

Installation Tools

Many calls to the Help Desk result in a request for some type of installation (printer drivers, new software, upgrades, patches, etc.). By using various software tools—for example, remote control mentioned above, as well as a product category referred to as ESD (electronic software deployment)—the Help Desk can fulfill a request without having to dispatch a technician or walk a user through a complicated process. See Chapter 9 for a more detailed discussion of ESD.

Call Tracking System

A midsize environment can receive hundreds of calls a month; a large environment can receive hundreds of calls each day. A call tracking system can serve many functions in addition to just keeping track of calls. It can route calls to the right person for resolution, schedule activities, set priorities, automatically escalate, generate reports on the types of activities, and track call history (both by user and by equipment or resource). See Section 4.5 for more on call tracking packages.

Service Level Agreements (SLAs)

Service level agreements (SLAs) represent a declaration to the user community of what type of service your Help Desk can provide, and how quickly it hopes to provide it. SLAs help to set the users' expectations, as well define the performance criteria upon which you, your staff, and your Help Desk organization will be judged. Service level agreements are discussed in detail later in this chapter.

User Surveys

While reports from your ACD system and call tracking software can give you all kinds of statistics, they often don't tell you if your customers are satisfied. It can be very helpful to periodically survey a sample of users who have called your Help Desk and ask them a small handful of questions.

The survey can be done in person, over the phone, or via e-mail. A sample survey might include questions like

- Was your initial call to the Help Desk answered by a person or by voice-mail?
- If your call was answered by voice-mail, how long was it before you received a call back?

- How long did it take before your problem was completely resolved?
- Did it require multiple visits to your desk or multiple phone calls to resolve your problem?
- Did the analysts who worked to resolve your call act in a professional and courteous manner?
- Overall, how would you rate this specific call to the Help Desk (using a scale of 1 to 10, with 10 being perfect)?
- Please feel free to make any additional comments, complaints, or suggestions you may have regarding the Help Desk.

Regardless of the results, the act of taking the survey will help users to believe that you are concerned about the quality of service being delivered. After each survey, statistics should be compiled and decisions made about what the results indicate, and what actions should be taken to improve service levels. If surveys are done periodically (every two or three months), you can evaluate trends and patterns.

Monitoring and Managing

Of course, even with all the tools available to make an effective Help Desk, it is still up to people to make it work. A good Help Desk has a supervisor that understands customer service, knows what it is like to work as an analyst, and can juggle and adjust multiple priorities and reassign resources. They must ensure that the calls are resolved in a timely manner, and that nothing—neither calls nor issues—falls into a black hole.

4.2   Help Desk: How Do I Staff One?

It is important to remember that a Help Desk is essentially a complaint desk—people only call when there is a problem. As such, callers to the Help Desk are likely to be frustrated and impatient. Accordingly, one of the most vital prerequisites for Help Desk analysts is their interpersonal skills. The staff on the Help Desk has to be sensitive to callers' needs; remain calm, mature, polite, and professional; and demonstrate confidence. The last item is of particular importance. If a caller to the Help Desk feels that the analyst is not qualified or capable, the caller is likely to become more frustrated. On the other hand, if the caller believes (whether it is true or not) that the analyst is confident and capable of finding a resolution, the caller will immediately feel better. Confidence is contagious.

The Value of a Help Desk

Your Help Desk staff could be the single most important resource you have to help ensure that users look favorably on IT. After all, a user is likely to appreciate and value a quick, courteous, and helpful response to even the simplest question a lot more than they would appreciate major upgrades and investments to your infrastructure.

In addition to interpersonal skills, individuals at the Help Desk need to have skills in whatever technologies they are supporting. Since you're unlikely to find someone who knows everything, it is important that they are also resourceful enough to find solutions to problems they haven't seen before, and be able to think through problems and explore alternatives on their own.

Specific Considerations When Hiring for a Help Desk

Chapter 2 covered staffing and recruiting in detail, but when hiring for a Help Desk, you should also consider the following:

- Perform the initial screening via telephone interviews. This will give you some feel for the candidates' "telephone personality."

- Develop a set of representative questions that might come into the Help Desk, and see how the candidate handles them. The questions should be ones that don't draw on technical skills exclusively, but also allow you to get a glimpse as to how the candidate thinks through troubleshooting, and how she reacts when the answers aren't clear-cut.

- Look for evidence that the candidate can learn on his own. Have all his technical skills been developed through formal training or self-taught?

- Is the candidate prepared for full shifts answering phones?

- If the candidate sees the Help Desk as a stepping stone to a higher-level position in IT, you and she should agree on a minimum time commitment at the Help Desk before such a transfer is possible.

Size of Support Staff

It is not possible to give an exact formula for how many people you need at your Help Desk. The answer varies with the number of calls that come in a given period, your service level targets, how long each call takes, and so on. A Help Desk that has multiple shifts will obviously need more analysts than one that runs just a single shift. You'll probably need to be flexible in your staffing: you'll want more analysts during peak periods, and fewer during quiet periods. Statistics from your ACD and your call tracking software can help you evaluate call patterns.

Staff Burnout

Taking calls at the Help Desk for eight hours a day can be exhausting and may be a short path to quick burnout. Consider rotation of assignments with other positions. Or schedule the shifts so that each analyst has some time away from the phone—perhaps to research questions that might normally have been escalated to some sort of second level. Section 3.2 discusses staff burnout in more detail.

4.3 Service Level Agreements: What Are They and How Do I Define Them?

When a user calls the Help Desk, they're hoping for immediate service and resolution. Of course, that may not be possible in all cases—a technician may have to be dispatched, it may be a problem that has to be researched or escalated to a specialist, and so on. If it is a hardware problem, a part may need to be ordered. When this happens, the user will usually ask, "How long will it take?" *Service level agreements* (SLAs) give you, and them, the answer.

Specific Issues

Service level agreements are your targets for delivering service. There can be many different types of service level agreements. For example:

- System uptime
- Hours of Help Desk operation
- How many rings before a phone is answered, or how long before a voice-mail message is returned
- Time until call resolution
- Turnaround time for creating an ID
- Turnaround time for password reset
- Turnaround time for repairs
- Turnaround time for obtaining new hardware
- Turnaround time for installations and/or moves

Positive Values of SLAs

By defining and publishing your service level agreements, you can help reduce anger and frustration—yours as well as the users'. For example, if you tell users that it takes 24 hours to create an ID, you are likely to get users in the habit of requesting them in advance versus those emergency requests that come on Monday mornings because human resources never informed IT about the new hires.

There will always be exceptions, emergencies, and special cases, but published service levels can be an enormous help in taking a support organization from constantly being in crisis mode. Of course, it is important that the service levels you set be ones that you can meet and that are reasonable for the user community. For example, don't tell users that voice-mail messages will be returned within 15 minutes unless you have a very high degree of confidence that you can do so consistently. On the other hand, promising a return call in 24 hours may be a target that you can meet, but one that your users are likely to find unacceptable.

Ask for Help from Your Staff

When setting service levels, solicit input from your support staff, as well as users, as to what is reasonable and what is feasible. Then, before publishing your service levels, have your staff work with them for a while to see how well they meet them. Then, when you are confident you have service levels that are both reasonable and feasible, let the users know. Post them on your intranet, or distribute them via e-mail. Afterwards, monitor how well you're meeting them. They are not carved in stone. It's okay to adjust them if they are not working. And you may need to add to them as your support organization takes on additional responsibilities or types of services.

4.4 Training: How Do I Arrange for User Training?

There are many options available for user training. The ones you choose to use depend on the size and budget of your organization, as well as the skills you need to develop in your users.

In-House Classes

If you are able to have your own training staff and facilities, you can tailor course content, schedule, and class size exactly to your needs. The costs are readily identifiable in terms of staff and equipment needed for the training room.

Third-Party Training Providers

These organizations can provide quality training in popular skill sets. The downside is that they are somewhat inflexible in regard to schedules and curricula.

Alternatively, you can usually arrange (at an additional charge) for these providers to deliver classes customized to your needs. Training providers usually have a staff of professional and highly experienced trainers, and the curricula for many classes usually adhere to outlines established by the appropriate vendor (e.g., Microsoft) in order to maintain their authorizations.

Computer-Based Training (CBT)

Computer-based training (CBT) generally refers to a software application that trains the user in a particular product set. These applications are often multimedia based, and sometimes include exams to gauge the students' progress and adjust the pace accordingly. On the plus side, CBT can be very inexpensive (once you buy a CBT package, you can generally use it for an unlimited number of students), very flexible (students can use it at their convenience, rerun specific portions, or jump ahead as needed), and convenient (no travel or time away from the office required). On the other hand, students cannot ask the instructor questions and may rush through the program if it doesn't hold their interest. Students may also hold CBT in less esteem than a formal instructor-led course.

Web-Based Training

Training on the Internet can simply be another flavor of CBT, or it can be more like an instructor-led class (except that the students and instructor are all at their own desk). As a result, the advantages and disadvantages of Web-based training can be a combination of the pros and cons of these alternatives.

Choosing

Before choosing a particular method of training or a particular provider, you can usually ask for the opportunity to sample their offerings. Most training providers will let you attend a class, or preview CBT or Web-based offerings, at no charge. Additionally, most providers have volume discounts available.

4.5 Call Tracking: How Do I Select a Call Tracking Package?

In a small environment that only receives a handful of Help Desk calls each day, the activity could be tracked through any number of simple means (whiteboard, spreadsheet, etc.). However, in larger environments that receive thousands or tens of thousands of calls per month, a more sophisticated solution is required.

Call Tracking Software

Call tracking is a software category designed specifically for managing large volumes of calls at call centers. (This category includes more areas than just traditional corporate IT Help Desks.) There are call tracking solutions that are available for a few hundred dollars, up to those that may cost a few hundred thousand dollars. Since most offerings are licensed based on the number of concurrent users, however, the size of your staff may be the greatest factor in determining how much your implementation will cost. There are a surprisingly large number of offerings in this product area. A good resource to start narrowing your search is the Help Desk Institute (*www.helpdeskinst.com*). This organization, which you may want to consider joining to keep abreast of developments in the area of support services, can be a good resource to learn about call tracking software offerings.

Specific Issues

There are a variety of factors to consider when evaluating this category of call tracking packages:

- Ease of customization. Some packages can be customized using a point-and-click type interface; others require scripting.
- Client, server, and database platforms supported.
- Auto-escalation (beeper, e-mail, etc.).
- Integration with your e-mail environment.
- Ad hoc queries and reports—the ability to define and generate customized reports.
- Integration with PDAs—to allow technicians to download their calls to a handheld device.
- Access from a Web browser interface. This could be helpful for technicians who work from nonsupported platforms (e.g., Mac) or to allow techs to access the database from any workstation without having to install the full client software package.
- Integration with third-party desktop management tools (Microsoft's SMS, Intel's LAN Desk, etc.).
- Integration with third-party knowledge base packages.
- Ability to build an internal knowledge base of calls.

- Support for international use. If your organization will use the package in countries outside the United States, you may want to make sure the package can be configured for multilanguage support, and that the vendor has a presence in the countries you will be operating in.

- How usable the package is "out of the box." You may not have the resources available to dedicate for customizing the package to your exact needs.

- Extent of the implementation effort in terms of time, training, and need for consultants.

The Value of Selecting Appropriate Help Desk Software

Selecting a Help Desk package is a critical decision since you will be using it for several years. In addition to the standard practices of checking references, investigating the vendor, and so on, you should also consider getting the input from some (if not all) of the staff that will be using the package. You may want to solicit their assistance in narrowing down the field of candidates to a few finalists. And, when you're down to deciding among the last two or three vendors, you may want to have some of the staff sit in on the vendor demos so that they can see how the packages operate and ask questions.

4.6 Further References

Web Sites

- *www.helpdeskinst.com* (Help Desk Institute)

Books and Articles

- Bruton, Noel, *How to Manage the I.T. Helpdesk, Digital Press, 1997.*
- Czegel, Barbara, *Running an Effective Help Desk,* 2nd edition, Wiley, 1998.
- Czegel, Barbara, *Help Desk Practitioner's Handbook*, Wiley, 1999.
- Jaffe, Brian D., "Taking the Measure of Customer Service," *PC Week*, June 5, 1998.
- Jaffe, Brian D., "Maturity Is a Help Desk Prerequisite," *PC Week*, February 7, 2000.
- Laub, Lori and Navtej Khandpur, *Delivering World-Class Technical Support*, Wiley, 1996.
- Tourniaire, Francoise, and Richard Farrell, *The Art of Software Support: Design and Operation of Support Centers and Help Desks,* Prentice Hall, 1996.

Managing Projects

CHAPTER FIVE

What You Will Learn

- What a "project" is and how you get started
- How to set up a project team
- How to conduct project meetings
- How to fund projects
- Ways to carefully keep track of your project

Introduction

As an IT manager, your life is likely to revolve around projects—some small, others that are enormous. Projects are an integral part of corporate life; this chapter discusses how they are conceived, organized, funded, tracked, and executed. Project management is a complex and formal management science (although it is often more art than science); you won't need all that complexity and formality, though, to run most successful IT projects.

5.1 Initiating Projects: How Do I Get Started?

You won't go too long as an IT manager without hearing the word *project*. "Project" is a catch-all word. It could be a relatively simple activity like getting new PCs for all the building's receptionists. It might be a more complicated venture, like deploying a systemwide software or operating system upgrade. Or it could be a monumental task, like implementing an ERP (enterprise resource planning) application throughout your company. A project might be staffed by a single person or a team of 75 from different organizations. It might be highly technical in nature, or not at all. Simple projects may require little planning, and all the key information is maintained in someone's head. At the other extreme, a complicated project may need special project software, along with group calendaring and scheduling to keep it all on track.

Your ability to manage a project so that it meets its goals, within the defined time frame, and within the approved budget, may be one of the single most important skills you can develop as an IT manager. Become adept at it, and the rest of the organization will consider you someone who can get things done.

Three "Laws" of Project Management

The following three "laws" of project management are supposed to be tongue-in-cheek. However, they prove true more often than not:

1. No major project is ever installed on time, within budget, or with the same staff that started it.

2. Projects progress quickly until they become 95% complete, and then remain 95% complete forever.

3. When things are going well, something will go wrong.
    a. *Corollary: When things can't get any worse, they will.*
    b. *Corollary: When things are going well, it is because you have overlooked something.*

The Value of Project Management

Project management (PM) has become a formal discipline and a widely practiced part of today's corporate life. While it is not necessary for you to become an
official "project manager" and get certified by the Project Management Institute
(there is such a thing, and it is the leading professional association of this emerging area—see *www.pmi.org*), it is useful for you to know some of the important
aspects of PM to help you in your role as a manager. Every manager has some
project management responsiblities, regardless of how those needs are defined;
it can be critical to your success to not only accept, but embrace these responsibilities. Take control of the projects in your business life and manage them
well—it will greatly be worth your effort.

Key Points about a Project

- There are five key elements about a project that you will need to answer: its
  objective, the *members* of the project team, the *length,* the *cost,* and who else
  within the company will be *supporting* it.

- Projects vary widely in size and scope, and they can start in a pretty innocent
  way: they might have no formal requirements, no specified budget, and only
  vague deadlines. On the other hand, the requirements, budget, and deadline
  may be virtually carved in stone.

- Your most important task as a manager of a project is to define a clear objective (or set of objectives) for a project. Don't do anything without first defining the goals, getting them agreed to by team members and project sponsors,
  and writing them down.

- Next, get assistance and sponsorship for your project. You cannot do a project alone; you will need help from other people, some perhaps from other
  parts of the organization.

- Having defined your objective, you next need to define the steps that will be
  required to reach that objective. These steps are called *milestones.*

Five Key Questions You'll Need to Ask—and Get the Answers To

1. What is the objective of this project?
2. Who will be on the team to help me accomplish this objective?
3. How long will this project take?
4. How much will this project cost?
5. Who else will support this project?

How Formal Do I Have to Get?

"Focus your time, energy and money tightly. You don't have to be very formal about it—not every good project manager uses Gantt charts, for example. But you have to manage your project carefully, regardless of how formally you do that. Whether you are installing a new phone system, taking over the management of a building, or deploying a fleet of brokers to evaluate a potential new marketplace, you have to systematically schedule your efforts and theirs. By managing your timelines, you can anticipate when your resources will be slack or overdrawn, when the project will slow down or intensify, and when you need to step in and rearrange things. You need this kind of information, or the project will overwhelm you."

—Peter Hansen
Principal, Hansen Realty, Berkeley, CA

These questions and their answers are discussed in detail in the sections that follow.

How a Typical Project Can Start

A project generally starts as an idea—either yours or someone else's. At the very beginning, a project is probably short on specifics. There's no framework for costs, time frames, or the resources required. In fact, as these areas begin to get quantified, it often happens that the project gets killed because it will take too long, or cost too much, or require too many staff members.

Once you have a project to manage, whether you gave it to yourself or someone else did, it's your job to manage it properly. Obviously, projects of different sizes are not all managed the same way. For the purposes of this text, we'll work on a midsize project. "Midsize" depends on your perspective, of course, but in this case, we'll say that about 10 people are on the project team, and that the project will last about four or five months.

Clearly Define the Project's Objective

But before you even get to setting up the project team or establishing time frames, let's talk about the project itself. First and foremost, the project needs a clearly defined objective. Objectives can take all kinds of shapes. But you can think of the objective as the achievement that will indicate your project is completed and successful.

The objective of the project must have several important characteristics. It must be

- Clearly defined
- Agreed upon by the important people related to the project (this group can include people not directly on the project itself)
- Written down

There are other issues that you will need to consider, but you must first define your objective, get it agreed to, and put in on paper.

Department versus Company Objectives

Carefully match your project's objectives to the company's overall objectives. It is best not to think of yourself or your department as an island, but instead think and act as if you are part of a dynamic organization. And define the objective of your project *within the company's overall goals.* This step sounds obvious, but often isn't done. And sometimes the connection is not obvious—and it is your job as the manager of the project to state it clearly. If your company is an auto parts dealer and you are installing a new upgrade for the phone system, many people in the company might wonder why they have to help, and how that activity helps them. You need to have the answers to those questions formulated.

Get Proper Sponsorship for the Project

Along with clearly defining the project's goals, you need to carefully define the political sponsors of your project. Perhaps your boss handed you the project; make sure that you clearly inform her that you will need her support soon. Maybe your boss's boss came up with this clever idea, and it got passed down to you. If that happens, find out as quickly as possible from the source of the idea how much help you are going to get when it comes to issues like funding, personnel, and so on.

If you created the project yourself, after clearly outlining its goals, set about finding out how much help you are going to get from others in the company. You almost assuredly need help from people outside your department, and you will probably need help from people higher up than you on the corporate ladder. Find out how much help that is going to be before you start making any significant decisions or commitments.

Your project may actually be a pet project of the company president or other high executive. If so, having this type of sponsorship and backing can be enormously helpful to you in eliminating roadblocks, particularly as you try to make use of resources from other parts of the company. If somebody "upstairs" wants everyone to have access to the Web from their homes, you're going to need a lot of personnel, time, effort—and money—to make it happen.

Project Milestones

Once you've defined the project's objective, the next step is to define the project's milestones.

You may want to think about what needs to be done to reach this objective. You begin to break the objective down into a few milestones. You don't need a lot of detail here, but break the project down into a few chunks so that you can begin thinking about the kinds of people you want on the project team, and maybe begin to develop some perspective on time frames, costs, and other resources. You may have enough knowledge about the project to do this on your own, or you may want to chat with some colleagues, your boss, or seek outside resources (books, Web sites, classes, consultants).

If the goal of the project is to install an upgrade to Microsoft Word on all machines in the company, and you are working for a 400-person company, you need to carefully plan how you are going to accomplish this task—and by when. While it may appear a simple task to someone from outside the department, anyone with much experience in IT knows an upgrade project like that can take an enormous amount of time and effort. Careful project management can be the key to success in this regard.

To further complicate the project concept, it is entirely likely that you, and many others on your team, will be involved with several projects simultaneously, each of a different size, each at a different point in its life cycle, and each competing for resources—including your time. Not only will you be coordinating the companywide upgrade to Word, you may also be overseeing the new operating system installation for a server, be involved in the purchase of a new companywide phone system, and serve on a cross-functional team evaluating the corporation's new health benefits package. And every member of the various projects you are working on is also working on other multiple projects themselves.

At the time you are defining the milestones, you should also identify the project's risks. These are items that could adversely impact a project's success (e.g., a vendor failing to deliver key components on time, or the inability to find someone with a particular skill set).

5.2 Project Teams: How Do I Set One Up?

IT projects often have personnel that work both within the department and in other areas of the company.

Candidates for the Project Team

Now you should begin thinking about candidates for the project team. Individuals'" involvement on the team can be quite varied. Some people may be dedicated to the project almost 100% throughout its life. Others may spend only a portion of their time on the project. Still others may only be involved with the project during certain phases of the project's life cycle. A project team will probably consist mostly of employees, but there may also be outside consultants if special expertise is needed.

Some Projects Benefit from a "Project Room"

For very large projects, you can assign individuals to deal exclusively with the administrative tasks like scheduling, keeping track of specific assignments, and documentation. For some projects, it has become somewhat trendy in the past few years to have a *project room* or *war room*. This room provides team members a place to work on the project that is separate from their regular work area. The idea of the war room is to keep members from being distracted from the project by their regular duties, and to increase communication (and hopefully productivity, quality, etc.) by having the team members near each other.

Lately, war rooms aren't complete unless they also include a whole host of toys (Koosh balls, hacky sacks, Nerf games, etc.), a whiteboard, an endless supply of munchies and soft drinks, and "open" seating—which is really a euphemism for cubicles—so that team members can easily communicate. Of course, the open seating is generally cheaper, too.

The first people you'll probably include on the team are the ones that spring to mind when you think about what it will take to achieve the project's goal. As you chat with these people, they will probably offer up suggestions of others that need to be involved. They will also offer you different perspectives on what it will take to make the project succeed. Some of the project's team members may be on your staff. Others that you'd like to include might be your peers, direct reports of your peers, and individuals from other departments—perhaps some that are senior to you.

Recruiting Other Employees for Your Project

For team members that report to you, it is easy enough to assign them to the project. But you can't simply go into other departments and assign individuals. You need to meet with those department heads and explain your project to them and what resources you're coming to them for. This may take a great deal of diplomacy—especially if the various department heads don't have much of an interest in your project. It's at times like this that you will need to call on your well-defined objectives, explain how those objectives fit in with the overall company goals, and be ready with an explanation of how your project positively influences the person you are talking with. When the objectives don't convince them, you can either re-evaluate your project and objectives, or call on your executive project sponsor to place a phone call or write a quick memo to help dilute the resistance.

Use of a "Kick-Off Meeting"

It may also be wise to enlist your boss when trying to demonstrate the value and importance of your project to other department heads. Often the senior-most executive who is "sponsoring" the project will call for a meeting, along with various department heads, at the beginning of a project. The purpose of a meeting like this is to make sure that all the various department managers are aware of the importance of the project, and to encourage them to commit resources to it as needed. A meeting like this, often called a "kick-off meeting," can be a critical success factor in a project.

5.3 Project Meetings: How Can I Make Them Productive?

Okay, now you have the project team, or at least the first cut at the project team. The first thing you want to get is do all the team members together.

Keys to Successful Project Meetings

- Set clear goals in your first project meeting: document the objective and scope of the project, how frequently meetings will be held, have minutes taken, and so on.

- Holding a successful project team meeting involves several simple but effective meeting techniques. Use these methods to increase the productivity of your meetings and your team.

- Don't forget that you are in control—and therefore responsible—for the success of both the meetings and the overall project. Watch both carefully.

Goals of Your Initial Project Meeting

At your first project meeting, you want to set some ground rules, establish some administrative procedures, and make sure that everyone is on the same page. Typically, you want to make sure everyone is very clear about the project's objective and scope. This is the perfect time to discuss the project's goals. You have already written them down, and this first meeting is the place for you to distribute them and make sure everyone buys into them.

At this same meeting you may want to establish how often and where the project team is going to meet. A regular schedule of a weekly meeting, at the same time, in the same room, is helpful—it sets a valuable routine.

Minutes of the Meetings

Have minutes taken so that there is no disagreement on items that were decided, tasks that were assigned, and so on. Minutes should also include accomplishments, areas of concern and problems, updates on time frames, and so on. The minutes should be distributed to all team members and project sponsors as soon as possible after the meeting occurs—and certainly before the next meeting. Taking and distributing minutes can be painful tasks that can be easily forgotten or ignored; they can also be critical to the long-term success of the project. As manager of the project, it is your job to make sure these tasks get done.

You may get volunteers to take minutes, or you may not get any. A popular technique is to rotate this assignment each meeting. Or decide that the person who shows up *last* for the meeting is the one assigned to take minutes—this is a clever way of making sure people arrive on time.

Among other things, the minutes ensure that everyone is aware of how the project is progressing. The minutes may also give senior executives an idea of when they need to get involved; they may decide to rally the troops, motivate, or buy lunch for everyone because a milestone is met.

Minutes can chart the progress of activities and tasks from week to week and serve as a reminder of things that need to be done. The minutes can also document who is responsible for each item. Too often, especially in large project teams, it is too easy for everyone to think "someone else" will take care of it. Although several people may be working on an item, it is important to identify a single person as being the one to take the lead.

Useful Meeting Techniques

At each meeting, review the minutes of the previous meeting. It's a good way to remind everyone about accomplishments, and to re-review any items that were still pending or unresolved at the end of last week's meeting.

In addition, stating the desired length of the meeting up front can be an effective technique for getting people to participate. If everyone knows that the goal is to finish the meeting in one hour, people will make more of an effort to get to the point (and will try to force those who don't to cut things short). Meetings held early in the day are more productive than those when people are tired after a full day's work; on the other hand, many critical project meetings are held at the end of the workday to assess the daily status of the project. When the meetings are held and for how long are critical decisions you need to make.

It is also a popular technique to schedule meetings to begin an hour before lunch or an hour before the end of the day. In this way, everyone has an incentive to move the meeting along. Of course, while it's nice to have a fast meeting, effectiveness and productivity have to be priorities. Don't sacrifice value for the convenience of short meetings.

Have Each Attendee Contribute

Make sure everyone gets a chance to speak. A popular technique is to go around the table and ask everyone to comment on their assignments, problems, accomplishments, and so on. At the close of the meeting, you may want to go around the table a second time and give everyone a chance to air their concerns. Often, during this phase, individuals will voice concerns about items that they're aware of, have observed, or heard about, but didn't mention before because it was outside their specific project role. And, if you hear many people expressing the same concerns, there's a good chance that this "concern" is an actual "problem."

Watch the Mood of the Meetings

Project meetings can get tense. For intense, stressful projects, you may want to strongly encourage a more casual atmosphere to help lighten the mood. Some managers offer various forms of relief, such as little toys (Slinkies, Nerf balls, etc.), while other managers like to pummel their subjects with weapons (Koosh balls, water guns, etc.)—of course this should all be done in the spirit of fun, not punishment. Like the rotating minutes, you may want to rotate a job of bringing some refreshments (like donuts, bagels, etc.) to the meeting.

Control the Meetings and the Project

Regardless of how you run your project meetings, it is important that you maintain careful control of them, as well as the project as a whole. It's your project and your meeting. It's important that your team knows that and respects that. Yelling and disciplining probably won't be effective in any situation, but especially for those who report to you only for this project.

One especially effective way for managing team members is simply by asking questions. Few people like to say that they didn't complete an assigned task on time—especially if they don't have a justifiable excuse. By asking some simple and direct questions (like a parent who knows their child is being evasive), you may be able to improve the performance of team members simply because they want to avoid the discomfort (or possible embarrassment) of being questioned like that.

5.4 Funding Projects: What Do I Need to Know?

Projects cost money, and IT projects typically cost lots of money because they usually require hardware, software, and special skills and expertise. When you run a project in IT, you almost always need to determine how much it is going to cost and who is going to pay for it.

Determining Costs

In general, when it comes to IT projects, the concerns are primarily about "hard" dollars. Hard and soft money are economic and budgeting concepts. The definitions may vary from organization to organization, but for the most part, "hard" costs are those that the company has to write a check for (hardware, software, outside consultants, etc.). "Soft" costs refer to costs that are less concrete (office space, use of existing staff, time, etc.). When corporate management wants to know how much a project is going to cost, they often only care about hard costs. However, at times, it may be advantageous to add in the soft costs (like when you're trying to make a project look more impressive in a press release or on your resume). In addition, referring to the soft costs will demonstrate to management that you are aware that use of existing resources costs the company money as well.

Your best source for determining a project's costs might be the members of the project team, or it might not. It was their expertise that led you to select them for the team; tap this same expertise to evaluate costs. However, it is very possible that team members may only be able to provide you with information about the technologies that will be required, but not the costs of these technologies. This isn't unusual. Many technical personnel are not interested in the business side of the technology. When you face this situation, you may have to contact the vendors and manufacturers directly to get estimates on the products your team members identified.

Estimating Costs: Go High

As a general rule, projects always exceed their initial cost estimates. As a result, it is not uncommon for project managers to inflate their cost estimates by factors of 10% or more. There are several reasons for this:

- When estimating costs, it not unusual for smaller, "miscellaneous" items to be overlooked as everyone focuses on the big expenses. However, these miscellaneous items can add up to a significant amount.

- If management balks at the total cost, the inflation factor provides you with some room to revise the estimate downward without (in theory) impacting the success of the project.

- If the cost estimate is going to be wrong, you prefer that it be too high than have it be too low. If it were too low, you would end up in the embarrassing position of having to admit your poor planning and shortsightedness, and ask for more money.

The inflation factor gives a project manager an opportunity to look like a hero if he can complete the project for less than was estimated. Then again, wildly padding your estimate simply to ensure you come in under budget can negatively impact your credibility in the eyes of management, as well as the credibility of the IT department.

Earlier in the chapter we talked about identifying the project's milestones and risk factors. Those costs that you have not been able to adequately estimate can be included as part of the risk factors.

Projects Always Cost More Than Is Estimated

There are many costs to include within any IT project. Besides the obvious costs of hardware and software, others common costs to consider include vendor support costs, travel, installation costs, annual licenses and maintenance, physical plant expenses (raised floor, air conditioning), training, telecommunications, books and manuals, user group fees, trade shows, software utilities, test equipment and environments, parallel testing, incentives for project team members, consultants, and so on. And don't forget some money for the Nerf balls, munchies and sodas, and pizzas for working during lunch or late into the night.

Capital Expenditures and Expense Items

The last consideration when considering project costs are the differences between capital expenditures and expense items. A *capital expenditure* is for an item that will have a useful life of several years—like a piece of hardware. Some companies consider software to be a capital expenditure. An *expense item* is something whose value is gone almost immediately. (See the next chapter for a more thorough discussion of this and other budgeting topics.)

Examples

The monthly cost for a leased line, for example, is an expense item. The value of the money spent each month disappears in 30 days. If the useful life of a $10,000 computer is expected to be five years, accounting principles of capital depreciation allow you to spread the cost over the life of the equipment—in this case five years. So, even though the company may have to write a check for the full amount when it buys the equipment, the impact of this purchase on the company's books may only be $2,000 that first year and in each of the subsequent four years of the device's expected life.

You'll do yourself a big favor by checking with your accounting and finance department to get an understanding of your company's policies in regard to capital expenditures, depreciation schedules, and so on. Armed with this, it is within your best interest to group your project's costs into three categories: capital expenditures, expense items, and any recurring costs that will continue after the project is completed (e.g., maintenance contracts, telecommunication costs, etc.).

Exactly Who Is Going to Pay for It?

If the company is going to pay for all the costs you've estimated for this project, someone has to figure out where the money is going to come from. More than likely, the company's budget as well as your department's budget have already been set. And unless someone built enough padding into either of these to cover your new project's expenses, it is likely that your project may cause your department, as well as others, to go over budget.

This dilemma may not be the problem it initially seems. If corporate management approves your project and costs, then the various department heads will have your project as a ready justification when they have to explain their overruns. If the project is being sponsored or initiated by a very high-level executive, she may direct you to charge all of the project's costs to a special department code that she is responsible for, which alleviates everyone else's concerns about their own budgets.

Chargeback Codes

Some companies may choose to set up special "chargeback codes" for projects so that it is easier to track the total costs. This is especially true for very large projects. For smaller projects, individual departments may be instructed to "eat" the costs as part of their regular budget. It is important that you know how upper management wants to pay for the costs associated with your project so that there are no surprises, and that your project doesn't make enemies among other department heads at the same time you're trying to develop allies.

In larger corporations, certain projects may be assigned accounting codes of their own. This not only means that other departmental budgets are not impacted by the project, but it also presents a convenient way of tracking the project's costs. Then again, when such a special code exists (sometimes jokingly referred to as a "slush fund"), it can be awfully tempting to use it for items that have a tangential relationship to the project.

Justifying the Costs

No matter who initiated the project, sooner or later you're going to have to defend the costs. If you're the one who initiated the idea for the project, you may have to justify the project even before you know the costs.

The most efficient means of justifying your costs is to try to show a clear ROI (return on investment) for your project. For example, if you wanted to implement a pool of network modems for dial-out capabilities, you could easily justify the costs by demonstrating that the company will no longer have to pay for individual modems and telephone lines at each desk and workstation. (See Section 5.2 for more details on how to justify your project to other departments.)

However, project cost justification is rarely so cut and dried. More often, the justification consists of a variety of intangibles that are hard to quantify. In the modem pool example used above, you could also cite that it would improve security since connections in/out of the network would occur at a single point that could be better monitored and controlled.

First, here is a list of the more clear-cut justifications:

- Improved productivity and efficiencies (faster and/or cheaper)
- Reduced costs (fewer dollars/resources needed to accomplish the same task)
- Meeting changing demands of the marketplace (e.g., the introduction of the Euro)
- Less waste (materials, time, resources)
- Reduced head count (in these more politically correct times, it is better to phrase this in other more sensitive terms: "reallocation of existing staff to other company areas" or "eliminate the need to add to staff")
- Compliance with legislative regulations (tax laws, environmental issues, safety regulations, etc.)

Next, here is a list of the more nebulous intangible benefits:

- Increased advantage over competition

- Improved customer relations
- Improved company, product, brand awareness
- Higher quality
- Improved staff morale
- More convenience (for staff, customers, business partners)

Think of the project's justification as the answer you give to people when they ask, "Why should we do this?" and later when they ask "Why are we doing this?"

5.5 Keeping Track: How Do I Keep Track of My Project?

The bigger your project, the harder it is to keep track of who is doing what, how long different tasks will take, and so on. Earlier in this book, several techniques for project management were discussed (project meetings, minutes, etc.). But these techniques provide more snapshot-type information and fall short of giving any perspective about the "big picture."

Although there are many software tools available for project management, one in particular has become the predominant choice: Microsoft Project has become very popular for managing projects of almost any size.

Gantt Chart

A *Gantt chart* is a chart that tracks time along the horizontal axis. The vertical axis lists all the tasks associated with the project, their start and end dates, and the resources required. See Figure 5.1 on the next page for an example of a Gantt chart that can be generated from Microsoft Project.

When you print out the Gantt chart for a particular project, you and every member of the project team (along with anyone else who is interested) can see the real scope of it. Gantt charts rarely fit on a single page, by the way, so it is not uncommon for the entire report to require a whole wall to view when all the pages are taped together.

Microsoft Project

Simply entering your project's information into Project is a valuable exercise in itself. It forces you to think of the specific tasks needed, their dependencies on other tasks, and the times and resources needed. As you do this, Microsoft

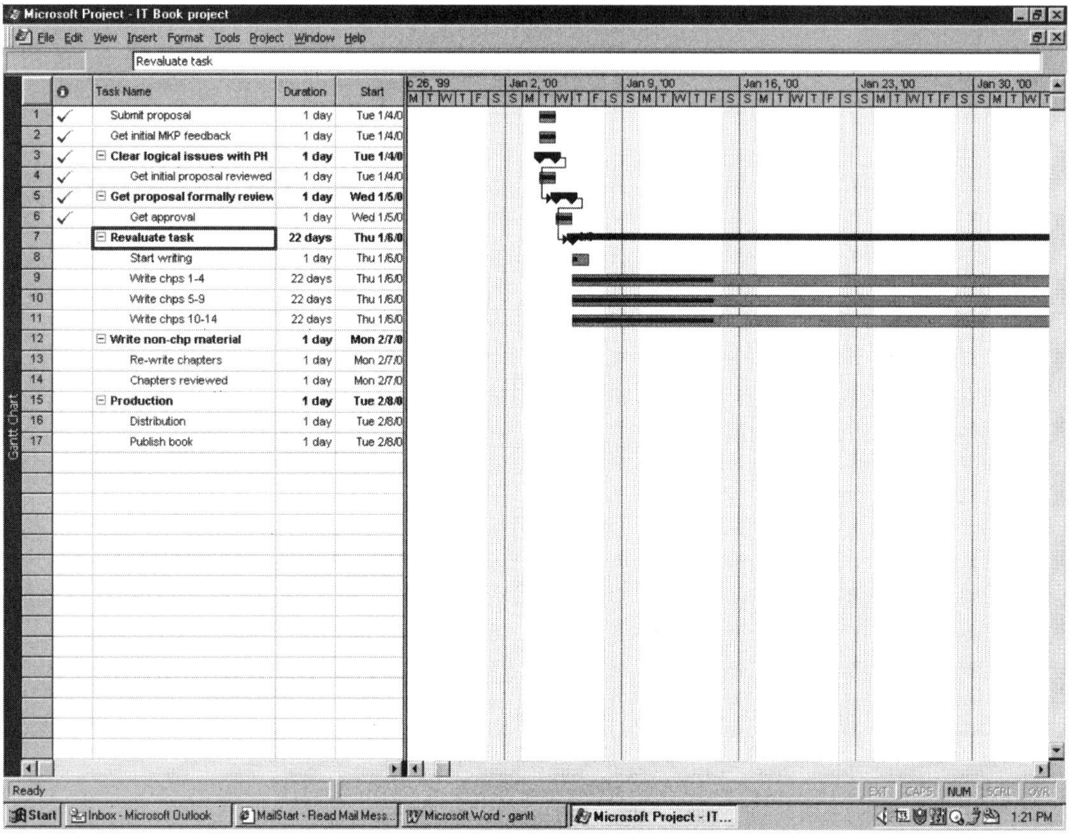

Figure 5.1   A Sample Gantt Chart

Project will alert you when the left hand doesn't know what the right hand is doing. For example, if you've overallocated resources, or if time constraints are being exceeded, Microsoft Project will let you know. By defining to Project which tasks can occur simultaneously, and which must be done sequentially, it is easy to make changes to any portion of the project and have all the dates and resource allocations updated automatically and see what the impact is.

Microsoft Project is a very inexpensive tool for the value and assistance it provides. If you've never used it before, it is to your benefit to find a few hours to familiarize yourself with it first. However, remember that Project is simply a tool, and a tool's effectiveness depends on your use of it. On the other hand, remember that *you* are running your project, not Project.

5.6 Further References

Web Sites

- *www.pmi.org* (Project Management Institute)

Articles and Books

- Bender, Stephen A., *Managing Projects Well,* Butterworth-Heinemann, 1998.
- Hallows, Jolyon E., *Information Systems Project Management: How to Deliver Function and Value in Information Technology Projects,* Amacom, 1997.
- Kerzner, Harold, *Project Management: A Systems Approach to Planning, Scheduling, and Controlling,* 6th ed., Wiley, 1997.
- Lewis, James P., *Team-Based Project Management,* Amacom, 1997.
- Lewis, James P., *The Project Manager's Desk Reference: A Comprehensive Guide to Project Planning, Scheduling, Evaluation, and Systems,* McGraw-Hill, 1999.
- Pennypacker, James S. (Editor), *The Principles of Project Management*, John R. Adams (Introduction), Project Management Institute Publishers, 1997.
- Taylor, James, *A Survival Guide for Project Managers,* Amacom, 1998.

Budgeting

- What a budget is and what its key components are
- How the whole budgeting process works
- What the difference is between *capital* and *expense* items
- Whether leasing or buying is better
- Key budgeting factors to consider

CHAPTER SIX

Introduction

As a manager, one of the things you have to manage is the money your department spends. And since IT departments often have one of the largest budgets in the organization, many eyes will be on your budget. This chapter will help you minimize, and deal with, raised eyebrows over those eyes.

6.1 Budgeting: What Are the Key Items in a Budget?

Every company keeps track of items a bit differently and may use different names, categories, and groupings. The best way to get started with a budget is to review the previous years' budgets for your department. Budgets are historical records and are (in most cases) carefully tracked documents—somebody in your company is always watching the money.

Sample Budget Items

First you need to consider all the different items your department could spend money on. Below is a list of potential items for your budget.

Personnel	Hardware	Software
Salaries	Upgrades	New software (applications, operating system, utilities, etc.)
Benefits	Maintenance	
Recruiting (agencies, ads, etc.)	New equipment	
	Leases/rentals	Maintenance/support
Bonuses/overtime	Replacement components	Upgrades
Education/training		License renewals
Consultants/temporary help		

Telecommunication services	Supplies	Travel and entertainment
Dial-up lines	Printer consumables (paper, toner)	Conferences
Leased lines	Backup tapes	Off-side travel to branch offices/new sites
ISP services		

Miscellaneous	Depreciation	Physical plant
Books and subscriptions	Hardware	Data center services
Membership dues for professional organizations	Software	Furniture
Postage		
Duplication		

Outside services	Overhead
Disaster recovery	Telephone
Off-site tape storage	Rent
Service bureaus	Utilities

6.2 Budgeting: How Does the Process Work?

Budgeting is the process of assigning specific amounts of money to specific departments within a company for a single fiscal year.

Frequently, the fiscal year that a budget tracks is *not* the January–December calendar year. The year that the budget tracks can be *any* 12-month period, although it generally begins on January 1, April 1, July 1, or October 1. Regardless, the 12-month period for your budget is called the *fiscal year*. If the fiscal year is not the same as the calendar year, you identify the fiscal years by the year in which it ends. For example, if your fiscal years go from July 1 to June 30, fiscal 2002 would refer to the budgeting between July 1, 2001, and June 30, 2002.

If you are new to management, you will quickly discover that the budget process and all its attendant processes are critical to you and your department's success. Regardless of how important your role in the company is deemed to be, unless that importance is backed up with financial support, you will find getting *anything* done to be a very difficult task.

In this chapter we discuss the general issues behind such topics as how and when a budget is generated, capital expenditures, leasing versus buying, and key factors you need to watch out for when doing your department's budget.

When Does Budgeting Start?

In general, the budgeting process begins 2–3 months before the start of the fiscal year. At this point, you begin to develop your first draft of the budget, estimating the amount of money you plan to spend during the upcoming 12 months. You prepare this budget based on the past year's spending as well as factoring in growth. Also include projects that you know your department is likely to undertake.

Ideally, you should have conversations with other department heads to see if you can learn about their upcoming needs and projects that might impact your spending. Depending on your company and the business that it is in, you may want to also include discussions with key partners, clients, suppliers, and customers. Similarly, it couldn't hurt to take a closer look at your company's chief competitors to try to learn about their use and plans for IT.

Other Reviewers for Your Budget

Most likely you'll be reviewing this first draft with your director or vice president. In general, it is a good idea to get as many eyes and minds involved with your budget as possible. You don't want to overlook anything. It is also a good idea for you to get your direct reports involved in the process. Solicit them for ideas about projects they know about, things they'd like to get done, and so on. In all likelihood, involving your staff in the budget process will benefit both of you—not only will they appreciate the opportunity, they will most likely offer up some items that you had neglected to think about. At the same time you are collecting the expected dollar amount for your budget, you want to make sure you note the need. You'll have to refer to this information when it comes time to explain, justify, and defend your budget. See the subsection below on "Getting Approval: Defending Your Budget."

How Close Should You Cut It?

It is general practice to *overestimate* your budget to a certain degree. While this style *sounds* dubious from a practical perspective, it is so widely practiced that you need to address the issue directly when you present your budget. Most experienced managers are expecting an overestimation.

It is important to understand that the practice of overestimating is a very common one and well understood by both sides. If you consciously do *not* overestimate (and many managers do not), make a point of bringing this up during budget discussions with your supervisors.

There are several benefits to overestimating:

1. It gives you room to cut if upper management asks to reduce spending.
2. It gives you room for those unanticipated expenses that invariably crop up.
3. It increases the likelihood that you'll be within budget for the year—which could be a critical factor in determining your bonus or merit increase.

In either case, you need to carefully research your material before making a formal presentation. Many managers—IT and non-IT alike—do not do their homework before making a formal presentation of a budget. This lack of preparation shows.

In general, the budget may be approved by your CFO or executive committee right around the start of the fiscal year. However, it is not unheard of for the final approval to be delayed until a month or two into the new fiscal year.

Getting Approval: Defending Your Budget

As you prepare your budget, it is entirely likely that you'll have to present it or defend it in some fashion during the year. While there may be great temptation to review each item, line by line, this is usually not warranted or welcome—though this is not an absolute, it pays to know your audience.

More likely, you'll probably want to give a high-level overview of your budget—using more words than numbers. It is best to couch these explanations in business terms, as opposed to IT terms. Don't try to explain why three programmers are needed for the e-commerce project. Instead, explain the value of the e-commerce project to the company, and that the cost of the programmers is the means to that end. Be prepared to explain how budget reductions may impact various goals and projects. For example, time frames may be expanded, or functionality will be sacrificed. It may be appropriate to make references to last year's budgets and projects as a comparison.

When presenting your budget, not only are you providing information and letting your audience see what they're getting for their money, but you're also trying to give them a level of confidence in you, so that they have a comfort level that you know what you're doing.

Don't be surprised if your budget goes through several iterations. The powers that be may kick it back and ask for reductions or more explanation. You may be asked to eliminate certain projects so that those costs can be recovered, or you may simply be asked to reduce it by a fixed amount or percentage.

Reports from Accounting

During the year, your Accounting department will probably furnish you with monthly reports of your department's year-to-date spending. You should look closely at these reports—it is not uncommon for data entry errors to occur where another department's purchase is charged to your cost center, or for one of your own purchases to be charged to the wrong category.

The report you get from accounting will probably have several columns for each category:

- Budgeted amount
- Actual amount for the month
- Actual amount year-to-date
- Variance against budget—an over/under amount indicating how well you are doing compared to the expected amount based on your original budget
- Variance against last year—an over/under amount indicating if you are spending more or less for the same items as last year

Your Accounting department may be able to give you reports of different formats based on your needs. Detailed reports can usually be requested if you have questions about information in summary reports.

Revising Your Budget

During the year, you may have one or two opportunities to revise your budget. These revisions are often referred to as forecasts, reforecasts, or updates. These revisions can be used to

- Include projects that were not expected during the initial budgeting process
- Eliminate or reduce costs for projects that were canceled or scaled down since the initial budget was proposed
- Update estimates based on other changes (e.g., vendor pricing, expansion, size of projects)
- Demonstrate anticipated cost reduction as a result of (management-ordered) belt tightening

Each opportunity to revise the budget is a chance to deliver a more accurate estimate. Your initial budget is essentially a 12-month projection. However, a mid-year revision is 6 months of actual costs and only 6 months of projection.

6.3 Capital vs. Expense Items: What Is the Difference?

Whenever you spend money on something, you'll have to consider if it is a capitalized item or expensed item. A *capital expenditure* is for an item that will have a useful life of several years—like a piece of hardware. Some companies consider software to be a capital expenditure.

Alternatively, an *expense item* is something whose value is gone in a shorter period of time. In general, Accounting departments give IT equipment an estimated life of 3–5 years; the equipment used on an assembly line in a factory might have a life of 10–20 years.

Because there is more paperwork involved in tracking a capitalized expense for each year of its useful life, there is generally a minimum dollar amount for capitalizing items. For example, a computer cable might be useful for 10 years, but since it only costs $25, it would not be capitalized. The minimum amount for capitalizing varies from company to company. Figures of $500, $1,000 or $1,500 are not uncommon—check with your Accounting department.

Examples

A *software support agreement,* for example, is an expense item. The value of the money spent each year only lasts for the 12 months of the agreement. If the useful life of a $10,000 computer is expected to be five years, accounting principles of capital depreciation allow you to spread the cost over the life of the equipment—in this case five years. So, even though the company may have to write a check for the full amount when it buys the equipment, the impact of this purchase on the company's books may only be $2,000 that first year and in each of the subsequent four years of the device's expected life.

You'll do yourself a big favor by checking with your Accounting and Finance department to get an understanding of your company's policies in regard to capital expenditures, depreciation schedules, and so on. Armed with this, it is within your best interest to group your project's costs into three categories: capital expenditures, expense items, and any recurring costs that will continue after the project is completed (e.g., maintenance contracts, telecommunication costs, etc.).

There are several gray areas with capital and expense items. For example, some companies capitalize software, while others don't (see sidebar). Some may capitalize the software that is required to make a piece of hardware useful (e.g., the operating system). Some organizations will capitalize consulting services if they are bundled with the sale of hardware.

Software: Capital or Expense?

In 1999, the American Institute of Certified Public Accountants adopted a new set of accounting rules regarding software. These rules became part of the Generally Accepted Accounting Principles (GAAP), which all public corporations must comply with. Specifically, the new rules, called SOP-98-1, specified that:

- "Purchased off the shelf software, systems development and systems integration costs are to be treated as assets capitalized."

- "Planning, operations, and implementation costs for all internally developed software may be expenses as a current holding cost and need not be capitalized."

Source: Strassman, Paul A., "GAAP Helps Whom?"
Computerworld, December 6, 1999

Items to Watch Out For

For items that are capitalized, you will see the cost for each year of the item's useful life charged to your budget (usually in a category called depreciation). The Accounting department usually has software, frequently called a "fixed assets application," to track the cost and depreciation of capitalized items.

The example above said that a $25 cable wouldn't be capitalized because the cost was too low, even though it had a long useful life. If you place an order for 1,000 cables, you still would not capitalize the cables (even though the order totaled $25,000) because individually they cost so little. However, some companies may still choose to look at the total order so that it can be capitalized. Taken to an extreme, this philosophy would mean that a very large order of paper clips would be capitalized—even though this is clearly inappropriate.

6.4   Lease vs. Buy: Which One Is Better?

One of the discussions you're likely to have about acquiring hardware is "lease versus buy." Leasing computer equipment carries with it essentially the same pros and cons as leasing a car (see Table 6.1 on the next page).

Details of Leasing

When you lease something, you are essentially renting it for a specified period of time. In general, you make arrangements to purchase a piece of hardware, but the leasing company makes the actual purchase. The leasing company is then the owner, and they lease it to you. Over the period of the lease, the total lease payments will total slightly higher than the purchase cost. This difference is a result of the rate charged by the leasing company (essentially interest).

During the term of the lease (which is generally several years) you are responsible for the hardware, its maintenance, upkeep, and so on—just as if you owned it. You will generally make monthly or quarterly lease payments. It is important to note that lease payments are treated as an expense item, not as a capital asset. The reason is simple: you don't own the equipment that is being leased.

Crucial Details

At the end of the lease, you have several choices:

- Terminate the lease by sending the equipment back to the leasing company.

Table 6.1   The pros and cons of leasing.

Pros of Leasing	Cons of Leasing
Predictable payments for the life of the lease could ease administration.	Extra effort during purchasing to coordinate activities between leasing company and equipment vendor.
Allows companies with limited cash flows, or lines of credit, to obtain expensive equipment.	Complications if equipment is upgraded during the life of the lease: Should the upgrade be leased or purchased? If leased, it needs to be coterminus with original lease. If purchased, have to remember not to send the upgrade back to leasing company at lease's end.
Allows for predictable and planned turnover of equipment that is regularly replaced (e.g., PCs).	If you're leasing a high volume of equipment (like PCs in a large environment), there is an additional effort to track inventory precisely so that equipment can be located at end of lease to be returned.
	The packing and shipping of equipment being returned at the end of a lease could be burdensome.
	If you charge equipment to the department where it is used, it could require extra effort to properly code each lease invoice.

- Extend the lease (although you should be careful that the new lease payments are based on the unit's current market value, not the original purchase price).
- Buy the equipment. Often you can do this for a very low cost—like $1.00—or for its current market value.

Keep in mind you generally have to inform the leasing company of your plans 90 days prior to the end of the lease.

Who Makes This Decision?

Lease versus buy is not a decision that IT should make alone. In fact, it is a decision usually made by the financial departments with input from IT. Very often, the decision will be based on whether or not the company can better accommodate the costs as a capital expense or an operational expense.

6.5 **Budgeting: What Are Some Key Factors I Should Consider?**

There are a number of key factors that you should consider when budgeting.

Growth

In general, the IT workload grows each year. Even if the company's growth is flat, and the general cost of technology continues to decline, it is likely that the need for, and use of, IT resources will continue to grow. This could include items like faster line speeds, more server power, and more disk space.

It is hard to determine an exact figure for each year's growth. Often it is no more than a best guess. But, before making your guess, you should examine how the IT workload has grown in the past, and learn about upcoming activities and projects that the company, or other departments, have planned that might impact the demand on IT.

Technological Change

Technology changes. This is a fact of life that makes this industry so fascinating and frustrating at the same time. When you buy a new piece of equipment, for example, a server, it is safe to say that you'll be able to upgrade it over time to get more out of it as growth demands. You'll be able to add memory, disk space, and perhaps additional processors. Eventually, there will come a time when it really doesn't pay to invest more money into this device, either because the technology has changed (e.g., new generations of processors) or the cost of new equipment is relatively inexpensive. Regardless, you need to anticipate this. While technology does change fast, you need to be able to forecast the need to upgrade it, and its eventual obsolescence and replacement.

As equipment gets replaced, you're likely to be questioned for the need. Be prepared to explain, to users who have little understanding of technology, why you're buying a new piece of equipment to do the same job as the piece of equipment you bought three years ago.

Staff

The turnover rates of IT personnel vary tremendously. Staff that works with the latest and greatest technologies may not last more than a year or two. PC technicians may also last a short time as they seek to find opportunities beyond the Help Desk. Your company, salary and benefits, each employee's goals and objectives, and their overall happiness with the company—and with you as their manager—are all factors that will influence your staff members' decisions to stay with the company.

Even though your staff may seem quite content, you should assume that there will be some turnover. You may not be able to predict who and when, but you can probably estimate the number of people that will leave. As you try to best-guess the turnover, you need to estimate what it will cost to recruit their replacements—headhunters, newspaper ads, Web postings, and so on. And when you're thinking that some employees may actually leave you, you might want to also throw some money into your consulting budget to provide for interim staffing while you recruit new employees.

Software Maintenance

No one knows *everything* there is to know about technology—that's why vendors offer maintenance agreements. This can be a significant factor for software—annual fees of 20% of the purchase price are not unheard of. Some packages are so critical to your environment that you cannot even consider forgoing support. Other packages will be less critical. Keep in mind that sometimes software vendors differentiate between maintenance and support. If so, "support" generally refers to being able to get assistance (phone, Web based, etc.) when you have a problem or question regarding the use of the software. "Maintenance" may be limited to your ability to get upgrades for the product. Make sure you understand what your vendor means by "maintenance" and "support."

Hardware Maintenance

Like software, some critical devices (e.g., a production server) may have very high levels of formal maintenance arrangements, while other devices (e.g., a modem) may go without formal support for a variety of reasons (e.g., it may be just as easy, or cheap enough, to simply keep a spare around).

Crucial Details

While software support and maintenance are often only provided by the original manufacturer, there are often numerous sources to go to for hardware maintenance. Factors to consider when looking at maintenance agreements for hardware include

- Days and hours of coverage required (9–5 M–F, 24 × 7, etc.)
- Response time guarantees (keep in mind that frequently the "response" time refers to how long before the vendor calls you back, not how long it takes for a technician to arrive on site)

- Plans for spare parts (if you contract with some vendors, they may offer to keep a locked cabinet of parts in your computer room so that they are always available to them)

- Whether the vendor and/or its technicians are certified

- Pricing: standard versus premium for extended coverage, or escalated response times

- Financial penalties if the vendor fails to meet promised service levels

Time-and-Material Contracts

Alternatives to maintenance contracts are *time-and-material* (T&M) arrangements. Under these arrangements, when you place a service call for a piece of hardware, the vendor will bill you for the technician's time and the parts that are needed—similar to a repair on your car. Because of the high degree of reliability of today's technology, it is entirely possible you will save money by forgoing hardware maintenance contracts and rolling the dice on T&M.

Risks with T&M

There are two risks associated with T&M:

- The repairs could be costly, and it is entirely likely that the cost of a single site visit for a repair will be more than the cost of an annual contract.

- Vendors usually give greater priority to calls placed by customers with contracts than to calls for T&M service.

If you go with T&M, make sure you set up the account with the vendors you will use. By establishing a relationship in advance, knowing your customer number and site number, and having the right phone number to call, you will expedite the process when you need to make a call.

Vendor Policies

Also inquire as to the vendor's policies regarding

- Hourly rates, overtime
- Minimum time charges
- Charges for travel
- Credit for defective parts that are swapped out
- Availability of parts

Warranties

The last choice for hardware support is the warranty that comes with new equipment. Warranties of up to three years are not uncommon. However, sometimes the warranty requires that you send the unit back to the manufacturer or bring it to an authorized repair center, although some equipment does come with an on-site warranty. But it is important to realize that most on-site warranties generally provide for a "best effort" for a "next business-day" response. Generally, vendors and/or their resellers offer upgrades for new equipment warranties to provide for higher levels of response.

When you're thinking about skipping a maintenance contract on a piece of hardware because the price seems to high, be sure to think about the cost to your environment and its impact on customers, users, clients, and business partners if that unit should go down. And consider a situation where a piece of equipment fails after business hours on a Friday. Your call may not even be handled until the following Monday, and a next business-day response would get you a technician on Tuesday. She may diagnose a faulty part, and its replacement has to be overnighted from the warehouse for delivery on Wednesday. In this case, you've been down for five days. Throw a few wrinkles into the situation—a technician who doesn't show, a misdiagnosis, out-of-stock parts, delayed deliveries—and your downtime could easily be a week.

6.6 Further References

Articles and Books

- Droms, William G., *Finance and Accounting for Nonfinancial Managers: All the Basics You Need to Know*, Perseus, 1998.

- Finney, Robert G., *Office Finances Made Easy: A Get-Started Guide to Budgets, Purchasing, and Financial Statements*, Amacom, 1999.

- Strassman, Paul A., "GAAP Helps Whom?," *Computerworld*, December 6, 1999.

- Thibodeau, Patrick, "Gov't IT Execs Seek Software Accountability," *Computerworld*, October 18, 1999.

IT Infrastructure Fundamentals

CHAPTER SEVEN

What You Will Learn

- How to take a useful inventory
- Ways to find out who your users are, and why this is important
- How to estimate and deal with downtime
- Ways to test new software versions
- How to manage your legacy systems
- What "TCO" and "asset management" are

Introduction

In the field of information technology, it is often easy to be distracted by the exciting developments in hardware, software, the Internet, and so on. However, as a manager, you also have to keep your eyes on those areas that aren't quite as alluring. While activities like tracking your total cost of ownership (TCO), inventorying your environment, and managing legacy systems may be items you're tempted to put off, you mustn't. In fact, it may be one of the first activities you want to tackle in your new role as an IT manager. A first-hand knowledge of the environment, its history, and operation can help you to better define needs and future plans, and avoid repeating mistakes that were made in the past.

7.1 Inventory: Where Do I Start?

You probably have more technology in your environment than you realize. And it can be very difficult to get a handle on it all. The value of carefully determining everything you are responsible for, however, cannot be overestimated. Not only do you define your liability, but you understand the amount of resources you have at your disposal. Every audit uncovers surprises; some are small, but sometimes you can find some hardware or an underused closet that can be of great value.

Not only is completing an inventory good for insurance purposes, but it's also good to include this type of information in a disaster recovery plan. For more details on developing a disaster recovery plan, see Chapter 14.

Start Big

In order to avoid being overwhelmed with information, you should start at the highest levels, and work your way down to more detail.

WAN Schematic

A typical WAN schematic (Figure 7.1 on the next page) includes site locations, type of connections (including backup communication facilities), carriers, and so on. You may also want to include types and number of servers, number of users, IP addressing, key contacts, and street addresses. The WAN schematic should be updated regularly and distributed to members of the IT department. It should be posted on the wall of the data center for easy reference. The network manager should have it posted above his desk.

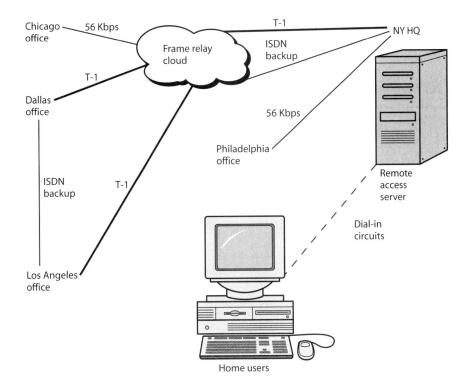

Figure 7.1 WAN Schematic

LAN Schematic

A typical LAN schematic (Figure 7.2 on the next page) drills down into the detail of a particular site from the WAN schematic. It should include the topology, location, and connectivity of switches, routers, and hubs. It should identify different types of cabling (copper, fiber, shielded, etc.). It can also include room locations for various network equipment, model numbers for key components, IP addresses, and so on. Like the WAN schematic, the LAN schematic should be regularly updated so that it is always current, and distributed so it is available for easy reference to all that need it.

Server Hardware Inventory

A server hardware inventory (Figure 7.3 on page 117) drills further down into the LAN schematic by documenting details of each server. An inventory can include basic items like processor type, memory, disk, function, and so on. But it can also include further details such as its backup cycle, what type of maintenance coverage was in force when it was purchased, whether it is a production or test server, and what users are affected by it.

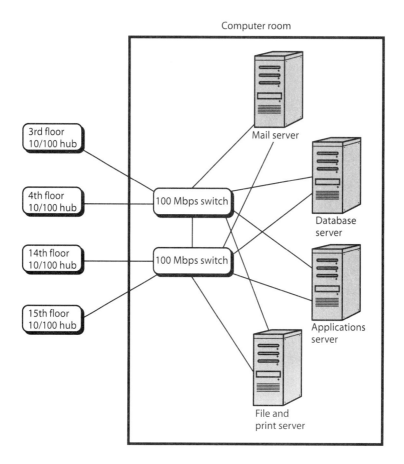

Figure 7.2 LAN Schematic

Server Software Inventory

A server software inventory (Figure 7.4 on the next page) looks at the details of the server from a software perspective. This can include items like operating system type and version, a list of applications that are running on it, backup, security, management, and BIOS version.

Communications Facilities Inventory

A communications facility inventory goes into the details of the WAN connections that were defined in the WAN and LAN schematics (Figure 7.5 on the next page). Items to track here include circuit numbers, circuit endpoints (including building and room numbers), carriers, type/speed of line (T-1, analog, ISDN, etc.), and phone numbers reporting problems. Although telecommunications in

Name	Manufacturer	Model	Function	Processor Type	Number of Processors	Disk Storage	RAM	Number of NICS	NIC Speed	Service Contract	Number of Power Supplies

Figure 7.3   Sample Server Hardware Inventory

Name	OS	Backup Software	Virus Software	BIOS Version	Database Software	Application (1)	Application (2)	Utility (1)	Utility (2)

Figure 7.4   Sample Server Software Inventory

Circuit Number	Endpoint (1) Location	Endpoint (1) Device/Port	Endpoint (2) Location	Endpoint (2) Device/Port	Carrier	Type	Phone Number for Service	Approximate Monthly Cost

Figure 7.5   Sample Telecommunications Facilities Inventory

the United States is very reliable, problems still come up. When a line goes down, you don't want to find yourself asking, "What line?" and scrambling to find out the circuit number and who you have to call to report the problem. And in larger environments, there are so many lines and so much activity in regard to adding, changing, and canceling them, it is quite easy to lose track. It is not unheard of for large IT environments to discover that they've been paying the bill on a line that they didn't know they had and had stopped using years ago.

Vendor	Sales Representative	Billing Representative	Support Center Phone Number	Account Number	Volume Agreement Terms	Web Site

Figure 7.6   Sample Vendor Inventory

Vendor List

You're going to deal with lots of vendors, and each will have several contacts for sales, billing, technical support, and so on. Keep track of who you're dealing with and any special arrangements you have. See Figure 7.6 above for a sample vendor inventory. Some vendors you'll call so often that you'll have the phone number memorized. For others, like vendors of legacy equipment, that you only speak with once a year or so, this inventory will be very helpful.

Support Services

When there's a hardware failure you should know immediately where to turn to find out how to call for service, including phone number and account number, and what levels of coverage you're entitled to. See Figure 7.7 on the next page for a sample inventory. It is particularly important that the information be current, distributed, and posted. You don't want to wait until there's a component failure to learn that the support provider's phone number changed, or that your contract expired.

Write It Down

The inventory documentation should be in a very readable format. The use of diagrams, charts, schematics, and so on is very effective. Infrastructure documentation should be updated and distributed regularly. Although documentation of this sort is considered valuable, many environments don't have it because IT workers often have little interest in creating documentation. However, not only is the documentation important, but the process of having your staff collect the information and create the documentation can be of value in itself. Naturally, you should work towards making the process of collecting this information as efficient and as natural to your organization as possible. These days, on-line forms and various other data-collecting means are often stored on the company's intranet site.

Vendor	Support Center Phone Number	Account ID	Account Password	Equipment Serviced	Terms of Coverage	Contract Start Date	Contract End Date

Figure 7.7   Support Service Inventory

Consider collecting all these various types of documents (schematics, inventories, etc.) and putting them together in a binder of some sort for each member of the team. This way everyone knows where the information is. Some of the documents should be posted on walls (data center, wiring closets) and bulletin boards so that they are all available for immediate reference.

What You May Find

An inventory can uncover under-/overutilized resources, potential problem and risk areas, and resources and facilities that were assumed to be working but may not be. It may uncover technology that is outdated and no longer needed, or that needs to be upgraded. Or it may uncover resources providing similar or identical functionality that can be combined. It can also help you to feel comfortable that your staff has a good perspective on their environment.

Define Your Scope

Of course, you also need to be careful about being overwhelmed with documentation and information. For example, as an IT manager you may want to know what version of software is running on your server, but you probably don't need to be aware of every patch that's been applied—although your LAN manager might need this information. Similarly, if there's an inventory of workstations, you may only choose to see the summary of information—perhaps broken down by department, location, or type of equipment.

If your staff is reluctant to do documentation (which is fairly normal for people in IT), you need to demonstrate how important it is as a way of encouraging them to keep it current. You can post schematics on bulletin boards and on the walls of the data center so that it is used as reference material by the rest of the staff. Use the documentation in your memos and presentations to corporate management. And when you're staff is discussing various issues with you, bring out the documentation and refer to it. Ask them to explain what they're talking about using the documentation they've given you.

An excellent way to determine the scope is to create a disaster recovery scenario in which you have to bring the entire IT infrastructure up after a major failure (like a fire, earthquake, or hurricane; see Chapter 14). If you can walk your way through the entire recovery scenario, then your scope is complete. If you find yourself guessing at some of the elements of your IT infrastructure, then your scope needs improvement.

7.2 Users: How Do I Find Out Who They Are, and Why Is This Important?

This is a critical first step in being an effective IT manager. Do this step well, and then act on the information you gather.

Ninety-nine percent of IT managers have the same user group: everyone who works for the same company that they do! In some cases, IT managers have clients or customers outside the corporation. Some companies have their IT staffs perform some "customer-facing" services, often on a short-term basis. A client might need several new PCs hooked up, for example, or a small network put in place. But these are often one-time events, and long-term IT service needs are addressed in different ways. In general, though, the "core audience" of an IT staff is the employees of the corporation they all work for.

Therefore, everyone has the same ultimate goal: to maximize the short- and long-term profit, and health and wealth of the company. It is imperative that you keep this goal in mind; in many conversations in the future, you (and the person you are talking to) are likely to forget it.

Find Out Who Your Department Thinks Its Users Are

It is important to note that some people consider the term "user" to be inappropriate. Because IT is essentially a service organization, some find the term "client" or "customer" to be more representative of the relationship. Don't quibble, keep focused: *who are the people your department is trying to serve?*

- This can be a simple voice poll; ask your people while you are discussing other matters with them. Keep it informal. Formality will come later.

- They will most likely reply that their users are a small subset of the company; they may reply that their users are mostly "in Accounting" or "Tom S., who calls me all the time." While these are true, they are not the entire story. If your users are customers, or business partners, find out who they are, where they are, and what their relationship is with your company—and what they want out of the relationship.

Find Out Who Your Boss Thinks Your Users Are

This data is useful for two reasons:

1. You find out what he thinks your job is.
2. You find out where some political issues lie.

If your boss's perception of who your users are varies radically from yours, you have a serious problem that you must correct immediately.

Having spoken to your team and your boss, now canvass the rest of the organization. Contact the leads of the major departments of the company. Obviously, size matters. If you work for a 10-person start-up, talking to all the key players will not take long, nor will it be a major effort. You still need to prepare, but you can do it in a short amount of time. If you work for a Fortune 500 corporation with divisions around the globe, on the other hand, canvassing your users is going to require some careful sampling.

Find Out Your User's Needs

In either case, it is imperative that you and your department have a clear definition of who your users are. And once you know who they are, you need to meet with them, establish a relationship, and ask them some questions about their needs.

Use these sample questions:

1. How well does IT satisfy your needs?
2. What services do you currently get from the IT department?
3. Which services do you need/would you like that you are not currently getting?
4. How do you envision the use of information technology in your department?

Ask these questions of the key department managers in your company. Tell them you are trying to align your department's functions with their needs. They may look at you funny, but then they will reply to your questions.

After this initial meeting, work to establish a continuing dialog and relationship with key users and departments. This might be an ongoing process, or it might be facilitated through periodic meetings, perhaps a few times a year. The meetings can be somewhat informal:

- Ask about the department's plans for the short and long term. You're likely to learn of possible challenges and opportunities of mutual benefit to your department and the user's.

- Tell your users and clients about short- and long-term plans for the IT department.

- Ask where IT has fallen short, where it's met expectations, and where it's exceeded expectations.

- Ask your users and clients about IT technologies they've read about, or how they believe it is being used in other organizations that would be worth investigating.

- When it's time to prepare annual budgets, be proactive in giving department heads some general cost estimates for common items: workstations, laptops, servers, and so on. Invite them to contact you to review costs for special projects they are considering for the upcoming year.

What you are trying to do is establish a relationship with the users and customers. Remember that in the beginning, the most important asset you may bring to these discussions will probably be a set of ears.

7.3 Downtime: How Do I Estimate, Schedule, and Announce It?

Downtime is a fact of life. With a little bit of luck, and some careful planning, your downtime will be both minimal and planned—it is the unplanned downtime that has the severest impact on you, your users, clients, customers, and partners, and the reputations of your department and team.

As much as we try to avoid downtime, sometimes it can't be helped. It might be a critical upgrade (either software or hardware), or a scheduled power outage, or perhaps you're relocating your data center.

Minimizing

While downtime can't be entirely avoided, there are several steps you can take to minimize impact. First, accurately estimate the impact. If you're upgrading a router, perhaps only the users in remote offices will be affected, and the local users can continue unaffected. Or if you're doing maintenance on your e-mail environment, your users can continue to use the core business applications. If the core business applications are down, perhaps users will be able to continue to work on their word processing, spreadsheets, and e-mail in the meantime. So, when estimating the impact, you need to consider *who* will be affected and *what functionality* will be affected. Lastly, you need to consider the *duration* of the impact.

Estimating

When you try to estimate how long downtime will last, there are several components:

- The amount of time it takes to bring the systems down from production mode to off-line or maintenance mode.
- The amount of time required to perform the work that necessitated the downtime.
- Time required to test the work that was done.
- Time required to undo the work that was done, if the tests indicate failure, or to restore to a premaintenance state.
- Time required for bringing the systems up into production mode.
- And, just a little bit more time for good measure. Better to overestimate your downtime and return the system to the users earlier than you announced than to underestimate the downtime and have users frustrated that the system was not available when you said it would be.

Scheduling

Sometimes factors outside your control may determine your downtime. Your local electric utility may tell you of their plans to replace the transformer on the corner, or an upcoming holiday weekend may be the only opportunity that provides you with enough time to perform the work you need to do.

But, in general, the very nature of planned downtime usually means that you can decide when the systems will be brought down. Once you've estimated the "who" (will be affected) and the "what" (functionality will be disrupted), you can take the estimated duration and grab your calendar to schedule the "when" of your downtime.

First consider the "who" and "what." If the downtime will only affect a portion of your users, or just a portion of the environment's functionality, you may be able to schedule it at a time when these users are not in, or when the affected functionality is not required. Most often, downtime is scheduled outside of business hours. It is generally preferred by IT professionals to schedule downtime as soon as possible after the end of business hours, as opposed to just prior to business hours. By doing so, there is more time available in case a crisis delays bringing the systems back into production mode.

When you consider your users, make sure you include your customers, clients, and business partners who also use your systems in some fashion. And be sure to consider more than your living and breathing users. Even though there may be no hands at the keyboards at 2:00 in the morning, the data center operators may have scheduled batch jobs to do critical invoice processing at that time.

Assemble all these parameters together—who, what, and when—and you may find that the calendar doesn't allow you any downtime. In these cases, you need to make some judgment calls and determine when the downtime will have the least impact. Lastly, before you announce your decision, you should contact representatives of key departments, and possibly business partners and customers, to see if they have any special activities planned at the time you'd like to take the system down.

Announcing

When it comes to announcing downtime remember that, in general, the longer the downtime you have planned, the sooner you should begin announcing the downtime. And you probably need to announce it several times. Announce an hour of downtime two weeks in advance and users will likely forget. Announce a weekend of downtime a day in advance, and you're likely to have users gunning for you because of the short notice. Of course, sensitivity to downtime varies from environment to environment—based on size, industry, hours worked, criticality of IT systems, and so on.

You can use various means of announcing the downtime—memos, e-mail, and voice-mail broadcasts. Choose a means, or combination, that you think will be the most effective for your users and your environment.

The announcement should be worded briefly and contain several factors:

- Overview reason for the downtime (maintenance, upgrade, etc.)
- Date and time the system will be unavailable
- Who will be affected and what functionality will be disrupted
- An acknowledgment/apology for the inconvenience

7.4 Testing: How Do I Test New Software Versions?

Whether it's software you developed in-house, or software you bought from a vendor, testing new versions is an important step. The fear with new versions of software is that you'll risk your existing stable working environment for the features and enhancements of the new version.

For certain types of software (e.g., word processing), you may be able to roll out a new version to a very small portion of your user community in a controlled test. For other types of software (e.g., mail, operating system, core business), a rollout may be more of an all-or-none type effort. In certain cases, an upgrade may be effectively a one-way process—that is, the only way to back out of the upgrade is to restore the entire system, including data, to a preupgrade state. Not only does this require time, but it could mean a loss of work in regard to the data that users have to re-enter.

Create a Test Environment

In either of these cases, testing plays a very vital role. To ensure that you fully test software, you should have a test environment—a separate hardware and software system designed specifically to allow for hardware and software testing. A test environment, sometimes called a production test environment (PTE), is a distinct system, apart from your regular, working system, which is called the production environment. Depending on the type of software you are testing, the test environment might consist of a small server that closely approximates your production environment including application software and a test copy of your database.

Having an environment specifically for testing has numerous benefits:

- It allows you to get a feel for what the actual upgrade process is like, and the difficulties you might encounter in performing the upgrade.
- It allows your users to test the new software and get exposure to it before it becomes production.
- It allows you to assess the impact on performance.
- It allows you to try out back-out procedures.
- It allows you to test the new features of the software to see if they work as promised.

In general, a test environment allows you the luxury to evaluate and test the impact of new software on your environment, without disrupting your production environment. Of course, even the best test environment is of little value without sufficient time and procedures to effectively test. Still, even the best test environments are only close approximations of production environments.

7.5 Testing: How Do I Test on a Production System?

No matter how much testing you do, eventually you still have to move the new software to production, and no test environment will be an exact replica of the production environment. There may be differences in hardware, users' activity, and so on. When you upgrade your production environment, you want the upgrade process to include some tests for success. This might include

- Installation and customization testing
- Running programs and procedures (perhaps vendor supplied) to ensure the upgrade process was complete, and the system is as it should be
- Running some production batch job
- Having users test the applications
- Comparing pre- and postupgrade statistics and information to ensure the integrity of the system

In a large environment (perhaps with multiple locations and/or multiple servers) it may be possible to perform the upgrade on only a portion of the environment. Most vendors realize that it may not be logistically possible to upgrade an entire environment at once, and usually write their software to be compatible with its own earlier versions. This is usually true with software like operating systems and e-mail. If this is the case, you should consider selecting a specific site (or server) to be the first candidate to be upgraded. By doing so, you minimize the impact to the entire environment, you gain experience as you upgrade more and more of the environment, and you build the confidence of your users/ customers/partners as they see that the initial upgrades went well.

7.6 Testing: How Do I Create a Test Environment?

Too often, a test environment is cobbled together with outdated equipment that is lying around, and unlicensed software. And, in some cases, the system that results from this "technique" may be entirely adequate for the immediate purposes. However, as your company grows, and the organization's dependence on IT grows, it becomes increasingly more important to have a more rigorous test environment.

The test environment should essentially be considered a formal part of the production environment—similar class server(s), similarly configured, copies of databases, with current versions of software and utilities, and so on. If your shop does a significant amount of in-house development, the test environment will probably be regularly used by the programming staff before new applications are moved into production. Each time a problem is found in production that could have been detected—but was actually missed—it brings further scrutiny to your testing techniques. In an environment that regularly uses their test environment to test, this scrutiny can serve as an iterative self-correcting process to keep the test environment current and useful.

Finally, you may consider redundant environments—production versus test. These environments are essentially swapped (cut over) and repointed during an upgrade. A new software version is loaded on the test environment. Once the testing is considered successful, the data is moved over and the test environment is now considered production, and the previous production environment becomes test.

Legacy Systems: How Do I Manage These?

"Legacy" is a euphemism for "older technology" and could refer to software and/or hardware. Resources become "legacy" simply with the passing of time—there is never a specific decision to categorize something as legacy; it just evolves that way.

There are good reasons for keeping certain functions on legacy technologies. The cost of converting (particularly staff, consulting, training, new products, migration, disruption to the business, etc.) can be prohibitive. More importantly, a legacy system—as a result of years of updates, modifications, tweaks, patches, and so on—may be performing its function perfectly well. And, strange as it sounds, it may be impossible to find a more technologically current solution that can provide the same level of performance.

How is that possible? Corporations have current needs, sure, but they often have needs that have been identified and addressed years in the past—with solutions that matched the problems very well. To create a new solution to an old problem is often asking for trouble—especially if an "old" but perfectly functioning solution exists. Stories abound, for example, of personal computer users still using old Intel 386 machines. Should these users upgrade? Depends on their needs, but most of these people are very happy with the solutions their systems provide them. (Imagine the learning curve for a user going from MS-DOS 3.0 to Windows 2000 in one step!)

Supporting Legacy Systems

As you would expect, the big fear corporate IT managers have in regard to maintaining legacy systems (regardless of the reason they are being maintained) is support. Vendors go out of business, are acquired, merged, and sold. Through all these machinations the vendor may lose interest in providing support to a product it no longer sells. Additionally, you may find it difficult to hire staff who has interest, or expertise, in your legacy technologies.

There's no simple solution, but there are some guidelines that can smooth the inevitable bumps in the road:

- **Documentation:** Have your staff document as much as they can about the legacy technology. Get your hands on every manual (multiple copies, if possible) the vendor ever produced on the product. Consider looking in bookstores for books by third parties.

- **Third-party support resources:** The original vendor may continue to provide support for the technology, but more out of a sense of obligation than a desire to provide quality customer service. Support from a third party might be more expensive, but they may also be more interested in your business than the original vendor.

- **Training:** If still available, send your staff (and possibly even consultants) to training. In addition to the training, you may make valuable contacts among other students and the instructors.

- **Peer support:** Join user groups, discussion groups, and subscribe to any newsletters, journals, or e-mail lists that cover the legacy systems you have.

- **Staff assignments:** Look at your staff. Some might be attracted to the excitement of being involved with new technologies. Others might prefer the comfort and stability of an assignment focused on established products.

- **Varied assignments:** For those whose job consists of supporting legacy systems, consider rewarding them by giving them the first exposure to new technologies and assignments.

- **Team assignments:** Instead of assigning one or two individuals to supporting the legacy system, consider spreading the assignment over a larger team (along with other assignments). This will help reduce your risk if a key individual leaves.

7.8   TCO and Asset Management: What Are They?

In the past couple of years, two phrases that have garnered a lot of attention for IT managers are "asset management" and "total cost of ownership" (TCO). Many people use these phrases synonymously—and while they are similar, they are not identical.

Both of these phrases are most often used in reference to personal computers. It is important to realize that with a population of several hundred or several thousand desktop computers in a company, it can take an enormous amount of resources to support them. As such, there are many hidden costs associated with these devices, their use, and their support. Accordingly, there can be significant savings in effectively managing these devices.

Total Cost of Ownership

Total cost of ownership refers to the fact that there is a lot more related to the cost of the personal computer beside the price of the hardware and the software. There are many studies about the true cost of a personal computer, with annual TCO figures ranging from $3,000 to $12,000. It is open to endless debate where the true number is—and it seems obvious that the figure can vary from company to company.

On top of the cost of the hardware and software, additional items that factor into the TCO include

- Cost of support (staff, consultants, vendors)
- Network facilities (servers, applications, cabling, routers, hubs, etc.)
- Training
- Administrative (purchasing, inventory, auditing, etc.)
- Money costs (capital, depreciation, etc.)

Some analyses have taken TCO to a very detailed level and have included

- Consumables (diskettes, toner, paper, etc.)
- Wasted user time (playing games, changing settings of fonts, colors, screen savers, etc.)
- Coworkers' time (when user A has to stop doing his job because user B asks him a question)

The important thing to take away from this is that there are a lot of costs and factors that are associated with desktop computers. As such, there are opportunities for savings by managing these costs—enter asset management.

Asset Management

With all the costs mentioned above, and probably more, it is important for an IT manager to keep a careful watch. If TCO is the costs associated with computers, then asset management refers to what you do to keep those costs down. This can include everything from policies and procedures to technology issues. Some of the most popular asset management techniques include the following:

- Maintaining hardware and software standards. The fewer the number of technology products in your environment, the easier it will be to support, maintain, and administer.
- Taking advantage of vendor discounts for volume purchases.
- Outsourcing functions that can be done less expensively, or better, to others.
- Using tools to automate repetitive procedures.
- Investing in electronic software distribution tools so that the technical staff doesn't have to visit each workstation to deploy software and/or upgrades.

- Employing disk cloning technology so that newly purchased computers don't have to be loaded manually with software.

- Proactively checking for problems (virus checking, system monitoring, etc.).

- Using dynamic host configuration protocol (DHCP) to automatically assign IP addresses.

- Having your hardware reseller preload your standard disk image on your workstations when they ship, so that they can be deployed immediately to users upon receipt.

- Providing effective training for IT staff and users.

- Using inventory tracking software.

- Using Help Desk tracking software.

- Implementing restrictions so that users can't change system configurations and cause adverse impacts.

- Defining and setting appropriate hardware and software defaults.

- Providing support personnel with resources (reference materials, vendors' support lines, etc.).

- Tracking software usage (frequently referred to as license metering) to ensure that you're not paying for more licenses than you need, nor risking being underlicensed.

- Performing upgrades only when they are deemed necessary and you've tested them to be reliable, versus every time the vendor makes an upgrade available.

As you can see, most of these tools are designed to reduce the demands on the Help Desk and/or the number of interruptions (i.e., problems) that users encounter. This is because the most expensive factor related to desktop computers is the labor—whether it's the cost of the staff at the Help Desk, or the cost of the user's time when system problems prevent them from working.

Of course, if you're going to be implementing asset management techniques to reduce your TCO, you'll want to know if you're having any success or not. Most of the asset management techniques listed earlier cost something to implement—either in terms of hardware/software or staff time, and so on. Obviously, you don't want your TCO costs to outweigh the cost of implementing asset management. Most TCO and asset management gurus recommend that you first take some time to assess your own TCO as the very first step. This can be a rather tedious and often complex process (and of course, there are many consultants who are eager to help you with this). However, the findings can be eye opening—as they'll show you where your TCO dollars are going. Armed with this information, you can make a value judgment as to which asset management techniques are worthwhile for your needs. Then, you can periodically reassess your TCO as a way of measuring your progress.

7.9 Further References

Web Sites

- *www.computerworld.com/home/features.nsf/all/980914tcolinks* (This link has a great number of asset management and TCO links.)
- *www.gartner.com* (for Gartner's research analyst reports on TCO)
- *www.metagroup.com* (for Meta's research analyst reports on TCO)

Articles and Books

- Cortada, James W., *Best Practices in Information Technology: How Corporations Get the Most Value from Exploiting Their Digital Investments,* Prentice Hall, 1997.
- Jaffe, Brian D., "One Manager's Look at TCO," *Computerworld,* November 17, 1997.
- Jesse, Chris, *A Journey through Oz: The Business Leader's Road Map to Tracking Information Technology Assets,* Kendall/Hunt, 1999.
- Lewis, Robert, "The Winding Road to TCO Includes Calculations That Are Both Tricky and Useless," *InfoWorld,* November 3, 1997.

Hardware

What You Will Learn

- How to get current information on functionality and pricing
- How to evaluate products and vendors
- What issues are involved in buying desktop computers
- How to choose specs for desktop PCs, laptops, and network computers
- What the difference is between a workstation and a PC

CHAPTER EIGHT

Introduction

Hardware technology is advancing. Each day brings new buzzwords, acronyms, and faster processors. What you buy today will probably be with you for several years, but you can't be sure the manufacturer will still be around at that time. One of the reasons the IT budget is so large is because of all the hardware you'll be buying. This chapter offers you specific information on how to make intelligent and cost-effective decisions on hardware.

8.1 Products: How Do I Get Current Information on Functionality? On Pricing?

At the rate companies are being formed, acquired, and merged, and the rate that new products are being introduced and developed, it is impossible for any single person to be fully aware of all that is available in the marketplace. IT trade journals may help, but even they can't keep up. Hence the need for journals that specialize in various segments of the market (LANs, communications, AS/400, NT, Unix, etc.).

So how do you stay on top of it? There are a variety of resources to use. In addition to the trade journals, there is the Web, trade shows, vendor representatives, e-mail, consultants, and so on. For the most part, you have to make very little effort to gather information. The effort will be in trying to filter it, digest it, and turn it into information that you can use effectively.

It would be a full-time job trying to stay on top of industry developments. But you already have a full-time job managing your IT department, and staying abreast of industry events can only be a fraction of your time. You'll eventually have to figure out what works best for you—everyone absorbs information differently.

Remember, you're not in this alone. Your staff should contribute a great deal to this effort. They are the ones who will be working with the technology, hands on, day to day. They should be the ones most in tune with what's going on in the marketplace.

Vendor Representatives

You should invite key vendors to come in and meet with you once or twice a year. This could be specific product vendors, or system integrators, or resellers. Let them tell you of new product announcements, changes in product lines, what their other customers are doing with technology, and so on. You can share with them your upcoming plans for the department, the company, and your customers. These meetings can be in your office, perhaps with key members of your staff, or some vendors may whisk you away to their "executive briefing center" for the full dog-and-pony show, complete with smoke and mirrors. While you may not get any specific useful information from these meetings, you can use them to establish and reinforce a relationship. You never know when some tidbit of information that is shared today is just the nugget that's needed to help resolve a need six months from now. Invite your vendors to put you on a mailing list so that you're kept aware of any key announcements, seminars, demos, and so on.

Trade Journals (Print and Electronic)

There are probably hundreds of sources of printed journals and newsletters in the IT industry. Many are free, others are very expensive. Start with some free ones. Publishing groups like Ziff-Davis (*www.zd.com*), CMP (*www.cmp.com*), and IDG (*www.idg.com*) produce some of the most popularly read journals in the industry—some free, some for pay. You can usually apply for the free ones right on the Web.

You probably won't have time to really read any trade journal in full. At least glance at the headlines. It'll help to keep you aware of what's going on, and you never know when you'll spot an article that addresses a problem you've been struggling with. Avoid getting bogged down in journals that don't match your level of responsibility (e.g., too technically oriented) or about topics that have no relevance to your department's functions. If you spot an article that you think one of your staff should read, rip it out and send it to them. Not only will you be sharing information, but you'll be letting them know that you're involved.

Many trade publications have e-mail services that send out regular, often daily, e-mail messages. Sometimes these contain the latest news reports; other times they offer brief synopses of full articles that appear in print. Sign up for those that work best for you.

The Web

The Web can be a great resource if you know what you're looking for. Otherwise, it is likely to overwhelm you with information. Use the Web to visit vendor Web sites for product information, announcements, and so on. Use search engines when you're looking for some information, but aren't quite sure where to get it. Most IT trade journals have Web sites with current information, and there are outlets that are publishing IT news for the Web only (no print), like *www.cnet .com* and *www.planetit.com.* In addition to news and product information, the Web can be an incredible resource tool. Organizations that are responsible for technology standards (e.g., ANSI at *www.ansi.org* and IEEE at *www.ieee.org*) have Web sites. And there are sites that offer valuable reference information to the IT professional (e.g., *www.whatis.com*, *www.webopedia.com*). You may also use the Web to subscribe to e-mail-based mailing, or join newsgroup discussion threads.

Trade Shows

Just as there are trade journals dedicated to specific segments of IT, there are trade shows that cater to similarly specific areas. Between vendor representatives, junk mail, and trade journals, you'll probably learn about the ones that are pertinent to you. Unfortunately, trade shows are usually only held in the large metropolitan areas, and often the travel expense prohibits many IT professionals from attending them.

For the most part, trade shows are all identical in structure: most prominent is the exhibition hall where vendors pay large amounts of money for booths that have more square footage than many homes. The prominence of the exhibition hall is followed by the speeches—usually by major figures in the industry. Then there are the seminars, conferences, and panel discussions. And lastly, there are the hospitality suites.

The various speeches, usually including a handful of "keynote" speeches, often get the most coverage, which usually means they need little of your time. While they might be entertaining, especially with a particularly dynamic speaker, it is unlikely that they will offer any groundbreaking news.

Visitors to the exhibition hall usually enjoy the opportunity to talk directly with vendor product developers, executives, and technical staff. The exhibition hall usually offers an opportunity to touch and feel—especially nice for recently announced products—and often to try out a product. However, some exhibit visitors find that some of the products they see being demonstrated never actually make it to market. While the exhibits of the larger vendors may be the most alluring, you may actually find that the smaller vendors' booths (often tucked away in the back of the hall or on another floor) are of greater value. After all, there are lots of ways to get information about the large vendors, but your radar may not otherwise detect the smaller vendors. And you never know when a small vendor has just the utility software or hardware doohickey that is the perfect solution for your needs.

The seminars, conferences, and panel discussions can be very valuable. A trade show may have several of these going at one time. Very often, the people who host these and participate in them are IT practitioners just like you. The topics may be about a recently completed project, management strategies, or the pros and cons of different technologies. The attendance at these sessions is usually small (less than 100 people), and they frequently conclude with a question-and-answer session. This up close and personal format in a session of interest to you can be very valuable.

8.2 Products: How Do I Evaluate Them?

When evaluating products, be it hardware or software, the first thing you want to make certain is that the product does what you need it to do. With most products, you usually arrange for the opportunity to evaluate the product in your environment. Thirty-day evaluation periods are quite common, and they are often extended to 90 days just by asking. Sometimes, you can even arrange for the vendor to provide some on-site expertise to help you. If you are offered this kind of help, grab it! It usually speeds up the evaluation process since you can speed by all those bumps in the road that usually arise when you try a new product for the first time.

Important Issues to Consider

In addition to the overall functionality, there are some other items to consider when evaluating a product:

- Will the product scale to meet the size of your environment? When considering an enterprise-wide application (e.g., e-mail), your test bed will probably be quite small. However, the results may be very different when the product is deployed throughout your organization.

- What does the rest of the market think of the product? Is this one considered a leader, an up-and-comer, a has-been, or a never-will-be?

- What type of support will you be able to get for the product? Can you buy into premium support programs? Is training available for your staff? What is the labor market like for skills in this product?

- Does the product integrate well into your environment, or will it require specialized interfaces? Does the product adhere to industry standards? Or is it based on proprietary technology?

- What is the cost of the product? In addition to the sticker price, think of the costs for support, implementation, training, prerequisite hardware/software, conversion/migration, and so on.

- Ask your staff if they've used this product in previous jobs.

- Ask resellers if they sell much of this product, or what their other customers think of it.

- If you're evaluating hardware or networking technologies, you may be able to arrange to evaluate the products at the vendor's site, instead of arranging for the logistics of delivering and setting up a test bed in your environment.

The more complex, expensive, and specialized the hardware, the more elaborate and detailed your investigation and decision process should be.

8.3 Vendors: How Do I Evaluate Them?

The computer industry is maturing—there is less "let's figure it out as we go" now because there is a lot more "been there, done that." There are two important historical experiences that you can tap into to help you evaluate vendors:

- Past organization experience
- Past personal experience

Past Organization Experience

Your company and your department most likely already have extensive experience—good and bad—with a long list of vendors. If you have just joined your company, one of the first things you should do is find out who the company's informal historian is. If you are lucky, this person will be either in your department or at least near it.

Members of your department remember the department's experience with certain vendors and have experiences of their own. Take this data and make it yours. Don't accept it all as absolute fact, but don't throw it away, either. For certain vendors (a certain company from Redmond, Washington, comes to mind), you may not always have viable alternatives.

Past Personal Experience

If you have been in the computer industry any length of time, you will have direct experiences with all kinds of vendors. Use these experiences. But remember—the computer industry in particular, but the commercial world in general, is changing fast. If you had a bad experience with a particular vendor in 1997, factor it into your decision on which hardware to use, but don't eliminate this vendor from the consideration list. The hardware has changed, the company has changed, your needs have changed.

Set Up a Trial Experience

Buy something small, make your needs clear, and see how well the vendor performs. Tell a salesman that you need three CPUs on site and installed by Friday.

If they are delivered as promised, the decision is easy. If the machines never arrive, and he never shows or calls, the decision is also easy. But if he calls on Thursday and says they won't be available until Monday, you get a feel for how he might respond to future requests.

Establishing and Maintaining Relationships with Vendors

As an IT manager, you are going to order a lot of hardware and software. You have a complex matrix of responsibilities that includes saving money for your company, getting the right resources to make the projects work, giving your employees the right tools, and making a series of overlapping deadlines that occasionally seem hopeless.

Try to balance all these needs with some perspective: there will be other projects, other deadlines, and other issues. Against this backdrop, act—and demand that your vendors act—with this view in mind. You are not buying one piece of equipment from a vendor (no matter how large); you are engaging in a relationship that will have many other important stages to it. Your goal here is not only to save money in the short term, although that is of course desirable. You are trying to create an environment where your success and your vendor's success overlap, so that not only can you save money in the short term on that five-laptop deal, but you can get a quicker response when you need that upgrade or a favor when that machine—which is now out of warranty—needs a replacement interface card.

Naturally, you'll act the same towards your vendor. If you say you need the new laptops Monday, and she has a shipment coming in Wednesday, evaluate your deadline; if you absolutely need them right away, find someone else. But if you can wait, or make do, tell her you'll wait as a favor to her—and because you believe the dates she gives you. Another vendor might tell you anything to get your business.

Finally, be careful not to get locked into long-term contracts (outsourcing or supplier) with vendors. Vendors need to provide the lowest price and highest quality—*all of the time.* Contracts that specify "sole source" are usually based on bad IT business decisions. Flexibility is the key.

Tell Your Vendors You Are Thinking Long Term

Remember that a vendor/client relationship is a two-way street. It may appear to be one-way, but it is in fact two-way. There will be times when you will be able to make or break a vendor's monthly quota, but there will also be times when you will need a modem delivered over the weekend or a copy of a new piece of software before it hits the stores. In both situations, it helps both parties to view the relationship as one that can help each other, rather than an adversarial one where only one wins at the expense of the other.

Use words to this effect the first couple of times you speak to vendors; for those people who are just job-hopping through, this speech will mean nothing. But to those people looking for business not only this quarter but also next year, you will quickly get their attention.

Reviewing Contracts with Vendors

Depending on the size of your organization and the size of the contracts (in monetary terms), getting formal legal help can be of great assistance in this situation.

If your company is not big enough to have an in-house lawyer, have the contracts reviewed by a legal consultant. Regardless, you should read the contract and be able to understand the following:

- What exactly am I agreeing to?
- What exactly is my liability and rights?
- What exactly is the vendor's liability and rights?

In many contracts the up-front portion contains some very standard legalese that may go on for pages—issues of confidentiality, warranty, liability, applicable laws, and so on. This is the part you really want the legal experts to look at. They know if anything here is putting the company at risk. They will alert you to

- Any wording that they are virtually forbidding you (i.e., the company) to agree to
- Terms that they are uncomfortable with (for these they should suggest alternatives)
- Terms that they are uncomfortable with, but recognize you are unlikely to get changed (although they will suggest you at least ask)

You need to turn your attention to the section called "Terms and Conditions," also called Ts and Cs. As an IT manager, this is the section with the items that you are concerned about. This might have terms like

- Service level guarantees
- Specifications of hardware and software
- Support, maintenance, upgrade terms
- Ability to return/cancel if not satisfied
- Specific deliverables
- Associated costs, time frames, and so on

Everything is negotiable—don't feel that just because it is on a form that you have to accept it. You may end up accepting it, but at least know that you can ask for changes. Remember that whatever promises your representative told you are of no value unless they are in writing. If it is important to you, ask to have it included in the Terms and Conditions. Also, remember that by the time you get to the negotiating, your representative can virtually taste the commission he's making from this sale. He will do essentially anything to get you to sign—at this point he almost becomes an advocate for you to his own legal department. Take advantage of this ally.

Joe Auer has written many excellent columns for *Computerworld* regarding vendor contracts, negotiations, and so on. See the "Further References" section for this chapter.

What about Spending Limits?

Many companies have formal standards designed to determine which level of personnel can sign for how much. *If your company does not have these standards in place, they should get them installed right away. And if they have them set up, find out what they are.* This should not be very difficult; the first time you sign a purchase order for a million or two over your limit, you'll hear about it. Instead of embarrassing yourself and your company, find out in advance what your limits are.

And if they are too restrictive for your responsibilities—if you are required to keep the company's road warriors outfitted with the latest machines and you have a signing limit of $500—work aggressively with your boss to correct the situation quickly.

How Do I Find the Best Deal?

There are many alternatives for where/how to buy all kinds of technology products, and the best deal can be any of them—provided you have carefully defined what you need.

Price

While important, often this should not generally be your only criterion. Rank the other criteria below for each purchasing decision. (You don't have to create a formal chart each time you buy a widget. But it is a good idea to use all the items below when spending someone else's money. You'll end up making a wiser decision. Sometimes all you need to do is scribble some of these other factors on a notepad before you call a vendor or start surfing.) This is good information to have on hand when someone from accounting asks why you purchased brand X over Y, or used vendor Z. After all, as all the studies say, the initial purchase price ends up being a small portion of the total cost of ownership.

Service

This can be a valuable component of an IT purchase. Products are getting more complex and their maintenance requirements are getting larger. Treat the item and the service options or contract as equally important elements in the buying decision. One may appear to cost more than the other, and be more important in the short term, but over time, the value of each can even out.

Also consider serviceability. Are parts easy to get? Does one vendor have long hold times on their support line? Will you be able to find staff or training that can help maintain this item?

Long-Term Vendor Relationship

This issue is discussed in detail in the section above. Keep this goal in mind during all buying activities.

Performance

Not all computer hardware performs at the same level of quality, of course, but your needs may not always be to purchase "the best," either. Everyone wants the most for the money, but sometimes in the frenetic IT world, the "fastest right now," or the "one I can get installed tomorrow," instead of the "best," is the preferred option. IT managers, both men and women, tend to have an almost macho attitude towards hardware performance: "The bigger, the faster, the better performing, the more I want it." Take stock—that attitude may be costing you performance in the long term.

On the other hand, hardware performance is often easily quantifiable. Standards are common. And if a vendor starts touting the performance of his equipment using standards other than those used in the industry, take it as a sign that his equipment may not perform as well. If everyone knows throughput is the standard and you start hearing about a new measure, be wary. Ask about the machine's throughput and be ready for a quasi-explanation about why that standard may not be correct. Standards are not inviolate, of course, but they mostly exist for very good reasons—a lot of people tested various methods and arrived at the same conclusion.

Speed of Delivery and Availability

As often, or more so, than money, this item can be the deciding factor in important hardware decisions. The IT world moves very quickly, and a vendor's ability to move with it—and along with your schedule—is a critical factor. Like cost, you should carefully evaluate the importance of this issue on every buying deci-

Vendor Name	Price	Service	Vendor Relationship	Performance	Speed of Delivery
Acme	$210	One year guarantee; must be returned for service.	New vendor	12-port (have a 24-port model, which we probably do not need)	This afternoon
JONES & CO.	$220	$50/yr each for first five machines, $25 per machine after that.	New vendor	12-port model only	This afternoon, if the tech gets back from another job
Smith & Assoc.	$190	$25/yr, unlimited	We have used them successfully for other equip; should be able to leverage this history.	12-port model only, although 24-port model will be available in three weeks	Next week— they have to have it shipped from warehouse

Figure 8.1   Sample Evaluation Matrix for a 12-Port Baseline Hub

sion. Naturally, you want everything ASAP—who doesn't? But how much are you willing—and how much should you be willing—to pay for that speed? If you don't need something tomorrow, don't FedEx it; use (significantly) cheaper delivery options.

Train your vendors to think the same way. You need things delivered on your schedule. Sometimes that is this afternoon by courier, but sometimes that can be tomorrow, or after the weekend. Yelling about wanting everything as soon as possible dilutes your message and makes those times when you really do need the stuff this afternoon more difficult to deal with.

Finally, availability is a major factor in the speed of delivery. You may want the latest software upgrade the very afternoon it arrives at the reseller's office, but so do all her other clients. Keep in mind that getting that hard-to-find item will be influenced both by traditional speed variables such as distance, shipping method, and so on, as well as if the item is available.

If you purchase a large volume of certain products, you want to make sure that your vendor keeps adequate stock in their warehouse to meet your needs. You don't want to continually hear that they are back-ordered. Using FedEx won't help if there is no product available to be delivered.

How Well Does Each Vendor Meet Each Criterion?

For important purchase decisions, set up a simple matrix that allows you to compare all of your options. See Figure 8.1 above for a sample evaluation matrix.

An evaluation matrix does not make the decision for you, but it clearly outlines your options and locates them conveniently next to each other. A formal matrix like this is not required for every buying decision, and naturally the cost and the importance of the purchase will dictate how much effort you want to put into analyzing things before actually buying.

But seeing all the criteria and the items listed right next to each other can be of tremendous value when trying to determine how important the issue is for you, which vendor to use, and which equipment to buy.

It is important to note that the terms "vendor" and "manufacturer" may not be the same. Your vendor may be a VAR (value-added reseller) or a retail store—neither of which is the manufacturer of the hardware you're buying. It is unlikely you'll ever buy a Hewlett-Packard printer directly from HP. However, this is mostly to your benefit. Your vendor can make up for your manufacturer's shortfall. If Acme, Inc. (in the previous example) requires that you return the hub if it needs to be repaired, your VAR may agree to service the unit for you on site. This is a perfect example of where you can work your relationship with your vendor to your advantage. (See the discussion of VARs below.)

Where Can I Find the Best Deal?

You need to stay current with the new methods of conducting business. In the old days, buying and selling computers occurred in only a small number of places: directly from the company itself, from a local retail store, or from some member of that netherworld of OEMs (Original Equipment Manufacturers). Today, your choices are much broader, and they are changing all the time.

You have the following options for buying IT equipment:

- Web
- Catalogs
- Retail computer stores
- Direct company reps
- VARs
- Other contacts

Naturally, one new method of evaluating and buying products is the Web. This option is discussed in detail below. But there are others. Catalog ordering, a cousin of on-line ordering, is another method of buying products. And it can be a very effective means, especially for buying commodity products with a somewhat looser schedule.

If you have, or can find and establish, a relationship with a VAR or a retail store near your company, that is the best. A contact with a real live human being who is genuinely interested can often be much more valuable than any other benefit.

Buying Stuff off the Web

Buying things off the Internet offers several advantages:

- It's generally easier to find a wider range of options.
- It's generally easier to get more detail about the product.
- It's generally easier to find comments (pro and con) from other users/ purchasers of the product.
- Most importantly, items sold on-line are often (though certainly not exclusively) less expensive.

The disadvantages of buying stuff off the Internet are the following:

- You may not have an opportunity to establish a relationship.
- On-line vendors may insist on a credit card payment, as opposed to the corporate purchase order you prefer to use.
- It may be difficult to assess your delivery, warranty, and service options and rights.

If you need two routers by next Friday, and you have ordered 10 routers from this catalog company before and they delivered them on time for a great price, many IT managers will not go on-line to see if they can save 1 % in price or shave off a day—they will go with what works. On the other hand, if you need three laptops for new employees starting next month, you might go to the Web to see if you can beat the price. Your company and your department have hardware standards, so you are probably not going to experiment here: you know the machines you want, and the Web will let you search for the best price and the fastest turnaround.

Catalogs

You probably get more of these in the mail than you thought trees existed to print them all. Nonetheless, catalogs can have great value for IT managers trying to buy the right stuff for the least amount of money. A lot of catalogs are now morphing to Web-based vendors. By eliminating the printing and mailing of catalogs, they can save money and immediately change prices, specs, and so on, on the Web.

As mentioned above, think long term. Try to establish a relationship with a company over the course of time. If you can consistently deal with the same representative, that is even better. (Believe it or not, it is possible to do this. The turnover rates for phone reps at catalog companies is dropping as the catalog sales industry matures.)

Catalogs are useful for three reasons:

- You can quickly scan them to get informed about product categories. ("Just how many speech recognition software packages are there, anyway?")

- You can quickly scan them to get price information. ("How much is a new router going to cost me? I paid *X* last year for the one I have.")

- You can access them even if you are not connected or near your machine. This situation occurs more often than you would think—you have the time or the need to evaluate different products and you are not connected to a network. You might be stuck in a cab in a traffic jam or searching for something to look at on the plane. If you have paper catalogs ready to read at these common nonelectronic moments, you can get some useful work done.

Retail Computer Stores

Retail stores can simultaneously be the most convenient and most inconvenient source for computer products. If they have what you want, it may be the quickest place to get something in an emergency. However, they certainly lack the flexibility and motivation that your VAR's dedicated rep has. This is the most unreliable—and often the fastest—method of buying hardware. Selling computer equipment through retail channels has been tried many times in many places, and much money has been spent trying to make the concept work. But most people would agree that the system still needs work.

The principal advantages of buying from a store are

- It's fast. (If they have it, you can walk out with it.)

- It's tactile. (That means "you can touch it." This feature is not as important for something like a router or a hub, which looks like a stereo receiver, which looks like a Sparc station CPU, which looks like a pizza box . . . but it can matter if you are buying keyboards or mice.)

The principal disadvantages of buying from a retail computer store are

- Its inventory is limited. (They probably do *not* have what you are looking for in stock.)

- It's a retail operation. (Which means it has the trappings of traditional retail operations, like it is open only certain hours, there can be lines at the checkout counter, it can be populated with uninformed individuals trying to sell you things you don't want, and it can be difficult to find what you are looking for.)

Most corporate IT purchases are not made in retail stores. Professional organizations have sophisticated hardware needs that most stores are not prepared to meet. In addition, most corporation employees do not have the time to go shopping at a store for company purchases. However, there are few IT managers today who haven't ducked into a CompUSA with a credit card to buy a part or component in an emergency.

Stores have recognized those shortcomings, and they have begun to offer sophisticated alternatives to the "come-into-the-store-and-buy-the-item" options. As a corporate customer, you can call someone like CompUSA, and you will be given the choice of contacting an individual store or talking to a CompUSA sales rep. This rep will then be able to determine if the item you are looking for is in stock at your local store.

Direct Company Reps

This, too, can be a very effective means of getting the equipment you need. The advantages are obvious: most company reps are better informed about their product than salespeople with multiple product lines; the company has a better sense of how many items they have and, if they don't have one themselves, have an idea where one might be. The disadvantages are clear, too: if you need multiple items from multiple manufacturers (which you will much of the time, since there are so many things you need and so many manufacturers), you are going to have to make multiple phone calls. Also, company reps move through that job quickly, so talking to the same person over the course of a year is not a guarantee by any means. Company reps are usually very well versed in the products and associated technologies, and they can tell you how others use their products.

Many manufacturers prefer to sell their products through the "channel" (VARs, retailers) and simply don't have the resources to sell directly. It is common for manufacturers like this to have sales reps to keep you informed and educated about the product, but who really can't sell you the equipment.

Value-Added Resellers (VARs)

For many IT managers, VARs are the preferred means for purchasing many products. As the name implies, VARs resell other manufacturers' products. Because they have a very high volume, VARs often can provide excellent pricing and have enough stock to meet your delivery needs. The "value-added" refers to additional services that the VAR can perform for you (for a fee, of course). The VAR can preload software onto the PCs they will ship to you. They can install the additional memory in the printer before it ships, so that you're only receiving one item and don't have to do the install yourself. If you buy all your software through your VAR, they can help you keep track of your licenses. VARs usually have excellent contacts with the manufacturers, which may enable you to get detailed information you need before making a purchase decision, or when you need support.

If you have an order that consists of components from multiple manufacturers, the VAR can hold all the items until the entire order is complete. This saves you from receiving and storing multiple deliveries. A VAR is usually able to service virtually all the products they sell, which means you have fewer support channels to deal with. And, as indicated above, a VAR can usually augment a manufacturer's warranty/service offerings to something that is customized to your needs.

8.4 Desktop Computers: What Are the Issues Involved in Buying Them?

There are many places to buy a PC, and the best deal can be any of them—provided you have carefully defined what you need.

You probably won't be able to squeeze more than five years of life out of a PC. Sometimes it can be less than three. The driving force is that as the available hardware gets more powerful, applications are developed for them, and they just run too slowly on older units. In fact, some have said that with faster and faster hardware getting cheaper and cheaper, software developers see no need to write "efficient" code—hence, the birth of bloatware.

When considering workstations, think about the following issues:

- **Price:** This may be tough to judge with new models being announced almost weekly, along with price changes. Also consider leasing versus buying (see Section 6.4).

- **Service:** Many vendors, especially those selling to the corporate market, include on-site service as standard (or as an inexpensive option) as part of the warranty coverage. Also, check the quality of the tech support (24×7, hold time, expertise, etc.).

- **Long-term vendor relationship:** (See discussion above.) Will the vendor be around in three years? If you're tempted to buy no-name or "white-box" devices, you risk that the off-brand components may cause problems with future versions of operating systems and software later on.

- **Component consistency:** Corporate environments are often leery of equipment marketed at consumers, primarily because the manufacturer may switch brands of components depending on source availability and pricing. This leads to workstations that are identical in model number, but could be very different in regard to the makeup of the internal components. This can cause support headaches among your staff in regard to repairs, hardware drivers, configurations, and so on.

- **Performance:** With hardware specifications varying, and workstations priced as low as $500 and up to $3,000 or more, it is difficult to know whether to buy a bargain at the low end, or to buy at the high end in hopes of getting the most bang for the buck. There is no right or wrong answer to the question, which is in part financial and part philosophy of technology. The difference between the low end and the high end really amounts to how much useful life you get out of a PC. A $500 device might be considered a disposable that you replace every 18–24 months. On the other hand, a $2,000 unit should serve a lot longer. Of course, as the TCO model indicates, there's a lot more to the cost of a PC than the cost of the hardware (see Section 7.8).

- **User consequences:** Some users like getting new equipment (technology envy), even if the new hardware has no impact on how they do their job. On the other hand, some users fear the disruption of new equipment, thinking that they just got the old one working the way they like, and now it is being taken away.

- **Depreciation:** Your finance department may not like the idea of corporate assets being replaced too often—especially if it is replaced before it has been fully depreciated on the corporate books.

- **Availability:** If you go with a mail-order company, you only have one source for product. If you go with someone who sells through the reseller channels, you can go to another reseller if one reseller is out of stock.

8.5 Desktop Computers: How Do I Choose Specifications for Them?

First, define your needs. There are primarily six components to a desktop PC:

- Monitor
- CPU
- Disk
- RAM
- Modem/network connection
- Mouse/keyboard

Monitor

In late 2000, when this book was being written, 17-inch monitors were becoming the standard. Graphic artists and spreadsheet users commonly use 19-inchers; 21-inch monitors are seen at corporations, but they are less common. Monitors can have a long service life; a good 17-inch monitor can provide several excellent years of service.

Quality among the major brands is pretty good. You can buy cheap monitors, but you are taking a risk: the tube is the major component of a monitor and the one thing that typically goes out in a monitor. If you buy a monitor for under $300, it will easily cost you that much to get it repaired if the tube goes out.

Monitors with a smaller "dot pitch" (millimeters between pixels) will have a crisper image than a monitor with a larger dot pitch. The most common dot pitch specifications are .26 and .28. Monitors for high-end graphic artists will have smaller dot pitches. As the dot pitch goes down, the price goes up.

Flat-screen monitors are starting to become popular. Not only are they trendy, but they give back valuable desk real estate. However, they are considerably more expensive (easily running over $3,000 for the largest flat screens), and servicing them can be a headache for the IT manager.

CPU

These days, most CPU decisions translate into an issue of desirable speed of performance. Back in the old days—like three years ago—certain software would only run on a CPU of a certain power. That criterion is no longer really paramount. Generally, hardware has outpaced software: now, most software runs on most hardware. Keep in mind that if you buy the lowest-level CPU available (because it is the cheapest), it probably means it will be out of production very soon. On the other hand, if you choose the latest and greatest processor, you're probably paying a premium for "top of the line" and "latest and greatest."

While Intel still owns the lion's share of the desktop/laptop processor market, there is competition. AMD has been making processors for several years that are comparable in performance to Intel's. In fact, many home computers are sold with AMD chips. So far, compatibility issues do not seem to be any problem at all. And Macintosh computers are based on processors from Motorola.

A significant factor of a CPU's performance is the cache. The cache is very high-speed memory that can significantly impact performance. As the cache size increases, so does performance, and so does the cost.

Disk Space

Disk space is very cheap. Most workstations are offered with disk drive sizes ranging from 4 GB to 20 GB. The real demand for storage space on PCs is usually the software, not the data; 2–3 GB can be required just for the operating system and the applications. While you don't have to get the largest disk drive available, you should get a little more than you need. The job of replacing or adding disk drives in existing workstations can be very burdensome to your staff and your users.

Memory (RAM)

In general, more RAM will improve a computer's overall performance—but only up to a point. Define your users' needs. Some corporate users do not even run two applications at a time: giving them 256 MB of RAM is a waste of money and memory. On the other hand, power users can live and work in departments where you do not expect one: the guy in marketing who runs linked Excel spreadsheets, embeds objects into Word, and drops a Visio diagram into his presentation may need more RAM than the coder who spends all day hacking in Unix. Figure out what your users need and structure your delivery around that. With the delivery of Windows 2000, many IT managers considered 128 MB to be the standard for PC desktops (up from 64 MB for Windows 9x and 32 MB for Windows 3.1).

Similarly, Macintosh units may have hundreds of megabytes of RAM if they are used by graphic artists. A Mac user who is simply doing word processing and e-mail will have more modest RAM requirements. See Table 8.1 on the next page for a comparison of different memory types and technologies.

Modem/Network Connection

How do your users connect to the network? Are they mostly directly connected to your LAN? Are they dial-ups? Are they a combination of the two types? See Chapter 10 for details on data networks.

Here speed and performance do matter—especially for remote users, but really for all network users. As the Web grows even more complex and graphic intensive, the need for speed and bandwidth grows along with it. Users are very tired of the World Wide Wait. It is here that you can have a big impact with a small amount of effort. Users—especially nontechnical ones—are very frustrated by download times.

Technically, 56K modems are now the fastest modems that can be used over a telephone line; and they often do not achieve these advertised speeds when the user is logged on. There are several potential reasons for this, but a common one is that the receiving service does not accept 56K data feeds. Many on-line services are upgrading, but not every company accepts this speed. And if the service can support 56K connections, you have to establish a very high-quality connection in order to achieve this speed.

Almost every computer that is ordered by a corporation will also require a LAN connection. The corporate standard for desktop networking is 10 or 100 Mbps Ethernet. In general, this should meet the needs of the vast majority of your users for quite some time. There are also network cards that have fiber-optic connections, as well as gigabit speeds. Both of these are considered too new and too expensive for significant deployment, except perhaps in the data center and for the backbone infrastructure.

Table 8.1 Diffferent types of memory and technologies. (*Source: Computerworld*, July 24, 2000, page 66.)

Chip Set	Full Name	Primary Applications; Main Proponents	Speed	Advantages	Disadvantages
DRAM	Dynamic RAM	Older PCs with early Pentium, 486 or 386 processors	Slow	Least expensive RAM	Slow
SRAM	Static RAM	Cache	Three times faster than DRAM	Fast; retains data without power	Most expensive; chips are physically larger
EDO DRAM	Extended data output DRAM	Older PCs with Pentium CPUs	5% to 20% faster than DRAM	Superseded by SDRAM	Slow
SDRAM	Synchronous DRAM	Most common main memory for PCs; wide cross section of computer memory manufacturers	Fast	Prevailing memory standard; works with a wide variety of micro-processors; economical	Slower performance than DDR-SRAM or RDRAM; transfers data once per clock cycle
PC100 (PC133)	SDRAM for 100-MHz (133-MHz) motherboards	PCs with faster processors (PC100 in those up to 600 MHz, PC133 in those up to 1 GHz); Intel	Faster	Meets Intel specifications	
DDR-SDRAM	Double data rate-SDRAM	PCs with fast CPUs; memory manufacturers and Advanced Micro Devices Inc.	Faster yet	Next-generation SDRAM; transfers data twice per clock cycle	Higher cost than conventional SDRAM; slower than RDRAM
RDRAM	Rambus DRAM	PCs using new Pentium III Coppermine CPUs (700 MHz and up); Rambus Inc. and Intel	Fastest	Highest-speed commer-cial memory; uses fast bus, 2-byte data channel	Costs up to three times more than other chip sets; large die size; low production volumes
Flash RAM		BIOS, modems, also remov-able storage for devices such as PDAs and laptops	Fast	Retains data when pow-ered off; can be quickly erased and rewritten	Expensive
FRAM	Ferro-electric RAM	Memory in small devices such as PDAs, phones, and smart cards; Ramtron International Corp.	Fast	Uses very low power; retains data when powered off	Lower memory densities per chip

Keyboard/Mouse

This is another high-impact item. Always, always have a few spare mice and keyboards around. You will not be that famous if you have a mouse for a guy in accounting who broke his, but you will be very infamous if you don't have a spare one for the president's secretary when he stops by to replace the one he spilled onion soup on.

You may also need a few special keyboards or mice. The chairman may want a black keyboard and mouse to match his new desk. Some users may ask for ergonomic keyboards and devices (wrist rests, etc.) to ease fatigue. And the innovations in mouse technology keep moving along (thumb wheel, wireless, track ball, etc.)—don't be surprised if users ask you for them.

8.6 Laptops: How Do I Evaluate/Choose Specifications for Them?

IT managers need, as this book has said often, to carefully define the needs of users. If your company does not have people who travel a great deal, laptops may make no sense for your user base. A laptop's primary advantage is its portability; it allows the knowledge worker to be a mobile worker. Some users want laptops to do some e-mail or basic word processing while away from the office. Others may want their laptop for doing presentations. Many of the factors that go into choosing a workstation also apply to choosing a laptop.

If you have people who travel, though, you need to consider the following issues:

- CPU speed
- Screen size
- Keyboard size
- Battery life
- Memory capacity
- Disk space
- Overall size and weight
- Number/types of slots
- Integrated/modular peripherals
- Docking station/port replicator
- Service
- And, of course, price

Hardware has, for the most part, become commoditized.

CPU Speed

You lose CPU speed when you move from a desktop to a laptop. Desktops are always the fastest machines available; laptops lag six months to a year behind them. You lose speed but you gain portability. You can work on a laptop in an airport, but you can't even carry your desktop on the plane.

Screen Size

You can find laptops with screens that range from about 10 inches (diagonally) to 15 inches. Obviously, the bigger the screen, the bigger (and heavier) the laptop. For users who are just trying to do some basic e-mail and spreadsheet work while they travel, a small screen may be ideal. On the other hand, if they spend their days doing graphic design or will use the laptop to deliver presentations to clients, a larger screen is justified.

Keyboard Size

Smaller laptops usually have keyboards that are not quite normal size, or they may have special-function keys put in awkward locations, all in the name of saving space. Some users may find a cramped keyboard unacceptable. However, those two-fingered typists who normally hunt-and-peck their way through e-mails may not care.

Battery Life

The Holy Grail of batteries is the cross-country airplane ride—5 to 6 hours. If the battery can last that amount of time, it will garner 100% of the market. Unfortunately, no one has nabbed it yet. Do not believe the numbers listed in the specs in the ads; those numbers for battery life are only relevant if the user simply turns the machine on and leaves it sitting alone. If the user actually uses the machine, opens applications, saves to disk, and so on, the inflated numbers in the ads can be cut by one-half or one-quarter. Don't forget: the battery life is significantly impacted by the use of the computer and the power management configuration settings. As the use of the laptop increases, the battery life drops faster.

Memory Capacity

As with desktops, increased memory can improve the unit's overall performance and allows the user to run more applications simultaneously. This issue will allow you not so much to distinguish between manufacturers (they are close, although not identical) but between price categories. Memory capacity in machines is still growing, although it has reached levels that no one thought possible 15 years ago. (One of the quotes Bill Gates's legions of detractors use often is his jewel from 1986: "No one needs more than 640K of memory.")

Nonetheless, that was then and this is now. Because of the limited space inside a laptop, they generally have much lower limitations on the total amount of RAM that can be installed. On top of that, RAM for laptops can be considerably more expensive. How much money do you have to spend, and how much RAM do your users really need? All those famous users in your company who do not use more than one program at a time (there are more than you think, unless you work at a computer company) do not need massive amounts of RAM—they would be happier with a faster CPU or a bigger hard disk. Also, keep in mind that the maximum memory you can get into a laptop is usually much less than the maximum for a desktop.

Disk Space

With laptops, you generally don't have as much choice on the size of the disk space. You may have only one choice (i.e., no choice) or perhaps two. Like everything else with laptops, disk space is more expensive than it is with desktops.

Overall Size and Weight

This is an issue that can appear less important to the (typically nontraveling) IT manager than to her users. A couple of ounces or a pound may not seem much to someone who goes to a conference once or twice a year, but to a person who travels weekly with that bag over her shoulder, that number is important. Find out just how important it is to your user base. And remember, the "carry weight" (the amount pulling on that shoulder) is more than the weight of the laptop. It may include cables, adapters, the charger, and external devices (floppy/CD drive, etc.).

Number and Types of Slots

Laptops usually support a few slots for PCMCIA (Personal Computer Memory Card International Association). There are three different types of cards and slots for them. Type 1 cards are very thin and are usually used for additional memory. Type 2 cards are the most popular and are usually for modems and network cards. Type 3 cards are the thickest, and most often accommodate an additional disk drive. If a laptop has two type 2 slots, they can often be used together to accommodate a type-3 card. Your need for PCMCIA slots and cards will depend on the user's need for connecting additional peripherals and so on.

Integrated/Modular Peripherals

Many laptops have many features already integrated (modem, network port, CD drive). In other laptops you may need to add these components via PCMCIA cards and so on. In some laptops, the CD drive and the floppy disk drive share a bay, and the user swaps out the drives as needed.

Docking Station/Port Replicator

Many laptop users like to have a full-size keyboard and monitor, as well as a network and printer connection when they're in the office. Connecting and disconnecting these devices can be cumbersome each time. So many laptop vendors offer a docking station. Each of these external devices is connected to the docking station, and the laptop easily slips in and out, without the hassle of dealing with wires each time. A port replicator offers similar functionality, except that it is a much smaller unit that snaps on the back of the laptop. Not every laptop can support a port replicator or docking station. Check with your vendor.

Service

Laptops are more prone to problems, in part from being bounced around overhead storage compartments in airplanes, in part because the specialized technology inside makes them require special attention to configure. Many IT departments have had repeated success with one laptop manufacturer, and they stick with what works. The manufacturer knows this and tries to encourage it by allowing generous volume discounts, letting the company in on nonadvertised specials, giving them advance notice on upcoming products, and so on. Find out about service options available from your vendor. Is the technical support staff knowledgeable? How are repairs handled? Overnight exchange? Return to factory?

Price

This should not be your only, nor should it be your last, criterion for how to buy a laptop. Get a number and use it along with the other criteria mentioned above to make the decision. If you are buying multiple machines, factor in a discount. But try to achieve a number that you can use with other criteria to arrive at the machine you want to buy. Note: the average useful life of a laptop is still around 24 months. This should be factored into the price/value calculation.

Manufacturer and Model	CPU Speed	Screen Size	Battery Life	Memory Capacity	Overall Weight	Compatibility	Price

Figure 8.2 Product Decision Matrix

Product Decision Matrix

You can set up a decision matrix, like the sample in Figure 8.2 above, to help you evaluate all your choices.

Keep in mind that laptops are very attractive devices and are frequently stolen (there are numerous devices on the market for trying to deter and prevent the theft of laptops). All in all, the life cycle of a laptop may be significantly shorter than that of desktops.

8.7 Network Computers: What about Them?

Network computers, or NCs, are not history, but they are not seen as the saviors they once were. NCs are PCs configured only with essential equipment (no CD-ROMs, floppy drives, or expansion slots, for example) and maintained from a single central location.

For a brief time, these machines were to become "PC killers." They were projected by people like Larry Ellison of Oracle as being the new paradigm for personal computing. Unexpectedly, prices for personal computers plummeted. Perhaps this fall was related to the advent of NCs, perhaps not.

There is still a market for NCs—classroom networks, for example, where individual workstations can be conveniently connected to each other and to a source for their power and their applications. But the general corporate world no longer uses them in much quantity. There may be also useful applications of these types of computers in factory computing—where it is vital to isolate mission-critical systems from less production-hardened tools and applications.

To a certain degree, the technology that went into NCs is being used for remote access (e.g., Citrix Metaframe, Microsoft Windows Terminal Server). By using thin-client technology, companies can ensure that a user still gets high levels of performance, regardless of what computer is used, when dialing in from home.

8.8 Workstations vs. PCs: What Is the Difference?

Good question. The difference is somewhat in the eye of the beholder, is somewhat a matter of when the definition was made, and is somewhat a matter of who is making the distinction. In the ancient days of personal computing—in the late 1980s/early 1990s—this distinction was an important and valid one. Workstations were powerful machines with proprietary hardware and software, were generally networked together with other workstations, had complex installation and maintenance arrangements, and had significantly more computing power and huge price tags.

Personal computers were less powerful stand-alone machines with simple software, were easy to set up, not that tricky to get fixed, and had limited power and fairly modest price tags.

Originally, workstations were based on RISC (reduced instruction set chip) technology, usually running Unix, while PCs have been based on CISC (complex instruction set chip) technology, usually running Microsoft Windows. The concept behind workstations' superior performance was that the chips could operate much faster since they only supported a small number of instructions . . . but very efficiently. CISC systems, on the other hand, were slower since they were somewhat bloated by a very robust instruction set.

This distinction means much less today. Personal computers have large computing power, and "workstations" are not really different in price from expensive new personal computers. Most computers are networked together in some way, either through direct connections or over phone lines. Manufacturers like to call their powerful new machines "workstations," but what is new and powerful in February is often standard and underpowered by July.

Define your needs for a personal computer. Then get the best machine that fits those needs. If the salesman needs to sell you a workstation, let him—just make sure it is not more (or less) than what you need.

8.9 Further References

Web Sites

- *www.ansi.org* (standards organization)
- *www.cmp.com* (on-line publisher)
- *www.cnet.com* (on-line publisher)
- *www.idg.com* (on-line publisher)
- *www.ieee.org* (standards organization)
- *www.planetit.com* (on-line source for technology information)
- *www.techrepublic.com* (on-line publisher)

- *www.webopedia.com* (on-line encyclopedia)
- *www.whatis.com* (on-line encyclopedia)
- *www.wired.com* (on-line publisher)
- *www.zd.com* (on-line publisher)

Articles and Books

- Joe Auer has written many excellent columns for *Computerworld* (*www .computerworld.com*) regarding vendor contracts, negotiations, and so on.
- Sinclair, Joseph T. and Mark Merkow, *Thin Clients Clearly Explained*, Morgan Kaufmann, 1999.

Software

CHAPTER NINE

Introduction

You've heard of killer applications, but not killer hardware. That's because the real value of a computer system is the software. In other chapters of the book we examine the network operating systems software and enterprise resource planning (ERP) software. Here, we take a look at the desktop operating system (OS), Linux, as well as important issues to think about regarding software in large environments (deployment, testing, upgrades, etc.).

9.1 Software: How Do I Get Current Information on Functionality? On Pricing?

The Web is your best source for up-to-the-minute pricing data. Company brochures and literature are a close second. Most companies have both a Web and a paper version of product information. Web sites often include very detailed spec sheets about their products—often in PDF format so that they can be easily printed.

Of course, with highly complicated and sophisticated products (e.g., an enterprise resource planning system), it might be impossible for the vendor to provide comprehensive information in a glossy brochure. In cases like this it could require research, reference checks, vendor briefings, ad presentations, and so on before you fully understand the capabilities and functionality. Even then, you still might want to go through an evaluation or testing period before committing to purchase the item.

Getting information on pricing can be difficult—often impossible with many products, particularly those that are at the high end. While you can walk into any computer store and get the price of Microsoft's Word, getting the price for a product like Oracle's Financials applications is not as straightforward.

With high-end products like this, pricing includes such factors as licensing fees (number of users, number of sites, number of servers, etc.), the cost of optional modules in addition to the base software, and the type of hardware the software will run on. (In the mainframe world, for example, it is common for the cost of software to be dependent on the model number of the host computer.) On top of all these variables, it is important to realize that the price on these higher-end technologies is often very negotiable. As the pricing gets more complicated with issues like maintenance and support costs, vendor consulting, and so on, the more room there is to negotiate.

As you pursue software pricing, it is important to keep in mind that the cost of your project goes beyond the cost of the software alone—it includes items like hardware, maintenance costs, implementation costs, consultants, staffing, support costs, and training.

9.2 Desktop OS: How Do I Deal with the Various Versions of Windows?

There are basically six versions you need to worry about. They are listed here in order of release:

- Windows 3.1 (released in 1990)
- Windows 95 (released in 1995)
- Windows 98 (released in 1998)
- Windows NT (released in 1993)
- Windows 2000 (released in 2000)
- Windows Millennium (scheduled to be released late in 2000)

Windows 3.1 (Released in 1990)

This is a very old version that is no longer actively supported by Microsoft. It is different from other Windows products in some important ways, not the least of which it is old and even more difficult to use than you remember. You and your department should not be forced to support a 10-year-old product, regardless of how much your user likes it. If you have people still using this product, you need to tell them that you have established a company standard for operating systems and they are using a product that is not on the list.

You might get some pushback to this stance, so be ready with your facts. Even if the user wants to continue to use the software without any support from IT, you cannot agree to such a dinosaur on your network. Computers are mostly parts of networks, of larger user communities, and the user who balks at playing by the basic rules should be made to realize that the prices for such action could be severe. If they are using Windows 3.1, for example, they are not going to be able to use any of the easier-to-use, feature-rich systems that were created in the mid-1990s and that are in common use today.

Windows 3.1 is a 16-bit operating system; although there was a 32-bit extension available for it, it did not gain much acceptance.

Windows 95 (Released in 1995)

This is probably the most commonly used operating system around the world. This doesn't mean it is the best operating system. It is the most popular primarily because it was the one that was preinstalled on most PCs that were sold. Its improvements over Windows 3.1 were radical; its user interface has many

Mac-like features to it (the Mac "Trash Can" is the Windows 95 "Recycle Bin," for example); and it is significantly easier to use than its predecessor.

You should not be installing this OS on machines anymore (see the next version of Windows for more details), but many of your users might still use this version. In other words, you probably still need to support this version. Whether you decide to upgrade them to a newer version depends both on your needs and theirs.

Although Windows 95 was touted as a true 32-bit operating system, many purists dismissed this since Windows 95 retained a significant amount of legacy code from DOS and Windows 3.1. However, this legacy gave this version of Windows a great deal of backward compatibility for older applications (be they DOS or Windows 3.1 based).

Windows 98 (Released in 1998)

This version was not radically different from Windows 95. Many considered Windows 98 to be little more than a service pack upgrade to Windows 95. The OS includes some minor feature changes, and it was agreed that the product was more stable, but the fundamental behavior of the OS was the same as its predecessor. This aspect is not all bad news; many users like the added stability in addition to the familiarity of the previous version. As an IT manager with a keen eye towards the skill level of the entire range of your user base, you should never underestimate the importance of the learning curve when making decisions that affect this base.

Like Windows 95, Windows 98 was not considered a true 32-bit operating system.

Windows NT (Released in 1993)

Windows NT (which was sold in two flavors: workstation and server) was Microsoft's foray into the NOS (network operating system) category and the first true 32-bit version of Windows. The workstation version, as the name implies, is installed for end users on their desktop PCs. The server version was installed on a network file server, to provide for file-and-print sharing, as well as other network services.

This operating system was originally designed for corporations. It was intended to be a "Unix killer"—a product built to handle many users and many tasks at the same time. However, Windows NT did not gain any real foothold until version 3.51 in the mid-1990s. The last official version of this product was version 4.0. However, Windows 2000 (without the "NT") is considered by most to be NT version 5.0.

You could have many users using this OS. When released, it was by far the most robust and stable of the Window OSs and gained popularity as a corporate alternative to Unix. (So is Linux, of course. See Section 9.5 for a discussion of Linux.)

Windows 2000 (Released in 2000)

Windows 2000 is the latest version of Microsoft's true 32-bit operating system. Like Windows NT, it is offered in a workstation and server version. In fact, there are multiple server versions—with the primary difference related to the number of processors supported in the server. The release of Windows 2000 (originally referred to as Windows NT 5.0) was long delayed as Microsoft kept pushing back the expected release dates.

Windows 2000 (popularly called Win2K) is Microsoft's most reliable and feature-rich operating system ever. Although there were many features added to this product, the most heralded is probably the Active Directory—which serves as an enterprise-wide electronic directory for a wide variety of resources. Active Directory competes directly with Novell's NDS (Netware directory services), long considered to be the leader in the directory services category.

Windows 2000 is offered in several different flavors: Professional (targeted for workstations), Server (for small servers), Advanced Server (for large servers), and Data Center Server (for high-end mission-critical applications).

Windows 2000 Millennium (Scheduled to Be Released in 2000)

Windows Millennium is somewhat of an unplanned release. It had been assumed that Windows 98 would be the last release of the 16/32-bit operating systems, and that Windows 2000 would be the single product (albeit in different flavors) used on all PCs from home, to corporate, to servers. Although at the time of publication, there was little known about this upgrade, it is expected to provide several consumer-oriented enhancements (e.g., home networking, simpler setup, self-healing functionality, and more tools for dealing with digital media and entertainment).

9.3 Desktop OS: How Should I Decide between Using a PC and a Mac?

Like it or not, the desktop today is pretty much a Windows and Intel (Wintel) world. Although Intel has picked up some competition (e.g., AMD), Windows goes almost unchallenged in regard to the desktop OS. While Apple and its Macintosh product line have had its ups and downs, it generally has about

5–6% of the desktop market. Debates rage daily about ease of use, lower training costs, the value of using software everyone else uses, and so on. Given the
overwhelming numbers for the Wintel market share, though, it is difficult to
argue about which platform is the most popular.

When choosing an operating system, there are three questions you should
ask:

- What am I going to do with my computer?
- Which system do all the people around me—my fellow computer users—
  use?
- What do my customers need?

Which Applications Are You Going to Run?

In general, the primary factor leading to your decision should be the applications that you plan to run. Today, most software vendors are writing their applications for the Windows platform simply because that's what most users have,
and it makes sense to aim for the larger market share. In addition, many software publishers that develop their applications for the Macintosh platform are
also developing versions for the Windows platform.

Many programs are now developed for multiple platforms because the technology for doing so—the application development environments that have come
onto the market in the last 10 years—have dramatically increased the functions
available and dramatically decreased the cost of multiplatform development.

If you have one key application that you are going to run—say, you run a
small graphics company and your users will all be using a particular graphics
package every day—verify that the package's vendor is committed to the platform you choose.

But more importantly (you should do this regardless of which platform you
choose), ask about the cross-platform capabilities of the applications you are
running. Most applications not only run on different platforms, they generate
files that can be opened on other platforms. Word files generated on a PC, for
example, can be read in Word running on a Mac.

What Is the Rest of Your Community Running?

The Macintosh platform's strongest market has proven to be with those in the
creative community (graphic artists, desktop publishers, etc.) as well as the
education marketplace. Most individuals would agree that the Mac versions of

software products for graphic applications are better than the PC versions. The reason is that the Windows environment still seems to lag in areas like color calibration, fonts, and other important graphic capabilities. In most other PC environments, however, Windows is the dominant platform.

What Do Your Customers Need?

As we have discussed before, determining who your users are (and who their customers are) will make your job a much more productive and happier adventure.

Choosing operating systems is no exception to this rule. Consider what is the de facto standard for your customers. If a user community (the graphic arts department, or the elementary school you are supporting) runs on the Mac platform, it will make life easier for all concerned if you go with the flow and choose Macs for everyone. This will eliminate problems with sharing files, compatibility, and so on. It was also radically cut down on your training and equipment costs, since users can share their knowledge and their machines among each other.

9.4 Desktop OS: How Do I Deal with Windows OSs and Mac OSs in the Same Shop?

Supporting two platforms in one environment can be a difficult task with lots of headaches. Those few users who use the "alternative" OS will feel slighted because you don't choose their system as the primary one; the other group, in the majority, will not understand why you just don't define a standard and get on with it.

As the IT manager, your role is to pick the most efficient OS for your environment. Of course, you may not have a choice: some environments are going to demand two operating systems. But if you can, try to have only one operating system, regardless of which one you choose. Your life—and your user's life—will be the better for it.

Issues to Consider

While it is quite common to have an environment that is 100% Windows, you are less likely to find one that is 100% Macintosh. In other words, if you have Macs in your world, it probably means you're going to have a mixed environment. Here are some things you should know.

Need for Additional Support Labor

Most support technicians are skilled at either PC or Mac. While some may have knowledge of the other platform, it is rare to find an individual who has developed advanced expertise with both. If you need to support both, it is going to cost you.

Software and File Compatibility

While most applications run on both platforms, there will always be minor differences:

- Most vendors will generally develop for their preferred platform first, and then have the product for the other platform follow. This could lead to a lag time of 6–18 months before all of your users are running the same software. A year and a half is a long time in the IT world.

- In order to conform to the conventions and norms of the user interface for each platform, there will be subtle differences between the Mac version and Windows version of the same software. To experienced users (Excel wizards in the Accounting department, for example), these differences will be minor and will be easily overcome. To newer users, though, the differences between "Command-P" and "Control-P" might be a stumbling block. Mac users often get confused when suddenly having to face both a Control key and an Alt key—not to mention the second mouse button; PC users are often mystified at the prevalence of the Command key.

- There may be problems or issues when trying to share files between platform versions of the same product.

Different Software Versions

Having multiple versions of the same software may complicate your administrative burdens in regard to purchasing, upgrades, training, license tracking, maintenance and support arrangements, and so on.

Upgrades

Virtually every effort you make in regard to your desktop environment (upgrades, software distribution, support, etc.) requires a two-pronged approach—one for Mac and one for Windows. This issue can get complex quickly; it is already difficult enough to track everything, but now you have to track things in duplicate.

Enterprise Applications

If you have to support multiple platforms, you want to be sure that there are versions of key enterprise applications (e-mail, enterprise resource planning, etc.)

for both. Imagine how difficult it would be if you had to support two different mail environments.

9.5 What Is Linux and What Should I Do about It?

Linux is a public domain operating system; no company formally owns it. For the most part, Linux can be thought of as a public domain version of Unix. Linux was developed in 1991 by Linus Torvalds of Helsinki, Finland.

The first controversy surrounding Linux is its pronunciation—the accepted version has "Linux" rhyming with "cynics." "Line-x" is also heard often, though it is generally viewed as the "amateur" or "newbie" pronunciation. Below is a brief description of Linux's features.

Cost

Linux is often referred to as free. It is technically free, since you can download a copy from the Web at no cost. However, the word "free" here is more of a reference to "freedom" and your rights to use it than to the actual cost of the software itself. The "cost" of software is much more than the initial price you pay for the disks or the download.

Platform Versions

Linux is available for all major platforms including Intel, Sparc, Alpha, Mac, Amiga, PowerPC, Atari, and several others.

Source Code

The source code for Linux is readily available and posted on the Web. The idea behind Linux and its open source code is that it allows everyone to see how it operates, to find and fix bugs, and to enhance it as needed. This method of development—called "open source development"—allows Linux to become iteratively more stable and robust. This means that anyone with the interest, time, and skill can write new drivers, interfaces, enhancements, extensions, and so on for Linux. Of course, this flies in the face of other operating systems, which are proprietary, and whose source code is closely guarded by the company that owns it. Linux is distributed under the GNU General Public License, which guarantees the freedom to share copies and to change the software (but only if those

changes are also freely available under the GNU General Public License (*www
.linux.org/info/gnu.html*)). All updates to the *kernel* (the core components of an
operating system, as opposed to the *shell,* which are the elements that a user
interacts with) are approved by Linus Torvalds.

The Pluses

In addition to the benefits of this open source code strategy, Linux was archi-
tected with some distinct advantages. The core OS (the kernel) is modular. This
means that by using only the modules you need, you can keep the OS very
small—which greatly increases speed and increases reliability (by reducing
needless complexity). Because Linux is so efficient, it can be used effectively on
less powerful systems.

The Minuses

So, it's fast, it's reliable, it runs on almost any hardware platform, and it's cheap.
What's the catch? A few items have hobbled Linux's growth:

- Lack of drivers for popular hardware devices
- No support for clustered servers
- Limited support of symmetric multiprocessing (SMP) and RAID storage
- Complexity of integrating Linux into an environment with many other tech-
  nologies

A Bigger Minus

The biggest concern for larger corporate environments is, Where do they turn
for support and help when they have questions and problems with Linux?
   One answer, and one that has not seemed to satisfy corporate IT managers, is
the World Wide Web. Web sites and discussion groups for Linux abound on the
Web. But that seems to be little solace to corporate IT managers who want to
know exactly whom to call if their server crashes. Rushing to fill that need are
several vendors who sell (commonly for under $100) various "distributions" of
Linux. A "distribution" of Linux can be thought of as a package of modules that
have been preconfigured, often with a particular customer in mind (corporate,
consumer, etc.). Linux distributions are available from vendors like Caldera,
Red Hat, Slackware, and others. More important than their distributions is the
support available from these vendors. Many vendors include free support for

installation with the sale of their distribution. But for ongoing support, they offer various plans and programs to fit different needs. Support plans may be sold based on number of incidents, number of installations, response times, method of contact (e-mail versus phone), and so on.

The Biggest Minus

Okay, so you have speed, stability, versatility, affordability . . . and formal support arrangements are available. So why isn't Linux running on every computer in the world? The problem is with applications. The big problem is that many of the world's most popular software programs don't run on Linux (yet). The biggest stumbling block is the desktop application packages from Microsoft. However, as a file server, Linux is doing better.

As a result, until the suite of applications that most of the world uses runs on Linux, it is unlikely that Linux will gain popularity on desktop and home workstations. However, Linux is gaining popularity for servers that run Unix-based applications. This includes firewalls, database servers, and so on. In fact, recognizing the growing popularity of Linux servers, many major vendors (e.g., IBM, Oracle, Sybase, Corel, SAP) have, or have announced plans for, support for their product(s) on Linux.

9.6 Workstation Software Updates: How Do I Deal with These?

There are several ways to manage the distribution of software to workstations without having to visit each one individually.

Deployment

One of the most complicated issues related to PCs in the large corporate environment is the deployment of software. When there is a new software package to be implemented, or an update (no matter how minor) to an existing application, the manual distribution of files can be a very tedious and manually intensive process.

In a LAN-based environment, you might think that this problem would be moot by simply storing all the program files on a common server. By doing so you would essentially have only one copy of any program to update and worry about. Any change you made for one user would automatically become a change for every user.

The idea of storing programs on the server was a good idea years ago. In fact, some sites took the idea to its logical conclusion and even stored the operating system on the server. However, things have changed quite a bit, and that strategy is now being challenged for several reasons:

- It is not uncommon for programs to be as large as 50 MB, with whole suites going to several hundred megabytes. As such, the toll on the network to load a program has grown to be more severe. Imagine a large corporate environment with several hundred or thousand users, and each morning at 9:00 they all try to load their word processor over the network. Performance would drop to its knees.

- While some applications (like e-mail) require the network to be functional, other applications are perfectly usable without a network connection. By storing these packages on the local PC, the user can still continue to do some work even if the network or server is down.

- As programs have grown more complex, they have grown in size and the number of files. It is not uncommon for a single application to have several hundred files associated with it. And many applications share many of the same files. As such, it may not be desirable to do a single update affecting all users at once. It is not uncommon for an update of a single file in one application to cause another application to malfunction.

While the last item can be addressed to a degree with careful testing, the first items have led many companies to install application software on the PC workstation, not the file server.

This shifts managing the deployment of software to PCs, and it can be enormous. Even in a relatively small environment of 100 PCs, it is likely that there will be many different models of PCs with different capabilities and specifications for memory, BIOS, disk space, processor, peripherals, and so on. Each unique "flavor" of PC may result in minor variations in how (and which) software files, particularly those related to the operating system, are installed.

While the advent of a Plug 'N Play operating system (like Windows 95, 98, 2000, and Millennium), along with Plug 'N Play hardware, has made life somewhat easier, it has done little to ease the effort of deploying software to a large PC population.

To make the most of this situation, there are several concepts that many environments (small and large) have seized upon. They are gaining in popularity, and quickly becoming standard practice:

- Develop a standard disk image
- Select a disk cloning package
- Implement a software deployment tool

Develop a Standard Disk Image

Every site should create a disk image that will essentially serve as a way of ensuring that each PC's software configuration is as similar as possible. This can reduce a technician's troubleshooting time significantly. The disk image will include the following features.

A Directory Structure for All Programs and Files

This is the directory structure that will determine where programs and files will be stored. While many environments use each application program's defaults for most directory choices, it is likely that you will have to do some customization, particularly for the directories that hold documents and data files.

An Installation of the Most Common Programs Used

Many programs, like e-mail and word processing, will be installed on virtually every PC in the company. Other applications, like an inventory management program or a human resources application, will be much more limited. Depending on circumstances you can choose not to install these on each PC, or to install them and then "cripple," or hide, them from users who don't need them by deleting a pertinent file or icon. In this way, the more laborious effort of installing the software on each PC is simplified because it is the same for each user. Afterwards, the unnecessary applications can be quickly removed for those users who don't need them.

Drivers for Common Peripherals Used in the Environment (NICs, Pointing Devices, etc.)

The standard image should include drivers for popular and common peripherals that are used. This can include network interface cards, printers, pointing devices (e.g., mice), and so on. In this way, if a workstation's peripheral is changed, the drive is immediately available. An alternative to this is to have all drivers stored on a network server where they are easily accessible to be copied to the workstation as needed.

Preset Program Preferences That Are Applicable to the Environment

Most programs have many, many preferences and options that allow the user to customize the look and feel of their program. While many of these can be left to the user's discretion, there are also many that should be set by the IT department. For example, in Microsoft Word it makes sense for IT to set the default document directory, default printer, and AutoSave feature—to name just three. It is best for IT to carefully review each option and determine if the default setting should be changed.

Select a Disk Cloning Package

A standard disk image is a great way of ensuring consistency in an environment with many PCs. However, the image is only a blueprint. It does not provide a way to easily build each PC's disk to match the blueprint's specification. The amount of software on a PC can range from several hundred megabytes to several gigabytes. Even an automated install of all that data can take a fair amount of time.

A disk cloning package uses very sophisticated techniques to quickly copy large amounts of data in a fraction of the time it would take using conventional methods. Once the master disk image is made, it is possible to duplicate it to other PCs in a matter of minutes. In larger environments, where there is a constant influx of new PCs arriving at the loading dock, a disk cloning package can save an enormous amount of time. And, since it creates an identical duplicate, it virtually eliminates any errors that might crop into a manual effort. Popular disk cloning packages include

- Symantec's Ghost
- Imagecast IC3
- PowerQuest's Disk Image
- Altiris's RapiDeploy

It should be noted that Microsoft has had some issues with disk cloning. Microsoft has particular concerns about the cloning of the NT operating system. In particular, a normal installation of NT creates a unique SID (security ID) for each PC. By using a cloning tool, each PC would end up with the same SID as the master image—thereby defeating some of the security aspects of NT. Some of the vendors of cloning software have addressed this by creating a unique SID when they are used with NT.

Implement a Software Deployment Tool

While a standard disk image, along with a cloning tool, ensures that everyone has a similar software configuration when a new PC is deployed, it does nothing to help with updating software or adding software.

There are numerous tools available to help with the deployment of software:

- Microsoft's SMS
- Novell's ZEN works
- Veritas's WinInstall
- Wilson WindowWare's WinBatch

These tools operate in a very similar fashion by allowing you to "script" the installation process for a software update—be it as complex as a new company-wide application, or as small as an updated printer driver. While the packages provide assistance for creating scripts, it can still be a complex process. Many of the tools allow you to consider many variables and circumstances when a script runs. For example:

- You may code a script to check that the target PC has enough disk space before running.
- You may code the script to run only on PCs that meet minimum hardware and software requirements that you define.
- You may want the script to take different installation steps based on certain circumstances. For example, if the script is to copy a file to the PC, you may not want it to do so if a newer version already exists.
- You may choose whether the script runs automatically or by user selection.
- You may be able to determine what time of day the script runs.
- You can choose what action the script should take if the installation fails.

As you can see, a script can be a very effective tool, but complex to use. Since a single script may get used hundreds or thousands of times within an environment, it is best if the job of writing and maintaining scripts is given to individuals who have an attention for detail and careful testing.

While a single script may take a fair amount of time to develop, the value it returns in deploying software—in identical fashion—to an entire PC population is enormous.

Without the use of the ideas and tools mentioned above, the effort to deploy software is reduced to an essentially manual one. As the number of PCs in an environment grows, it could easily require a small team of technicians to do the software deployment effort. However, the effort and manpower can be reduced significantly by using the techniques and tools that are readily available. When used effectively, not only can these ideas make the job easier, the end result is likely to be far superior to a manual effort.

9.7   Software Licensing: How Do I Deal with It?

"Software pirating" refers to the use of software that hasn't been fully paid for. Software pirating is also referred to as bootlegging, with more than a passing reference to the trafficking of alcohol during Prohibition. Illegally copied and unlicensed software is estimated to cost the software industry $11 billion per year.

Concerns about software piracy may seem like a small headache and a low priority compared to your other responsibilities. However, that headache can easily grow to a migraine and become your highest priority. There are numerous cases of small companies being subjected to a software audit based on a call to one of the software industry trade groups (e.g., Business Software Alliance or the Software and Industry Information Association, which is now a part of the Software and Information Industry Association) from a single disgruntled employee. Countless hours and resources have been expended by companies to deliver the documentation and proof of appropriate licenses requested. Companies consider themselves fortunate if it is decided that the illegal licensing discovered was unintentional, and that the company had been making a good faith effort to be legal. In cases like this, there may be no fines or punitive damages. But the company will have to pay the license fees for all the illegal software that was discovered.

In general, corporations seldom consciously engage in illegal activities. They also generally respect intellectual copyright laws. However, due to complexities of licensing agreements and the volume of purchase activity, it can be difficult for an IT manager to fully know if his company is properly licensed on all its software.

In fact, it is not unusual for a company to find out that it is actually overlicensed on some products and underlicensed on others. Very often, the individuals responsible for buying new computers make certain that each order for a new workstation also includes an order for all the standard software. However, since workstations are generally replaced after 3–5 years, it is entirely possible that the replacement units are also being ordered with new software licenses. Since the software license can be transferred from the old machine to the new, buying the license(s) for the replacement device is not necessary.

Underlicensing usually occurs with software that is not "standard" on every workstation. For nonstandard software, it is very easy for the purchase of the license to be overlooked and forgotten by the administrative staff. In such a case, the technical staff may seek to satisfy a user's request and install an unlicensed software copy, and neglect to inform the administrative staff to purchase the license.

The process of keeping track of software licenses is often referred to as *software metering*. There are some general guidelines that you, as an IT manager, should be aware of in order to avoid putting your company at risk for copyright infringement.

- Understand that when you buy a software license, what you are actually buying is the right to use a copy of the software. The vendor is the actual "owner" of the software.

- Read and understand the licenses that come with your software. License terms can change, so review them periodically.

- Don't expect to be able to negotiate a change with your software's vendor, although very large organizations may have some success here. If the software you are buying is not an off-the-shelf or shrink-wrapped package, you'll have better chances.

- Be aware of concurrent license terms (which refers to how many people are actually using the software at the same time) versus nonconcurrency (which refers to how many people have access to the software, regardless of their use of it).

Road Warriors

For roaming and traveling users, some licenses allow a single license to be installed on each workstation the user has (e.g., the one in the office, the one at home, and the laptop in her briefcase), as long as these copies aren't used by others, or concurrently.

Buy vs. Lease

In some cases you "buy" a license, which is yours essentially forever. In other cases, the license is "rented" and must be renewed every few years.

Maintenance Plans

In addition to buying a license, some vendors sell upgrade or maintenance plans (not unlike the ability to buy extended warranties on a home appliance) that entitle you to upgrade (at little or a reduced cost) to newer versions of the software as they come out. While there is considerable doubt about the value of these plans for your new VCR, the value of them in regard to software depends on how often the vendor expects to provide new versions, and how often you expect to be interested in these newer versions.

Keep in mind that a vendor may also offer a "support" program, which entitles you to technical support on a product but does not include providing you with no-cost upgrades. Alternatively, buying into a plan for upgrades may not include free support. Check with your vendor as to what you are buying before you buy it.

While you probably won't be able to negotiate the terms of the license, it is entirely likely you can negotiate a volume discount based on the license quantities you intend to buy.

Contact the Legal Department

Let your company's legal resources review the terms of any software license you buy. In all likelihood, your company's lawyer will say that the license has numerous unfavorable terms, and that he recommends against entering into such an agreement. However, he is also likely to add that he recognizes that there is no real alternative.

Keep records of your license purchases: quantities, dates, vendors, and so on. For licenses that need to be renewed periodically, keep track of the start and end dates, and the same for support and upgrade plans. Make sure that everyone in IT is fully aware that it is against company policy to pirate software.

Advise users that it is against company policy to bootleg software, and any unauthorized software will be immediately deleted when found. (This is a nifty little policy to have around when you encounter games that people have copied from their home PCs.)

Get Organized

Whenever possible, consolidate all your software purchases. Many large software retailers have systems in place designed to help companies keep track of their license purchases, their obligations, expirations, and so on.

In a crisis or emergency situation, you may feel that the only solution is to install a copy of a software package that hasn't been paid for. If you choose to go this route, you should ensure that a proper license is ordered and purchased at the same time.

Track Your Software

In addition to the above guidelines, there are several tools available to help you track software use in your environment. Software metering packages keep track of how software packages are used in your company. Metering software is generally installed on your LAN's file server(s) and keeps track of which users are using which packages, how often, and when. You can reconcile this information with the records from your software reseller to make sure you have purchased enough licenses for the actual use.

Another tool at your disposal is inventory software. Inventory software can automatically detect what software is installed on each workstation. This data is stored in a database that you can query and generate reports from. Again, this information can be compared to the information from your metering tool, as well as your purchasing records. In IT, software that is no longer needed is rarely removed from the environment. With inventory reports, you can see what software is on each PC, and use it to remove old versions, as well as unauthorized copies.

9.8 Further References

Web Sites

- *www.bsa.org* (software licensing and piracy)
- *www.caldera.com* (Linux distribution)
- *www.imagecast.com* (disk cloning software)
- *www.linux.org* (Linux resources)
- *www.linux.org/info/gnu.html* (GNU General Public License)
- *www.linuxresources.com* (Linux resources)
- *www.powerquest.com* (disk cloning software)
- *www.redhat.com* (Linux distribution)
- *www.siia.net* (software licensing and piracy)
- *www.slackware.com* (Linux distribution)
- *www.symantec.com* (disk cloning software)
- *www.veritas.com* (software distribution tool)
- *www.windowware.com* (batch automation software)

Articles and Books

- Zachary, G. Pascal, *Show-Stopper,* Free Press, 1994. An excellent book on Microsoft's building of NT.
- Pfaffenberger, Bryan, *Linux: Clearly Explained,* Morgan Kaufmann, 1999.
- Rizzo, John, *Macintosh Window Integration,* Morgan Kaufmann, 1999. This is an excellent book, almost 600 pages long and including a CD, that discusses everything you would ever want to know about this topic.
- Stephenson, Neal, *In the Beginning . . . Was the Command Line,* Avon Books, 1999.
- Young, Robert, and Wendy Goldman Rohm, *Under the Radar: How Red Hat Changed the Software Business and Took Microsoft by Surprise,* The Coriolis Group, 1999.

Data Networks

CHAPTER TEN

What You Will Learn

- What data networks are
- What the difference between database, application, Web, and file and print servers is
- How to configure a server
- What the difference between MS Windows NT/2000 Server, Novell Netware, and Unix systems is
- What the important issues in LAN and WAN design are
- What the key LAN and WAN technologies are
- How to manage and expand LANs
- The important issues to know when designing a WAN
- How to manage WANs
- How to install, manage, and expand a cable plant
- Whether you need remote access
- What the advantages and disadvantages of telephone remote access are
- What the advantages and disadvantages of direct line remote access are
- What the advantages and disadvantages of Web-based access are
- What remote users see when they log in
- What the key issues of network security are

Introduction

One of the core functions of IT is getting data from one place to another. From client to server, from coworker to coworker, from New York to Los Angeles, from workstation to printer. Wherever your data has to go, it needs a network to get there.

Data networks refer to the collection of technologies that get data from one computer to another. The technologies include clients, servers, routers, switches, topologies, protocols, hubs, and cable (copper or fiber). Within these categories you'll find the usual issues of cost, performance, and industry standards. To make things more complicated, you can combine all the variables in many different ways.

Since you can't walk into a retail store or call up your value-added reseller and order a LAN, it is up to you to make decisions about the various technologies and components, which ones you want to use, and how you want to put them together.

10.1 Servers: What Is the Difference between Database, Application, Web, and File and Print Servers?

In general, the data network is what gets data between devices (printers, servers, workstations, etc.). Very often the data is moving to and from a server. A *server* is a generic term that really means little more than a resource that is shared and can be accessed by multiple users (be it humans, or other devices).

There are multiple types of servers that might exist in any IT environment. It is entirely possible for a single device to provide all of the types of server applications discussed below. Of course, this is likely to tax the resources of a single box, not to mention the fact that it would be very difficult, if not impossible, to tweak the configuration parameters of the server to provide the optimum performance for all functions.

File and Print Servers

File and print servers are the most basic types of servers and were the first servers to arrive on the scene. File and print are two different functions, but since they are so fundamental, they are often referred to together.

File Servers

These are central devices that store different types of files (data, application, etc.), which users can share. In their most basic form, users can access the data stored on a file server—and manipulate its contents—as easily as manipulating the contents of their own workstation's hard drive. Of course, file servers provide some management capabilities such as security and central backup in addition to the file-sharing services.

Print Servers

While file servers allow users to share files, print servers allow users to share output devices. When users send files to print, the requests go first to the print server, which in turn sends them to the printer—which might be attached to the printer server directly or via a LAN connection. While file servers offer security as an added value, print servers add functions like being able to set priorities and manage multiple printers.

Database Servers

To understand a database server, it is important to realize that a database does not stand alone, but is managed and controlled by a database management system (DBMS), which is a very sophisticated software program. Popular DBMSs include DB2 from IBM, Oracle, Informix, SQL-Server from Microsoft, and Sybase. When your customer service staff is entering data from customer orders, it is the DBMS that maintains the database's indices and integrity, monitors user access privileges, audit trails, transaction logging and rollback, and so on. The overhead, in terms of processing power, for a DBMS can be enormous.

As a result of the demands of a DBMS on overall performance, a DBMS—along with the data—often resides on its own server(s). Very often, the most powerful servers in a data center are the database servers.

Application Servers

In the client-server model, most of the processing function for the application occurs on the server, with the client portion of the software sometimes doing little more than collecting keystrokes and displaying screen contents. The actual logic of the application, including data querying, selection, and sorting, as well as procedure flow, occurs on the application server.

It is important to recognize that simply putting an application on a server doesn't necessarily make it an application server. A file-sharing server (see above) could have an application program (e.g., Lotus 1-2-3) on it. However, when users execute this application, the program is loaded to the user's local workstation. This means that the user is limited to the processing power of his own desktop, and the processing power of the server will go underutilized.

Web Servers

Application and database servers each run a specific type of software that allows the server to do its job. A Web server is no different. A Web server runs software that allows it to respond to various types of requests (e.g., those conforming to HTTP and FTP protocols). Chapter 11 has a more detailed discussion of Web servers.

10.2 Servers: How Do I Configure a Server?

Configuring a server includes the hardware configuration as well as the software configuration. Obviously, there are infinite parameters based upon the hardware and software you plan to use, the size of the operation, the specific needs and priorities, and so on. In fact, configuring the network operating system alone, which may have hundreds of parameters that can be set and tweaked, is the subject of entire books.

In this section, we'll talk about some high-level considerations when you configure the hardware for a server. We'll cover processor and memory, disk space, fault tolerance, backup, and support.

Processor and Memory

What processor you have in your server, how many of them, along with the installed memory, will be the primary impact on the device's performance. Your application vendor(s) should be able to give you some guidelines on these parameters based upon number of users, scale of environment, number of expected transactions, and so on. Many servers now can support a minimum of two processors, with others available for four, eight, and sixteen processors. Remember, adding more processing power may not do much if your application is I/O (i.e., disk reads and writes) intensive.

When considering the various trade-offs for your initial configuration, keep in mind options for later expansion. After all, it is likely you'll have this server for several years. It may not always be your primary machine, but you should be making a purchasing decision based on the fact that you will be using it in various capacities for at least three years.

Adding memory or an additional processor is a generally simple task, although as with any hardware upgrade check with your NOS (network operating system) and application vendors to see if the software will support, recognize, and take advantage of the additional hardware. Upgrading a processor—say, from one speed to another—may not be that simple. It may require changing more than just the "chip"; it may require changing the system board, or more. Your hardware vendor may not even support changing the processor. In multi-

Table 10.1 Units of bytes (approximate).

Unit Name	Abbreviation	Exponential Equivalent	Number of Bytes
Kilobyte	KB	10^3	1,000
Megabyte	MB	10^6	1,000,000
Gigabyte	GB	10^9	1,000,000,000
Terabyte	TB	10^{12}	1,000,000,000,000
Petabyte	PB	10^{15}	1,000,000,000,000,000
Exabyte	EB	10^{18}	1,000,000,000,000,000,000
Zettabyte	ZB	10^{21}	1,000,000,000,000,000,000,000
Yottabyte	YB	10^{24}	1,000,000,000,000,000,000,000,000

processor servers, you may have to upgrade all the processors at once since the vendor, or NOS, may not support a mixed processor environment.

Also keep in mind that the law of diminishing returns applies to adding processors. Each additional processor will, at best, increase performance by slightly less than a factor $1/N$ (where N is the number of processors in the system prior to the upgrade). For example, taking a server from one to two processors may give you close to twice the performance. Adding the third increases it by no more than one-half, the fourth by one-third, and so on.

Disk Storage

Whatever your estimate for disk storage is, be confident that you are underestimating. Disk usage has exploded. When PCs first became popular, hard drives for them didn't even exist. And a few years later, the initial PC hard drives were merely 5 and 10 MB in size (see Table 10.1 above). Now, PCs are routinely configured with 10 GB of disk storage, and more. Similarly, server storage has gone from a few hundred megabytes to tens, if not hundreds, of gigabytes. And it is not uncommon for corporate data centers to have several terabytes (1,000 gigabytes) of storage.

When considering disk storage, look for high-performance and high-reliability configurations. Consider configurations that will let you easily add storage, replace drives, and so on without extended downtimes. It is becoming increasingly common to be able to perform these functions with no downtime.

Fault Tolerance

Virtually by definition, a server is a critical resource—it is a central device that is serving multiple users. Therefore, you want your servers to be up and available as much as possible. However, things do go wrong, hardware does fail, and software does crash. *Fault tolerance* is the term applied to systems that can keep operating, even if a component fails. There are several steps you can take so that even if various components on your server fail, it still runs.

Redundant Power Supplies

Except for the smallest devices, all servers today are available with a redundant power supply option. The cost is relatively low, but the benefit is well worth it—power supplies do have a tendency to fail. If you have a redundant power supply installed in your server, the server will continue to run if either fails, allowing you to order a replacement for the failed unit and replacing it at your convenience. In fact, if your power supplies are "hot swappable," you can replace one without taking the box down (assuming that you have a redundant power supply installed).

Disk Drives

There are several options for fault tolerance with disk drives, including mirroring, duplexing, and RAID (Redundant Array of Independent/Inexpensive Disks). There are several different levels of RAID (see Table 10.2), and sometimes the definition may vary slightly by vendor. Each level of RAID is different in regard to performance, redundancy, costs, and so on. For a more detailed description of various RAID levels, see *http://www.acnc.com/raid.html.*

Regardless of which fault tolerance strategy you use, it is important to note that it may be possible to configure it through the hardware or through the software. For example, you may be able to configure your hard drives and controllers for mirroring. Or you can configure the operating system to do the mirroring. Depending on the hardware and software you use, you may not have both options. If you do, the choice of which way to go can be a difficult one. Some prefer to leave the I/O activity to the hardware devices—which are designed just for this task—and leave the operating system free to its application demands. Others, on the other hand, believe that the operating system should oversee everything that is going on. If you have the choice, discuss the options with your vendors and your network managers.

Redundant Network Interface Cards (NICs)

NICs are very inexpensive; if you have two in the server, you have redundancy so that you keep operating if one fails. In addition, you may be able to balance the network traffic across the two NICs to improve performance.

Table 10.2 Definition of RAID levels. (*Source: http://www.digidata.com/*).

RAID Level	Description	Data Reliability	Data Transfer Rate	I/O Request Rate	Application Strength	Cost
RAID 1	All data copied onto two separate disks	Very high; can withstand selective multiple disk failures	Data transfer rate is higher than single disk for reads, but does not offer load balancing	Twice that of single disk for reads; slightly slower than single disk for writes	General	Very high; requires twice as many disks for redundancy
RAID 2	Data striped across multiple disks with parity on multiple disks	Very high, can withstand selective multiple disk failures	High if error correcting codes are computed by hardware	Similar to twice that of single disk	General	High; requires multiple disks for redundancy
RAID 3	Data striped across all data disks with dedicated parity disk	Much higher than single disk; can withstand single disk failure	Highest of all types listed here for reading and writing	Faster than single disk, owing to parallel disk accesses	Video, prepress, medical imaging, and other large file applications	Low; requires only one disk for redundancy
RAID 4	Data striped across some data disks with dedicated parity disk	Much higher than single disk; can withstand single disk failure	High compared to single disk for reads but significantly lower than single disk for writes*	High compared to single disk for reads but significantly lower than single disk for writes*	Predominantly read oriented with few writes	Low; requires only one disk for redundancy
RAID 5	Data and parity striped across multiple disks	Much higher than single disk; can withstand single disk failure	High compared to single disk for reads but lower than single disk for writes*	High compared to single disk for reads but generally lower than single disk for writes*	Transaction processing with high read-to-write ratio	Low; requires only one disk for redundancy

* Write operations are slow in these cases because the controller must read parity information from a disk and recompute parity information for the disk before it writes information to the disk array.

Uninterruptible Power Supplies (UPSs)

UPSs protect your equipment in case of power surges, spikes, drops, and outages. With UPSs, many vendors offer a software package that enables the UPS to communicate with the server, and instructs the server to do a "clean shutdown" when there is a power outage and the battery is down to its last few minutes of power. A UPS is most often used to protect your server from damage from anomalies in your power line. Unless every device in your environment (workstations, hubs, routers, etc.) is also on a UPS, having a battery backup to keep your server up and operating will do little to keep your environment running when the power goes down.

Cross-Connecting

If you have multiple NICs in your servers, connect each to a different network hub. In this way, if a hub or NIC fails, you still have some connectivity to your network. You can do a similar configuration if you have redundant power supplies and multiple UPSs (see Figure 10.1). Lastly, if you do use fault tolerance technologies, make sure you periodically monitor the status of the various components. If one fails, get it repaired as soon as possible so that it's there to do its job when needed.

Clustering

The concept behind server clustering is to have several servers doing virtually identical work. If one server fails, the workload can be borne by the other servers in the cluster. This is a complex service since it requires a high level of integration among all the hardware and software in the environment. It requires special system software to balance the load among all the servers in the cluster and to shift the load accordingly when a device goes down. In addition, it requires that some resources (e.g., the databases) be shared among all devices in the cluster to ensure that each server has access to the most current data.

Backup

In truth, your first step towards fault tolerance has to be an effective and comprehensive backup strategy. Backup considerations are critical when configuring a server:

■ You may want to consider some type of central or consolidated backup strategy, as opposed to a backup strategy for each server and resource.

■ As you configure your disk storage, remember that the more storage you have, the more backup capacity you'll need, and the longer it will take to back up.

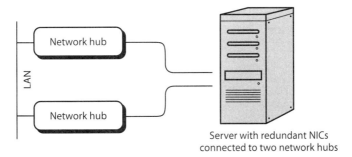

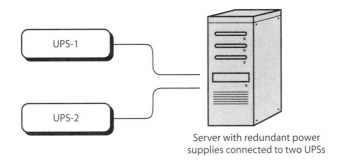

Figure 10.1   Cross-Connecting NICs and Power Supplies

- Consider your applications and databases. Check with the vendors about the integrity of backups that are performed when files are open. You may need to shut down the application in order to perform a backup that you can trust.

- You have to determine how long you should keep your data. In some environments, government regulations require data to be kept for many years. In other situations, your company may choose intentionally to keep a very short life cycle of data backup (e.g., e-mail).

- Give thought to the frequency and type of backup. Daily backups are common, although critical sites do almost continuous backups by mirroring their data environment to a remote site. When you think about how often to back up, you have to decide what types of backup to make: *full* or *incremental*.

- Lastly, be sure to have an off-site storage for some of your backups. In small shops, this might be a drawer in the home of the IT manager. In large shops, it could be a highly specialized and secured warehouse facility that is staffed 24 hours a day. The intent of off-site storage is to allow you some sort of recovery in case your facility suffers a catastrophe (fire, flood, or the proverbial plane crash) that destroys all your data. (See Chapter 14 for a discussion on disaster recovery.)

Support

Lastly, when configuring your server, consider what type of support is available from your vendor. Most hardware comes with a warranty, sometimes up to three years. Read the details. What is the response time? Is it available 24 × 7? Is it on-site service, or do you have to return the unit? Look into upgrading or buying service levels that fit the needs of your environment. If you have the skills and resources, you may want to consider just keeping some spare parts on hand to be used in the case of a component failure.

10.3 Server OS: What Is the Difference between MS Windows NT/2000 Server, Novell Netware, and Unix Systems?

Microsoft's Windows NT and 2000 Server products, Novell's Netware, and all the versions of Unix are a category of software known as network operating systems (NOS). Unix has been around the longest, Novell was the first to gain popularity in the corporate environment, and Windows NT 2000 Server is the most recent entry but has gained enormous ground.

Speaking generally, Unix is considered to be the best choice for very critical and large-scale needs. Novell's reputation for reliability and stability comes from its years of experience with a very large installed base. Windows NT Server (whose latest incarnation is called Windows 2000) is favored as the NOS that provides the easiest integration with other popular applications used in the corporate environment (e.g., those also from Microsoft). Windows NT Server is also favored by those trying to reduce the support headaches (e.g., finger-pointing) that can occur when an environment consists of products from multiple vendors.

Choosing among these three technologies can be very difficult. There are issues of performance, scale, reliability, support, administration, costs, and hardware and software compatibility that you must consider.

Hardware Compatibility

The issue of hardware compatibility is critical. In regard to hardware, Novell only runs on Intel devices, Microsoft NT Server currently only runs on Intel and DEC's Alpha boxes, and Unix runs on a variety of platforms (although that selection can be significantly limited by each Unix flavor's vendor).

Software Compatibility

Equally important is software compatibility. Your NOS choice should follow your choice of applications. If Novell's GroupWise is your choice for an e-mail platform, you'll have to run it on Novell's Netware NOS. Similarly, if you choose Microsoft's Exchange for e-mail, your only NOS choice is Windows NT or 2000 Server (at least for the server that will host the Exchange application).

10.4 LAN: What Are the Important Issues in Design?

A LAN (local area network) refers to the network that connects the devices in one geographic location, such as a single building. A LAN is based on any physical network technology designed to span distances up to a few thousand meters, although the "local" in LAN can sometimes be extended to include all the devices in a campus environment. As a general rule, a LAN's boundary is telecommunication facilities (T-1 lines, ISDN, etc.). These facilities are generally considered to be part of the WAN (wide area network).

Designing a LAN is like designing a house. It is dependent on needs, plans for future growth, and changes of use, and the definition of a good design can vary with changes and trends in the marketplace. The goals of a good LAN design should include the following:

- **Maximizing the efficiency of network traffic:** Moving the data from Point A to Point B as fast as possible.

- **Reliability**: A LAN is one of those things that no one notices until it fails to function.

- **Manageability**: So that you can see trends of growth and traffic patterns, as well as identify bottlenecks and problem areas.

- **Flexibility**: To be able to adapt to changing environment needs (not the least of which is growth), as well as the introduction of new technologies.

Of course, there is no black and white, right or wrong, when it comes to LAN designs. Like designing a house, there are many, many ways to do it—all of which can be right. Sometimes it is a matter of philosophy and personal preferences based on past experiences. Get as much help as you can, get as many heads into the process as you can. Tap all the expertise you know. Your VAR, vendors, staff, and others in the know can all help.

Location of Devices

The first consideration in designing a LAN has to be the location of all the devices. This will help you determine the layout of segments, and so on. This will also impact where you put your hubs since cable runs have distance maximums. Also consider the locations of your centralized resources (e.g., servers).

Traffic Volume

You then need to consider the volume of traffic. The volume might be high because of the number of devices or the types of data (low-volume e-mail versus high-volume animation files). In addition to the volume, consider the traffic patterns. Are most users only sending/receiving data to central servers? Or is there an expectation for a large amount of peer-to-peer sharing? Are these servers centrally located or spread throughout the environment?

Locations for a Hub and a Backbone

Armed with this information, you should be able to consider locations for a hub and a backbone. You should also be able to begin thinking about speeds, switched/shared, and so on. You'll want to work with your facilities staff regarding wiring closets and risers (for your vertical cable runs between floors). For wiring closets, you have to consider accessibility, security, ventilation, and availability of electricity to power any devices. For your risers and wire runs, you may have to deal with fire and building codes, drilling through walls and ceilings, and so on.

Budgetary Considerations

Then you need to consider your budget, need for speed, and growth expectations (traffic types and volumes, additional nodes, etc.). The more sophisticated LAN devices that offer the highest levels of performance and manageability are significantly more expensive than their feature-poor brethren. And certain cable types (e.g., fiber) are much more expensive to install than others (e.g., copper).

Moving Data: Gigabit Ethernet

Ethernet is by far the most popular way of moving data around a network. The industry considers it reliable and easy to work with. It has kept pace with the needs for more and more bandwidth by first providing speeds of 10 Mbps, then 100 Mbps, then 1 Gbps, and now there is development work being done to deliver 10 Gbps speeds. Gigabit Ethernet is primarily carried on fiber, but copper can be used for short distances (like connecting servers to hubs).

10.5 LAN: What Are the Key LAN Technologies I Should Know?

We discussed network servers in previous sections. Here, we'll discuss concepts regarding the network itself. This is the facility that moves the data between a personal computer in the Marketing department on the 3rd floor and the file server on the 70th floor.

Network technology is complicated. Don't hesitate to ask for help. Chances are that the VAR that is selling you your LAN equipment will provide some guidance and/or consulting expertise at little or no cost. The manufacturer of your key networking hardware may also be able to provide assistance in overall design to help you pick the best product for your needs and budget. Consider taking training classes on the related technologies and products. Ask your vendors for references of other customers using this equipment in a similar design—contact these references and learn from any mistakes they may have made.

Network design is a topic that is the focus of entire careers, so it isn't something that can be covered in a few pages here. Instead, we'll review some of the major technology concepts and the issues that have to be considered when implementing them in a LAN. You need to understand these concepts and principles to ensure that your vendor isn't over-/underengineering your design.

Architecture

A LAN's architecture refers to the overall layout of the LAN and how the parts are connected.

Topology

A network's topology is the way the various components are arranged and connected together. There are three popular topologies: bus, ring, and star (see Figures 10.2, 10.3, and 10.4 on the next page).

It is important to note that, in general, the actual topology really exists within the network hub devices themselves. For example, in the case of Token-Ring,

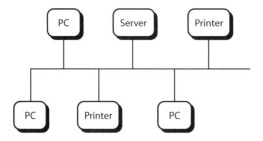

Figure 10.2 Bus Topology

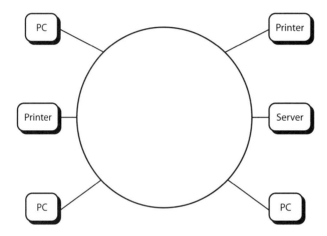

Figure 10.3 Ring Topology

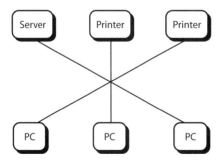

Figure 10.4 Star Topology

the "ring" exists in the hub even though the diagram might lead you to expect a large ring of cable. It is possible, and common, for a LAN to consist of several network topologies. For example, each floor of a building might use a bus topology to connect together all the devices on that floor, but the floors might be interconnected using an FDDI, which is a ring topology of fiber cable.

The Network Backbone

The backbone is the high-capacity portion of the LAN that carries/transfers data from lower-speed parts of the network that connect to it. On a small LAN, the backbone might be as small as a single piece of hardware in a wiring closet. In a large environment it could be a fiber ring that connects 30 floors of a high-rise. The backbone is the most critical portion of the LAN since its availability, performance, and reliability will most likely impact every user and every device on the network.

Ethernet vs. Token-Ring

The most popular technologies for devices to communicate on a LAN are Ethernet and Token-Ring. While there are devices to allow for interconnecting Ethernet and Token-Ring, it is important to remember that all the devices on any one segment of the LAN must all use the same technology.

Ethernet

Ethernet, which uses a bus topology, is the most popular LAN technology. Although there are several different Ethernet specifications, the most popular are 10Base-T (10 Mbps) and 100Base-T, also known as fast Ethernet (100 Mbps). 10Base-T is most popularly used for desktop and printer connections, although 100 Mbps is quickly being adopted for these uses. 100 Mbps is often used for server connections and for LAN backbones. Gigabit Ethernet (which provides speeds of 1000 Mbps) is a relatively new specification for Ethernet that is gaining popularity for backbone and server connections.

Ethernet uses CSMA/CD (Carrier Sense Multiple Access with Collision Detection protocol). When an Ethernet device wants to send a message, it senses whether any other device is sending. If not, the device begins to transmit its first data frame. If another device has tried to send at the same time, a collision is said to occur and the frames are discarded. Each device then waits a random amount of time and retries until successful in getting its transmission sent.

Collisions are a critical factor in an Ethernet network's performance. Devices that interconnect LAN segments (like bridges, routers, and switches) do not transfer collision signals from one port to another. A collision domain is a reference to all the devices on a network segment that risk collisions with each other. In other words, a device only has to worry about data collisions with other devices in that same collision domain. Obviously, the fewer devices that exist in a collision domain, the lower the chances of a collision.

Token-Ring

Token-Ring is a star topology network environment that was popularized by IBM in the 1980s, with speeds of 4 Mbps and 16 Mbps. A special packet of data, called the *token,* travels around to each successive node on the ring. When a node wants to send a message it first waits for the token to come around, and then appends its data packet, along with the destination address. As the token and data travel the ring, they are seen by each workstation until it gets to the destination device, which then changes the token to indicate that the message has been received. When this indication gets back to the originating device, the network is now available for the next device to send a message.

Hubs and Concentrators

Regardless of the topologies, protocols, and types of cable you choose to use, you'll need to buy hardware to connect all these devices together. Most of these will be "hub" devices. A hub (sometimes called a concentrator) is a generic term that refers to a piece of hardware that passes data among the network nodes (e.g., printer, workstation) that are connected to it. With each, you'll have choices to make.

Chassis vs. Stackable

A chassis device is an architecture that refers to the hardware design of the hub. In general the chassis is the "shell" that contains various components (power supplies, processors, host modules). The advantage of a chassis device is that the configuration can be easily altered by swapping components as needed, and if a component fails, it can usually be replaced with minimal disruption to the environment. On the other hand, the up-front cost of the chassis itself can make this architecture expensive if the environment it serves is not large enough to fully populate most of the chassis's slots.

Stackable devices are an alternative solution for the chassis architecture. Stackable devices (so named because they can be easily stacked on top of each other, but are often rack-mountable as well) don't require the up-front investment of a chassis. They are available with small numbers of ports (e.g., 8, 12, 24) and can be ideal for a small office or department. As the environment grows, additional units can be added. Stackables are inexpensive and convenient. However, they may lack some of the conveniences of chassis-based devices (e.g., redundant power supplies, high-end options, high-end management capabilities).

Passive vs. Active

A passive hub (a.k.a. "dumb hub") is a hub device that does nothing more than pass all the data and signals it receives to the devices connected to it. It is an inexpensive device for connecting network nodes. An active hub (a.k.a. "intelligent hub") adds value to its general function of interconnecting network nodes. This added value may be to regenerate the signal so that it can travel farther down the wire, or choose the best path, or some other network management functionality.

Shared and Switched

The more devices that are on a network segment, the slower the overall throughput there will be (of course, speed also depends on the volume of traffic). In an Ethernet environment, the more devices that exist, the greater the chances of collisions. In a Token-Ring environment, the more devices that are connected, the longer each device will have to wait for the token to become available before it can transmit data.

A LAN segment is said to be shared when all nodes attached to the hub "share" the available bandwidth. On the other hand, in a switched environment, each node connected to the hub can use the full amount of bandwidth available.

It is the type of installed hub that determines whether the bandwidth is shared or switched. Switched hub devices are more expensive than shared hub devices, but deliver superior performance. As the price for switches have dropped, many environments have begun to use them exclusively. Since it is the hub device that determines if the segment is shared or switched, there is no difference in hardware, software, or configuration between a node device on a switched segment, and one on a shared segment.

Wiring (Copper vs. Fiber)

The often-forgotten part of the network is the wiring. It is out of sight, buried in walls and ceilings. When considering cable choices, it is important to remember the biggest portion of a cable's cost is in the labor for its installation.

The primary consideration for wiring is whether to use copper or fiber. Most environments use copper where possible, and reserve fiber for where it is needed. The reason is that copper cable is cheaper to buy and install. Copper is also easier to work with, where fiber requires special equipment and skill to install. There is a more detailed discussion of wiring in Section 10.11.

Copper

Copper cable is often referred to as "twisted pair." Quite often, there is actually more than one pair—either because the technology being used requires it or for growth and/or redundancy. It should be noted that the "twist" is important. The two wires in a pair are twisted around each other to reduce electromagnetic interference. Often, the pairs (each of which is insulated) have additional shielding. This may be used to further reduce interference or protect from hazards, or because fire codes require it.

Copper cable comes in several different categories, with the most popular being category-5 (usually referred to as CAT-5). The specification for CAT-5 cabling currently provides for data speeds of up to 100 Mbps. Most organizations use CAT-5 from the wire closet to the desktop, and for some interfloor connections. CAT-5 is also being considered for use for short-distance runs for gigabit speeds. Keep in mind that when choosing a wiring specification, the increased cost of CAT-5 is generally inexpensive—the biggest cost associated with wiring is the labor to install it.

Fiber

Fiber cable uses the FDDI (Fiber Distributed Data Interface) protocol for transmitting data on fiber optic cable. Fiber's advantage over copper is that it can cover large distances (approximately 100 miles). In a LAN environment, the backbone is often FDDI for connections between floors or between buildings. On the downside, fiber is more delicate and often requires special installation concerns (particularly in regard to kinks, and to make sure the cable is protected from damage). In addition, fiber cable installation (particularly the connections and terminations) requires special skills, which also increases the cost of installation.

10.6 LAN: How Do I Manage One?

Ideally, managing a LAN should be a task that is done *proactively*. However, unfortunately, in practice it is often done *reactively*—when a problem occurs, you need to go find it and fix it. There are almost certainly problems on your LAN right now. If you connected a network monitoring device, you might see hundreds of minor problems that could be investigated—collisions, incomplete packets, time-outs, and so on.

Finding Problems

However, one of the frustrating things about managing a network is that, for the most part, it consists of copper wires. When data isn't moving, a close look at that copper won't reveal the cause, and it sure doesn't have a screen displaying error messages. However, you can buy tools that can look at the network and display error messages.

Chances are that most of the vendors of your higher-end network hardware (switches, routers, etc.) offer some type of management functionality that allows you to gather data about the network. However, very often this is information primarily related to the operation of the vendor's hardware. You can also buy products (e.g., Network Associate's Sniffer) that can connect to your network and allow you to examine the traffic, run traces, trap specific types of problems, and so on. Products like this are rather complex, though, and a complex tool in the hands of a novice is of little use. On the other hand, there are simpler tools (like those that can test and/or trace a cable to help determine where it is connected, and to see if it is wired properly or cut somewhere that you can't see).

Network Monitoring Concepts

There are entire categories of technologies to manage networks that might run thousands or tens of thousands of dollars. Some key concepts you want to be aware of when considering network monitoring solutions are the following:

- **SNMP:** Simple Network Management Protocol is a standard for monitoring networks. The SNMP protocol is used by virtually all networking devices. SNMP generally manages "events" like when a particular component fails or goes into an alarm condition.

- **RMON:** Remote Monitoring. RMON (two standards, RMON-1 and RMON-2) is an extension of the SNMP protocol. RMON collects information from different parts of the network (using probes if hardware based, or agents if software based) and presents them to the administrator. The advantage of RMON over SNMP is that while SNMP monitors events, RMON can provide and collect data for analysis, such as traffic statistics, bottlenecks, and so on.

With network monitoring tools, you can arrange for the software to send e-mail, or pages to beepers when certain events happen. You can also use them to generate reports and statistics on network usage.

10.7 LAN: How Do I Expand One?

The IT industry has always configured things with an eye towards growth, and LANs are no exception.

You may need to expand your LAN because of increased usage. Or you may need to expand it because the conference room that supported a single network node is now being turned into a project war room that needs to support 15 programmers, two servers, and three printers. Or due to your company's phenomenal growth, you're told that you're taking over another floor in the building you occupy. Or perhaps a building in another part of town.

To be sure that you can expand with minimal cost and effort, keep several ideas in mind:

Leave Room for More

On any device, always buy more ports than you expect to use. Give yourself about a 20% margin.

Multiple Wire Runs

The most expensive and difficult part of network installations and changes is the cost and effort involved in running the wire (copper or fiber). The cost is not so much in the materials of the wire, but in the labor of the installation—not to mention the disruption to your environment of having ladders all over the place as the electricians try to pull another cable. Whenever you have cable installed, consider having two or three runs installed. The incremental cost is very small (little more than the price of the materials), and it gives you additional wire when you need it (either due to growth, or to replace a connection that is failing).

Expect Your Needs to Grow

Expect your need for bandwidth to grow astronomically. With the explosive growth of Internet usage, the growth of file sizes (e.g., MP3, MPEG, JPEG, WAVs, executables), along with falling prices for high-speed connectivity and computers to process these files, you can expect network usage in your environment to skyrocket—even if your core business applications barely change. Don't be surprised to see your network traffic double every 2–3 years. Also, be sure to include the cost of forecasted bandwidth growth into each and every strategic, operational, and annual plan. Business units need to understand that this is a basic cost of doing business in the modern corporate environment.

Easily Upgradeable Hardware

Your network hardware is expensive, and you'll want to get a lot of life out of it. Look for devices that can be easily upgraded—either through software, firmware, or cards/components that can be easily swapped in and out.

10.8 WAN: What Are the Important Issues in Design?

A WAN (wide area network) refers to the network that connects the remote locations via telecommunications facilities (T-1 lines, ISDN, etc.). Unlike a LAN, a WAN can span large distances (such as cross-country). The network resources within the locations of a WAN, by the way, are generally considered to be part of the LAN.

Designing a WAN is very similar to designing a LAN: you have to consider geography, traffic flow, and volumes. One of the key differentiators in LAN versus WAN issues is that the vast majority of LAN costs are up-front capital expenditures of cable installation and hardware. On the other hand, the vast majority of WAN costs are in recurring charges for lines.

You'll want to examine the expected traffic load between sites. Very often, the volume of data is directly proportional to the number of devices. But this isn't a hard-and-fast rule. The data center may have just a few devices (compared to the thousands of computers at corporate headquarters in the next state), but the volume of traffic to the servers in the data center would be quite high.

Additionally, you need to consider the type of traffic between sites. If the only data going between the sites is e-mail, the volume of data will be rather low. However, if large data files are being transmitted (e.g., multimedia or database replication), it will be a very high volume.

Other factors to consider:

- The need for high-speed transmissions.

- The need for 24 × 7 operations.

- Backup/fail-over capabilities and facilities: The most critical connections need to be the most reliable. An analog, ISDN, or VPN might be sufficient backup. Or you may want to have multiple high-speed connections between your sites so that if one line fails the other continues to provide services.

- Installation delays: The more sophisticated the line, the more time your telecommunications vendor will need to install it. A simple POTS line could be installed in 1–2 weeks. However, higher-end lines (e.g., T-3) could take months. This could be critical if your WAN requirements are very dynamic.

Your telcos and vendors will probably be eager to help you design an appropriate WAN solution—often at little or no cost.

10.9 WAN: What Are the Key WAN Technologies I Should Know?

When designing a WAN strategy, it is important to know of the different connectivity options available to you. In general there are four types of options:

- Point-to-point circuits
- Dial-up
- Packet switching
- Cable modems

Point-to-Point Circuits

Point-to-point circuits, also known as leased, dedicated, and private lines, are facilities from telecom carriers that provide a connection between two locations. Point-to-point circuits can connect sites that are across town or across the country.

The primary advantage of a leased line is that it is always up, 24 hours a day. The cost is fixed and does not vary by usage. Since the line is dedicated, when there is a problem with the service the telephone company can investigate, locate, and resolve it (unlike a staticky dial-up connection, which is only resolved by hanging up and dialing again).

The most popular leased lines are T-1 and T-3. A T-1 line consists of 24 channels, each of which can provide 64 Kbps, for an aggregate throughput of 1.544 Mbps. A T-3 line is a leased line that provides data transmission speeds of 44.736 Mbps, via 672 circuits, each of which can support 64 Kbps transmissions. Quite often, a company will use a "fractional" T-1 or T-3. A fractional line is one that uses only a portion of the available channels. While this reduces the throughput, there is also a significant cost savings.

Dial-up Lines

Everyone is familiar with dial-up lines like the ones they have at home. While this is the most popular, recent advances have introduced other types, which have expanded the capabilities of dial-ups. Dial-up lines are somewhat less reliable than leased lines because each time you establish a connection you are using a different path through the telephone network. However, dial-up lines are more versatile since they can be used to establish connections to multiple locations, while leased lines only connect you to one place. Dial-up lines can also be significantly cheaper since you only pay for your actual usage (on top of a basic monthly fee).

POTS

The best-known and most popular type of dial-up line is called a POTS (plain old telephone system) line. A POTS line is what people have in their homes for their residential phone service. POTS lines are also used for fax machines and modems. Because POTS lines are based on analog technology, the highest-speed connection available is 56 Kbps—but even connections at this speed are rare. The advantage of POTS is its ubiquity.

ISDN

In the 1980s Integrated Services Digital Network (ISDN) began to become available. ISDN allows for digital transmission over standard copper telephone wire.

There are two types of ISDN: the Basic Rate Interface (BRI), usually used in homes and small businesses, and the Primary Rate Interface (PRI), for larger sites. Both types include a number of B (bearer) channels, which carry the actual data, and a D (delta) channel, which is used for signaling. A BRI consists of two 64 Kbps B channels and one 16 Kbps D channel, providing an aggregate throughput of 128 Kbps. A PRI consists of 23 B channels and one 64 Kbps D channel, for a total throughput of 1.4 Mbps. Note that the PRI's capacity is close to that of a T-1. However, since a PRI is billed based on usage and can be used to connect to multiple locations, it can be a more cost-effective solution. In fact ISDN lines are often used as a backup to a leased line circuit.

ISDN can only be installed at sites that are within a few miles of a telephone company central office (CO). Otherwise, expensive repeaters are required. As such, ISDN lines are not available everywhere. ISDN popularity seemed to peak in the mid-1990s. Lack of standards, expensive installations, and a relatively small gain in bandwidth for the home consumer (via BRI service) all helped to limit its growth. In addition, with the per-minute charges for ISDN connections, a highly used ISDN line can get very expensive.

DSL

Digital Subscriber Link (DSL) is a way of bringing high-speed connectivity to homes and small businesses over standard copper phone lines. Although DSL does run over existing residential lines, it is not quite dial-up. DSL provides an "always-on" connection to your service provider. Since it is always on, there is no dialing and no busy signals. In general, DSL is configured asynchronously (ADSL) to provide high-speed downloads (up to T-1 speeds) and slower-speed uploads (approximately 128 Kbps). In order to be able to use DSL, the home or business must be within a few miles of a telephone company central office.

Packet Switching

Packet switching technology breaks up a data transmission into small packets. Each packet is then transmitted through the network, generally on different paths, to the destination. At the destination, the packets are reassembled. One of the advantages of using packet switching is that if a portion of the network becomes unavailable (e.g., a resource or segment is down), the packets will find an alternative route through the rest of the network.

ATM and Frame Relay

The two most popular packet switching technologies are frame relay and asynchronous transfer mode (ATM). Frame relay speeds are available between 56 Kbps and 45 Mbps. ATM offers speeds from 25 to 622 Mbps. With ATM's high speed, it is often used for delay-sensitive applications like voice and video, in addition to data.

The actual packet switching networks are referred to as "clouds." Each of your sites has a line (usually a high-speed leased line) that connects it to the cloud. Then a private virtual circuit (PVC) is established through the cloud to allow your sites to connect to each other. Frame relay and ATM networks are provided by telecom carriers like AT&T and MCI Worldcom.

Virtual Private Network

An alternative to ATM and frame relay for a packet switching solution is the Internet. By using various security and tunneling techniques, a virtual private network (VPN) can be established via the Internet to connect sites. The advantage of VPN is significantly reduced costs. However, since the data is traveling over public facilities, specific transmission rates and security cannot be guaranteed.

Cable Modems

Cable TV companies all across the country are taking advantage of their infrastructure to deliver high-speed Internet access. This is a natural outgrowth of the fact that the technology that brings 100+ TV channels to your home has enormous bandwidth, and that the wire (right to your living room) is already in place.

Throughput via a cable TV system can vary by cable company and with usage. However, speeds are often in the range of 2 Mbps. In addition, the cost is fixed at a monthly rate, and the service is "always on."

Telecommuters are finding use for cable modems to connect to the office (as opposed to using dial-up or ISDN connections). In addition, cable modems can be a cost-effective ISP alternative for a small office. And a small remote office can combine the use of a cable modem with VPN WAN technology (discussed above) to establish a WAN connection with corporate headquarters.

10.10 WAN: How Do I Manage One?

Many of the same resources and facilities that monitor a LAN's operations (e.g., SNMP, RMOM) can manage a WAN. In addition, there are many third parties that will monitor your WAN for you. In particular, the telephone companies that can provide you with leased line and VPN services can usually provide you with 24×7 network monitoring and management. This of course comes at an additional price, but will probably provide you with a more sophisticated service than you could afford yourself.

10.11 Cable Plant: How Do I Install, Manage, and Expand One?

If you have always thought that all wires are created equal, managing a cable plant will show you otherwise.

What Is a Cable Plant?

The "cable plant" refers to the physical wire (be it copper or fiber) used in your facility that physically connects all the network devices (printers, workstations, servers, hubs, routers, etc.). In addition to the physical cable, the "cable plant" refers to the design of the wiring layout and all the components that are used within it (e.g., patch panels, jacks, etc.).

There are special issues related to cabling that make it unique among IT investments. These issues include the following:

- The cost of cabling is mostly in the installation labor, not the material.
- Once the cabling is installed in walls and ceilings, you virtually lose access to it.
- It is a capital investment that you can't take with you if you move to another office.
- It cannot be upgraded, only replaced.
- It may be the capital investment that outlasts all other IT capital investments.

Unless you are moving into a new facility, you probably already have a cable plant—and it was probably installed years ago. Your involvement with cabling may be limited to having new lines installed to accommodate growth—like when that corner office that used to support one executive is turned into a "bullpen" and now needs additional connections to support six programmers.

Designing Your Cable Plant

Designing your cable plant involves many factors:

- LAN technologies being used (ATM, Ethernet, Token-Ring, etc.)
- Distances involved
- Exposure to hazards (Are cables run through public areas where they are more prone to accidental damage, or in secured areas like locked wiring closets? Are they being run outdoors at all?)
- Bandwidth (or data transmission speed requirements)
- Existing networking equipment (such as NICs, hubs, routers, and switches)

- Local building code requirements (e.g., some cable may have to be fire retardant depending on where it is installed)
- Number of nodes per collision domain

Whether you are installing a new facility or expanding your existing cabling plant, it is a good idea to get some assistance. Since you probably won't be spending a whole lot of time on cabling issues, it is likely that you won't be current on the latest technologies and product offerings when a cabling project comes your way. There are consultants who specialize in this field and can help you with determining the best type of cable to use for your needs, which manufacturers offer the most reliable products, selection of components like wall jacks and patch panels, and so on. They can help you implement a system that is easy to maintain and expand, and can offer ideas and solutions to prevent your wiring closets from looking like a room full of spaghetti.

Ethernet Environments

Regardless of whether it is a cause or effect of its popularity, standards are in place to support Ethernet over a variety of mediums. For Ethernet environments, there are various cabling types you can choose:

- 100 Mbps Twisted-Pair, Type 100BASE-TX. Describes the two-pair variety of 100 Mbps twisted-pair Ethernet media.
- 100 Mbps Fiber Optic, Type 100BASE-FX. Describes the fiber optic variety of 100 Mbps Ethernet media.
- 100 Mbps Twisted-Pair, Type 100BASE-T4. Describes the four-pair variety of 100 Mbps twisted-pair Ethernet media.
- Thick Coaxial Ethernet, Type 10BASE5. Describes the thick coaxial variety of 10 Mbps Ethernet media.
- Thin Coaxial Ethernet, Type 10BASE2. Describes the thin coaxial variety of 10 Mbps Ethernet media.
- Twisted-Pair Ethernet, Type 10BASE-T. Describes the twisted-pair variety of 10 Mbps Ethernet media.
- Fiber Optic Ethernet, Type 10BASE-F. Describes the fiber optic variety of 10 Mbps Ethernet media.
- 1000BASE-CX. Describes twinax variety of 1 GB Ethernet.
- 1000BASE-LX for single-mode fiber of 1 GB Ethernet.
- 1000BASE-SX for multimode fiber of 1 GB Ethernet.
- 1000Based-T is 1 GB over twisted pair.

In all likelihood, you won't be using the coax varieties listed above unless you inherit an infrastructure with a large amount of these cable types. In general, IT managers are relying on twisted pair for wiring to the desktop and for short vertical runs between floors. Fiber is usually saved for longer runs that are beyond the limits for Ethernet or copper.

Twisted-pair copper is by far the most popular medium for Ethernet. It is inexpensive, easy to work with, and supports speeds up to 1 GB. Because of its popularity, there are many sources of products and components available for copper-based Ethernet, including network cards, hubs, testing equipment, and so on.

Fiber is probably the second-most popular for Ethernet. Its primary advantage is that it can span much greater distances than copper. However, fiber requires more care and skill in installation, and components for fiber are much more expensive.

Gigabit Ethernet

Table 10.3 provides a comparison between the distance restrictions for current Ethernet topologies and Gigabit Ethernet.

Currently, IT managers are looking at 1 Gb Ethernet as an alternative to other high-speed networking technologies (FDDI, ATM, etc.). Not only is 1 Gb faster, but it allows IT managers to simplify their environment by reducing the number of network technologies in it. Ethernet is easier to work with than these other technologies, and it is easier to find employees that are skilled in it.

Currently, because of the high price of hardware (e.g., NICs and switches), Gigabit Ethernet's use is being limited to servers and network backbones. However, it is reasonable to assume that, over time, prices will drop until there is barely a nominal premium for gigabit over 100 Mb. This is exactly what happened to 100 Mb components when it was introduced. And, just as vendors delivered 10/100 auto-sensing devices to smooth the transition, it is likely we'll see 10/100/Gb auto-sensing as well.

Even though gigabit sounds like more bandwidth than might ever be needed, IT managers should not dismiss it. History has shown that bandwidth demands constantly increase to meet (if not exceed) availability. As technology prices drop, and more and more applications are delivered, the bottleneck will often be the network. After all, just a few years ago an e-mail message consisted of just text. Then, attaching document and spreadsheet attachments upped the size of the attachment. Currently, with fast Internet connections via cable modems, DSL, and T-1, messages now include audio and video content. There's no reason to expect the growth of bandwidth demand to slow in the foreseeable future.

As you can see in Table 10.3 on the next page, it is possible to use single-mode fiber to achieve distances of 5 kilometers with Gigabit Ethernet. As such, this technology has potential for some WAN needs.

Table 10.3   Ethernet comparison. (*Source*: Gigabit Ethernet Alliance, *www.gigabit-ethernet.org.*)

	Ethernet 10 BaseT	Fast Ethernet 100 BaseT	Gigabit Ethernet[*] 1000 Base x
Data rate	10 Mbps	100 Mbps	1000 Base Mbps (1 gigabit per second)
Cat-5 UTP	100 m (min)	100 m	100 m
STP/coax	500 m	100 m	25 m
Multimode fiber	2 km	412 m (hd)[**] 2 km (fd)[*]	550 m
Single-mode fiber	25 km	20 km	5 km

[*] IEEE spec full duplex.
[**] IEEE spec half duplex.

Fiber Cable

Fiber cable is more costly, not only for the material, but also for the labor to install it. While tools and hardware are available from a variety of sources and catalogs to allow even a neophyte to work with copper wire connections, it requires special training and expensive equipment to work with fiber. Additionally, fiber is more sensitive and can be degraded by kinks, tight radii, and so on.

To make matters more confusing, the term "twisted pair" is somewhat generic. It could refer to two pairs or four pairs of wires in the same sheath. And the sheath itself may be shielded (STP—shielded twisted pair) or unshielded (UTP—unshielded twisted pair). The shielding refers to the outer wrapping that serves as a ground and can reduce the impact of outside interference on the data signal. It should be noted that STP is not a formally defined spec for Ethernet. STP is primarily used for IBM Token-Ring wiring topologies.

Twisted Pair

Twisted-pair LAN wiring is classified by categories (generally referred to as "CAT"):

- CAT-6 is not yet an approved standard, but is expected to be approved shortly and will support gigabit data speeds.
- CAT-5e is not yet an approved standard, but is expected to be approved shortly and will support gigabit data speeds.
- CAT-5 is approved for 100 Mbps Ethernet and 155 Mbps ATM.

- CAT-4 is approved for 10 Mbps Ethernet. However, this type of wiring is rarely used since it is approximately the same cost as CAT-5, which offers higher speeds. CAT-4 is also used for 16 Mbps Token-Ring environments.

- CAT-3 is commonly used for 10 Mbps Ethernet, as well as voice applications. While quite popular at one time, it seems that most environments are now moving to CAT-5 for both voice and data.

- CAT-2 is commonly used for 4 Mbps Token-Ring and is considered a low-speed medium.

- CAT-1 is generally found in residential environments for analog POTS (plain old telephone system) lines.

Cable Length Issues

It is important to remember that while cable can be purchased in almost any length, that doesn't mean it can be used for any length. As a general rule, CAT-5 UTP can carry signals for 100 meters (330 feet). Shielded wiring will extend this length (depending on the speed of the data rate). Multimode fiber extends the signal further, and single-mode fiber even further.

Connections

When considering your cable plant, it is important to note that although there is a connection from the computer on your desk to the server, it is certainly not one long continuous piece of cable.

Typically, the network card in your computer is connected to a patch cable, the other end of which connects to a jack on the wall. On the other side of the wall jack is a cable that typically runs to a wiring closet, where it typically terminates to the back end of a patch panel. On the front end of the patch panel is another patch cable (typically like the one connected to the computer), which connects to some sort of concentrator or hub. Coming out of the back of this unit is another cable (perhaps fiber, but oftentimes copper) that travels several floors (or perhaps across a campus) to another hub or concentrator in the computer room. Also connected to this device, finally, is the server that has the data you need.

Of course, depending on the size and complexity of your environment, a connection from the workstation to the server can be simpler or more complex. What is important to note is that the overall connection is no better than the weakest link. If, for example, all your cabling is CAT-5, except for the patch cable in your office, then you no longer have a CAT-5 connection. And, not only must all the cable conform to the CAT-5 specification, but each connection (including those made at patch panels) must also conform to the CAT-5 spec.

Managing a Cable Plant

As you might think, there really isn't much to the care and feeding of a cable plant on an ongoing basis. Unlike other IT resources, you don't have to perform daily backups of a cable plant, or apply bug fixes and patches to them. However, that doesn't necessarily mean you can "install it and forget it."

- Always maintain wiring diagrams, and keep them current. Post them where they can be easily referenced. For example, put a copy of each floor's diagram in that floor's wiring closet.

- Get in the habit of labeling both ends of cables. There are many offerings for this—everything from label makers to tabs with writable surfaces that can be attached to the cable ends. The label at each end of the cable should identify (1) where this end of the cable connects to and (2) where the other end of the cable is connected to. Depending on what the cable is used for, you may want to identify the room location it is connected to, or perhaps the specific device and port it is connected to.

- Keep wires organized. This is officially called "wire management." Bundles of wires should be held together. You can use tie-wraps for this (some are made of Velcro, which can be reused; others are made of plastic, which generally can't be reused). When bundling wires together don't make it so tight that there is no movement at all. By keeping it a little loose it ensures that the tie-wrap isn't cutting into the cable, and it also makes it easier if you have to trace a particular wire's path.

- Since wires are buried in walls and ceilings, and under raised floors, it can often be impossible to inspect them visually. There are many tools available to help you work without seeing. There are tools to help you trace and test. These can be invaluable in saving hours of guesswork or trial and error. Fluke (*www.fluke.com*) is a popular manufacturer of tools like this. A pair of walkie-talkies (or even cell phones) can also help your network analysts communicate when they are troubleshooting a wiring problem.

- Check on your wiring closets periodically. Your equipment in there may be generating a lot of heat. There may be a small water leak that is slowly dripping water on your equipment or wires. And it isn't uncommon for mice to gnaw on cable.

10.12 Wires: Can I Do without Them?

In recent years, standards and technologies have been developed for moving data without the need for wires. One example of this would be the use of cellular modems so that laptop users can connect simply by using their cellular phones.

Some companies have connected nearby office buildings using microwave. And, of course, satellites have also been used.

On the mobel front, pagers and cell phones have provided a certain degree of on-the-go connectivity. However, with the recent explosion of personal digital assistants (PDAs) and the interest in on-the-go Web connectivity, the demand for even more mobile access has grown.

Some recent attempts have included Palm Computing's Palm VII device, which allows users to send and receive e-mail from a handheld device. In addition, several models of cell phones provide users with some ability to surf the Web.

Wireless LANs

One of the technologies that is expected to have significant growth in coming years is wireless LANs. With IEEE standard 802.11b, users can achieve data transfer rates as high as 11 Mbps. Although the spec provides for 11 Mbps, which compares favorably with Ethernet's 10 Mbps, actual transmission rates can be half of that, or less. The cost of the hardware is very competitive with traditional wired products. And, in a new facility, the use of wireless can offer significant savings over the cost of installing a complete wiring plant.

With a wireless LAN, the standard network interface card (NIC) that is installed in a workstation is replaced with an NIC that acts as a transmitter/receiver. These NICs pass data to antennas that are strategically placed out of sight. The antennas then have hard-wired connections to the LAN's backbone.

In general, wireless devices can send and receive data if they are within 100 feet of an antenna. However, that limit can drop significantly if there isn't a direct line of sight to the antenna. Still, by strategically placing antennas so that there are overlapping areas of coverage, the distance limitations can be mitigated. Obviously, careful site planning and installation is a critical success factor to wireless LANs.

Wireless LANs are being used in college campuses so that students don't have to cluster around the perimeter of a room to be near LAN jack connections. And some organizations are installing wireless networking so that users can take their laptop from office to meeting room without having to fumble with disconnecting and reconnecting wires.

10.13 Remote Access: How Do I Know If I Need It?

"If you have to ask, you need it." That is a tongue-in-cheek way of saying, "Everyone needs, or will need, remote access." That statement is only a slight exaggeration. While there are some small companies that may not need remote access, almost every company does need it. At the very minimum, remote access allows your employees to access e-mail from home. At the other end of the spectrum, employees need access to all IT resources as if they were in their own office, even if they're in a hotel room in Kuala Lumpur.

Do you have users at remote locations, or are you about to have users at remote locations? Many small companies start with a small group of workers in a single location: a bread store, a development team, a group of telemarketers. Soon, however, as business picks up, their marketplace expands. They are no longer selling to the local bread consumer; they are eyeing customers two towns over and the big city 15 miles away. The new company is building software not only for the local ISP, but they have a tiny contract with an AOL content provider two states away. The telemarketing firm was so successful at selling the lots for the new development, they have won a contract to work on the next three developments—all in different states—for the developer. These companies all face significant challenges providing Internet and internal computer network access.

Three Key Choices

When setting up remote access for your users, you have three major choices:

1. Access over the telephone lines through modems
2. Direct line connections
3. Web-based remote access

The three options are not mutually exclusive—that is, you could provide all three if you think it is necessary—but the second option, direct line connections to branch offices, remote development sites, and so on, is a very expensive one. You will need to evaluate the needs of your users and work through your budget very carefully before springing for that method.

Before You Start Making Decisions

Back we go to the same old question: "What are the needs of your customers?" Some users will only be able to use telephone line connections because this method is by far the most convenient for them. Other users are going to scream at the slow speed and rickety connections that commonly plague plain old telephone system line access.

10.14   Telephone Remote Access: What Are the Advantages and Disadvantages?

This type of access is radically cheaper and much more commonly used than its direct line counterpart.

Advantages

The advantages of telephone remote access are clear: it is cheaper and more convenient.

Cheaper

The costs here are primarily in the hardware: you need to outfit your remote users with modems (a minor issue since most PCs sold now come with a modem preinstalled), and you need to equip your network with modems to handle the incoming traffic.

More Convenient

Sales reps in particular, big users of remote access, commonly need access to the network from multiple locations. Some sales reps are in one location all day, and others do not access the computer much during the day; but many more need complete access to the company network from the airport, from hotel data jacks, and other out-of-the-way places. You will have little or no success trying to convince these "road warriors" to use a direct line that is established somewhere—these users need access from many different locations.

Disadvantages

The disadvantages of telephone remote access are also clear: it is slower and the connections are not always reliable.

Slow Speeds and Small Bandwidths

Connections over analog telephone lines aren't likely to get past 33.6 Kbps. With some digital lines, you may approach 56 Kbps. If you can determine what your typical remote user is sending over their access, you can determine if this is an important consideration for you or not. If your remote users are mostly sales reps, for example, and they commonly use only e-mail, and at most they attach a Word or Excel document, speed of transmission may not be a critical issue. If you have a remote development team, however, and they commonly exchange chunks of code in enormous files, they are not going to want to be connected to each other over a phone line. It will not support their needs.

Spotty Connections

Telephone connections are notoriously spotty as far as data transmission goes: you can have a great connection one time, disconnect, and then have a terrible one when you try to reconnect. And, although they are improving to meet the needs of the digital age, the phone systems available in many hotels can be an enormous hindrance. For those users trying to connect to international systems over dial-up lines, the connection quality can be particularly poor because of the distance and the less sophisticated phone networks in many overseas countries.

Unreliability

This may seem an odd statement, but it is based in fact: your users are relying on someone else's network (the phone company) for access to your network. You have little or no control over that network. Some corporations do not have a minute-to-minute need for their employees to be connected; if some users cannot get on right now, they can simply try again later. Many other companies, however, have stringent data access needs that are severely compromised when a network crashes.

Dial-Up Variations

Try to determine just how stringent your data access needs are. If you need your users to be able to access your network 100% of the time, you may find that remote access over a telephone line does not provide the reliability you need.

Digital connections (e.g., ISDN, DSL) can address many of the negatives of standard analog dialog connections. However, you give up one very big convenience—the virtual total ubiquity of analog telephone lines.

10.15 Direct Line Remote Access: What Are the Advantages and Disadvantages?

Some organizations—especially large ones—already have large remote access networks in place. They use communication servers to connect terminals, modems, computers, and other networks together. These organizations are not debating the merits of telephone versus direct connections; they are figuring out ways of upgrading their systems.

You can get leased lines at various speeds from 56 Kbps up to T-1 (1.55 Mbps) and T-3 (672 circuits, each of which can support 64 Kbps transmissions, totaling up to 44.73 Mbps).

- T-1 is the most commonly used digital line in the United States, Canada, and Japan. It carries data at about 1.5 Mbps.

- T-3 is a leased line that provides data transmission speeds of 44.736 Mbps. A T-3 line consists of 672 circuits, each of which can support 64 Kbps transmissions.

If you are trying to decide between offering dial-up and direct line remote access, here are some positives and negatives of direct lines.

Advantages

The advantages of direct line remote access are its faster speed, more reliable connection, and greater control.

Fast Speed

Direct connections operate at multiples of the fastest telephone connection. A T-1 line offers connections that are 26 times faster than the fastest analog modem speed. This is a performance enhancement that is hard to argue with! If your users typically send large files, a direct connection will provide them with a much greater bandwidth and therefore a much more effective method of communication.

Reliable Connection

Direct connections are much more reliable than telephone ones. Since leased lines are point-to-point circuits (from point A to point B), the carrier that provides the lines can monitor, test, and ensure that it is free from noise or other impairments that might hamper performance.

More Control

Your users are always on your network—there is no need for them to "trust" someone else's reliability when accessing the network.

Disadvantages

The disadvantages of direct line remote access are primarily the cost and lack of convenience.

Cost

The costs of direct connections are exponentially larger than phone line connections. With direct connect, you have several cost issues:

- **Cost of the initial hardware:** Instead of the inexpensive modems needed for dial-up connections, a leased line will require you to purchase *routers,* which are considerably more expensive.
- **Cost of the leased lines:** Depending on speed and distance, a line can cost anywhere from a few hundred to a few thousand dollars per month.

Convenience

As mentioned earlier in this chapter, remote access needs vary widely. Some of your users could benefit greatly from a direct connection. But others might be so mobile that a T-1 line in one office might help the 5 local reps but be of no consequence to the 15 reps who travel.

10.16 Web-Based Access: What Are the Advantages and Disadvantages?

With access to the Internet becoming ubiquitous, many companies are looking at providing remote access to it. Assuming that the headquarters location has some dedicated connection to the Web, the big issue becomes "How do my remote users connect to the Web?" They might have a standard dial-up connection, a cable modem, a digital line, or perhaps a small office might have their own dedicated connection (and have the Web provide the connectivity across the country to HQ).

Users with cable modems in their homes, or digital connections, can get extraordinary performance. Of course, providing remote access via the Web raises higher security concerns than the other two options presented. Web-based access can also be used for connecting remote offices. Many telephone carriers have a product offering called Virtual Private Network in which data traffic between your locations is sent over the Internet, but using special encryption and security techniques that assure privacy.

DSL and cable modems offer another benefit in addition to their speed. They present "always on" access. "Always on" refers to the fact that the user doesn't have to go through any special connection process to access the Web. Users of dial-up modems are frequently frustrated while they wait 30–60 seconds for a dial-up connection to complete. Of course, on the downside of "always on" is the security risk. Since the workstation is always on the Internet, its files and data could be at risk. To address this, vendors are now marketing firewall software products for individual workstations. These function very much like the firewalls used by organizations to protect their network from the risks of the Internet.

Advantages

The advantages of Web-based access are its high availability, its infrastructure, and its lower cost.

Availability

Internet access for your end users is readily available, virtually anytime and anywhere. Continuous availability is the demand most users have now.

Infrastructure

Infrastructure is already built, and associated costs are only at the endpoints.

Cost Savings

Users only have to make a "local" connection to the Internet, which reduces costs. With dial-up, DSL, and cable modems, there are a variety of choices for accessing the Web.

Disadvantages

The disadvantages of Web-based access are potential security problems and a lack of control.

Security Concerns

Because the Internet is accessible to the public at large, there are always concerns about the security of data being transmitted. In addition, if your servers are connected to the Internet, there is the fear that some hacker, sitting in his apartment on the other side of the country, could be trying to infiltrate them. See Section 10.18 for security techniques that can address concerns about Internet connectivity.

Lack of Control

The Internet is not centrally owned or managed. If your data doesn't arrive, or you find transmission times to be slow, there is no one to call to complain to. Over time, the reliability of the Internet has improved. E-mail doesn't disappear into the ether with the same frequency as it did just a few years ago. Still, if manageability and control are important factors to you, an Internet-based WAN may not be the solution for you.

10.17 Remote Users: What Do They See When They Log In?

When dealing with road warriors and telecommuters, consideration has to be given to what users see when they log in. While the technology exists to make these users operate just like an in-office user, there are special concerns—slow performance, and a wide variety of PC equipment (particularly if users are planning to use their existing home PCs) that could be limited in its capabilities and is shared with the game-addicted teenager in the house. For these remote users, there are two types of connection scenarios: remote control and remote node.

Remote Control

With a remote control scenario, the only software that is installed on the end user's PC is the application that is required to establish the connection. Once the user is connected, she runs all the applications she needs off a server device. What makes remote control special is that the applications are loaded and run from the server, not from the user's PCs. As such, the specifications of the user's PC have virtually no bearing on performance. The only traffic that is passed between the remote access server and the PC are the screen images, user keystrokes, and mouse clicks.

An additional advantage of remote control is that application software does not have to be installed on the end user's PCs. Everything is done at the server. As a result, support demand is reduced since all configuration issues are really centralized on the in-house remote access server.

Remote control can be a highly effective remote access solution that simplifies administration, management, and support. However, the up-front cost of the server and software itself can be a deterrent.

Remote Node

Remote node is essentially the opposite of remote control. With remote node, the remote user's PC acts like any other PC on the internal LAN—with one critical difference: instead of a connection speed of 10 or 100 Mbps, the user is limited to the throughput of the connection type she is using. For a dial-up connection, this could be a paltry 56 Kbps.

One way of addressing the speed issues with remote node is to have the applications loaded onto the remote workstation. In this way, only the data is accessed remotely, while the software itself is loaded from the local hard drive. Then again, the local PC may not have enough capacity to house the applications.

The advantage of remote node is that there are little start-up costs associated with it. As long as you have modems and lines, you can get it to work. On the downside, the performance issue and the support issue related to supporting applications on a wide variety of PC types can be significant concerns.

E-Mail Synchronization

Remote access for e-mail presents some special concerns. Using the remote control or remote node techniques mentioned above, users can retrieve and send e-mail exactly like they do in the office. However, to do so requires that they be connected while doing so. Virtually all e-mail packages have an option that may be referred to as synchronization, replication, or off-line usage.

The way the process works is that a user can read e-mail and compose e-mail while they are disconnected from the network. Then, when they do connect, all the messages they composed are transmitted to the server, and in turn, the server sends to their workstation all the messages that have come in for that user.

The advantage of synchronization is significantly reduced telephone costs, since the time required to transmit messages between the laptop and the server is a small fraction of the time required for writing and reading messages. Plus, it allows users to deal with their e-mail at times when they don't have access to a telephone line (such as in a plane, at the beach, or in a dull meeting).

Except for training users how to use their e-mail while off-line, and how to replicate, there is little downside risk associated with this solution.

10.18 Network Security: What Are the Key Issues I Need to Worry About?

Obviously, with any type of remote access scenario, security is a vital concern—particularly if you're dealing with dial-up connections and/or access via the Internet. (Please see Chapter 13 for an in-depth discussion of security considerations.) With either the Internet or dial-up modems, to a certain extent your network is exposed to security threats from the entire world. As such, your standard network passwords may not be sufficient.

Other security techniques to use in a situation like this include the following:

Dial-Back

With dial-back security the device receiving the call will check the user's identification and then dial that user back at a preset telephone number to ensure that an intruder isn't using an existing user's ID to log into the system.

RADIUS

This acronym stands for Remote Authentication Dial-In User Service. Radius is a protocol that operates between the client and a remote access server. When a user attempts to dial in to a remote access device, the device first attempts to authenticate the user with a central RADIUS server. If the user is authenticated, the user is routed to the network; otherwise the user is disconnected. One of the advantages of the RADIUS protocol is that the organization can maintain a single database of authorized users. Alternatively, the organization would have to maintain this database on each and every remote access device in the network.

SecurID

Please see Chapter 13 for an in-depth discussion of security considerations, including several SecurID products.

Kerberos

Kerberos is a password scheme developed at MIT. The name, Kerberos, refers to a three-headed dog in Greek mythology. The idea behind Kerberos is to eliminate the need for passwords to travel on the network, where they might be intercepted by various network analyzers. With Kerberos, the user identifies himself to an authentication server, which then issues an electronic ticket that contains information about what services and resources the user can access. Based on the information in the ticket, the network services will either grant or reject the user's request for access. In addition, the ticket can be time-stamped so that it becomes invalid after a period of time.

PPTP (Point-to-Point Tunneling Protocol)

PPTP is a security protocol for allowing access to in-house resources via the Internet. In essence, it allows you to create a private "tunnel" over the Internet, giving you a virtual private network (VPN). This protocol is sponsored by Microsoft and other vendors. PPTP can be used for connecting a remote user to a host, or to connect one LAN to another. It is not yet certified by the IETF and is only available on networks served by Windows NT and Linux servers.

IPsec (Internet Protocol Security)

IPsec is a set of protocols for establishing private communications via the Internet. The data is encrypted using algorithms and a public key. In addition to encrypting the data, it authenticates the two end nodes in the communication session using the Internet Key Exchange (IKE) protocol.

10.19 Further References

Web Sites

- *www.3com.com* (networking hardware vendor)
- *www.acnc.com/raid.html* (detailed description of various RAID levels)

- *www. bluetooth.com* (industry trade group for mobile communications)
- *www.cisco.com/* (networking hardware vendor)
- *www.citrix.com* (remote access solution vendor)
- *www.digidata.com* (RAID controllers)
- *www.fluke.com* (for cable testing tools)
- *www.gigabit-ethernet.org* (Gigabit Ethernet Alliance)
- *www.lantronix.com/technology* (detailed reference information about standards, protocols, etc.)
- *www.protocols.com* (detailed reference information about standards, protocols, etc.)

Articles and Books

- Anderson, Christa, and Mark Minasi, *Mastering Local Area Networks*, Sybex, 1999.
- Fowler, Dennis, *Virtual Private Networks*, Morgan Kaufmann, 1999.
- Freed, Les, Frank J., Jr. Derfler, *How Networks Work*, Que, 1998.
- Marcus, J. Scott, *Designing Wide Area Networks and Internetworks: A Practical Guide*, Addison-Wesley, 1999.
- Marks, Kristin (Editor), *Handbook of Server Management and Administration 1999*, CRC Press–Auerbach, 1998.
- Palmer, Michael J., and Robert Bruce Sinclair, *A Guide to Designing and Implementing Local and Wide Area Networks*, Course Technology, 1999.
- Reed, Archie, *Implementing Directory Services (Enterprise Computing)* McGraw-Hill, 2000.
- Robichaux, Paul E., *Remote Access 24Seven*, Sybex, 1999.
- Sheresh, Doug, and Beth Sheresh, *Understanding Directory Services*, New Riders Publishing, 1999.
- Trulove, James, *LAN Wiring: An Illustrated Guide to Network Cabling*, McGraw-Hill, 1997.
- Vacca, John R., *The Cabling Handbook*, Prentice Hall, 1998.

Internets/
Extranets/
Intranets

What You Will Learn

- What the difference between the Internet, an intranet, and an extranet is
- Which of the three you need
- What you should put on your Web site
- How to design a server for Internet, intranet, or extranet uses
- What e-commerce is
- Specific examples of how the Web can help your company
- How to design a Web site
- How to register a domain name
- How to pick an ISP
- What issues to consider when connecting your environment to the Internet

CHAPTER ELEVEN

Introduction

Everywhere you go, you see and hear about the Web, the Net, I-this, and e-that. What kind of Web site do you have? Intranet or Internet—you have to slow down when saying either one so that people don't mistakenly hear the other one; type too fast and you'll capitalize the wrong one.

The Internet has changed society—not just for techies, but for everyone! It's a powerful tool that can do work for you, generate revenue, bring in customers, save money, and so on. That's a lot to do—no wonder there are so many different words for it. In this chapter, we take a relative respite from the fast pace of Internet time to try to help you get a solid understanding of the Internet and its potential value to you and your organization.

11.1 Internet, Intranet, and Extranet: What's the Difference between the Three?

It is important for most corporate managers to understand the difference between these three key types of Web sites:

- Internet—An Internet Web site is the one that a company makes available for every user of the World Wide Web to see (even though all these users may not be all that interested in seeing it).

- Intranet—An intranet site is a private site available only to those with the company or organization. Outsiders (defined as people without access to your proprietary network) cannot see material on your intranet.

- Extranet—An extranet site is similar to an Internet site except that it is specifically designed for use by the company's partners (suppliers, customers, etc.).

Companies can be connected and have all three, or they can have none. (If you don't have *any* of the above, you should consider getting your company connected soon.) The primary difference between the Internet, an extranet, and an intranet is who can access them, and which side of your firewall they are connected to. Aside from that, they are identical. They run on the same type of server hardware and software, they are all accessed with browsers (like Netscape Navigator or Microsoft Internet Explorer), and they can all be ingeniously—or disastrously—designed. Each of these types of Web sites are discussed in more detail below.

Internet

By now, we're all familiar with the Internet. This is the global connection between computers that allows individuals to send e-mail, make travel arrange-

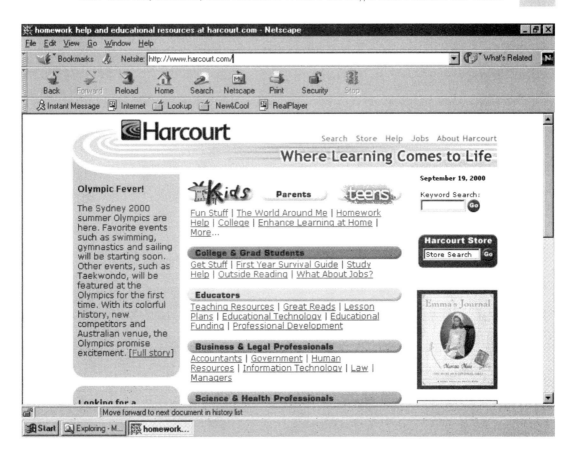

Figure 11.1   Harcourt's Internet Web Site

ments, order flowers, bootleg music, and so on, between people and companies all around the world. It is commonly called "the network of networks." The Internet (note the capital "I") is a public resource, which means that any user or server on the Internet can connect to any other user or server. No one "owns" the Internet, and that freedom gives individuals and corporations tremendous capabilities.

Companies set up Internet sites for a variety of reasons, including providing the ability to do e-commerce (see Figure 11.1 above for a sample Internet site). For details on e-commerce, Web sites, and other methods of using the Internet, see the sections following this one in this chapter.

Intranet

But what's good for the public is also good for the private or semiprivate. That's where extranets and intranets come in. (Note that extranet and intranet are not capitalized.)

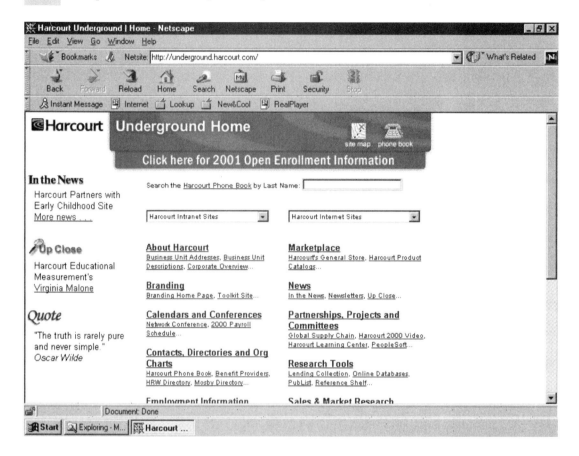

Figure 11.2   Harcourt's Intranet Site

If the Internet is for public consumption, then the opposite is true for an intranet. Intranets are for private use only. Typically, a corporation will create an intranet to replace those things that used to be posted on bulletin boards (both real and electronic), put in policy books, and distributed as memos. This can include various corporate forms (benefits, travel, office supply), lunchroom menus, job postings, and the phone directory. See Figure 11.2 above for a page from an intranet.

Advanced Features

More advanced intranets have greater functionality. For example, instead of allowing you to print out a form to request office supplies, you might be able to complete it on-line. At the click of a mouse, your request is automatically sent to the supply room, and the supplies are delivered to your desk. Along the same lines you might be able to reserve conference rooms on-line. Or you can change your W-4 tax withholdings and have the information automatically entered into the payroll and human resources databases. These are all items that are only accessible to people within the corporation; no one outside the company has access to this data.

A company might have multiple intranets. For example, each division or region might have its own. Or the engineers in R&D might have an intranet of their own where they can share information, and people in the Marketing department might have another.

Some companies will continually update their stock price on their Web page, as well as post information like press releases or other company- and industry-related news on the intranets as well. This can serve to keep employees informed and aware of goings-on relevant to the company, even while doing something as mundane as looking up a coworker's extension.

As we have already said, the only real distinction between an intranet site and an Internet site is whether they are accessed publicly or privately. This is determined simply based upon where you place the server. And that decision is a matter of cyber-geography.

Firewalls

If your environment is connected to the Internet, you probably have a *firewall.* (If you don't have one, you should immediately find out why not.) A firewall, as the name implies, is a device that prevents the rest of the world from getting into your network and seeing your company's financial information, e-mails, and lunchroom menus.

A firewall has two sides, as shown in Figure 11.3 on the next page. The one connected to your corporate network is called the private side, and the one connected to the Internet is called the public side. Therefore, in order to make your Web server an intranet, it has to be connected to the private side of your firewall. Move the connection to the other side of the firewall, and people all over the planet can start reserving your conference rooms. A more detailed discussion of firewalls appears in Chapter 13.

Extranet

While the Internet is public, and an intranet is private, an extranet is essentially a hybrid of the two: it might best be described as semiprivate. Like an Internet server, an extranet server is on the public side of the firewall. However, the content of the extranet server is specifically designed for a very limited audience. Typically, this audience might consist of a company's business partners such as their suppliers or customers. The company might post forecast information, projects available for bidding, or the status of orders on their extranet.

The distinction between an extranet site and an Internet site can get blurry. For example, if your local phone company has a site that allows you to examine

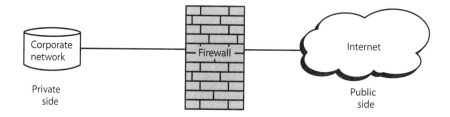

Figure 11.3   A Firewall between the Corporate Intranet (Private Access) and the Internet (Public Access)

your billing records on-line, you might be tempted to call it an extranet site because it is really only for their customers. But, since the customer base is so big, a large portion of the public at large would be using it. And this might be only a small portion of a larger Web site that has features for noncustomers also (such as yellow page information).

Nonetheless, there remain fundamental differences between the three types of sites: An extranet is for a select group of users outside your company. An intranet is for users only within your company. And any user can access your Internet site.

Since an extranet exists on the public side of a company's firewall, it is up to the company to take steps that ensure that only authorized parties get access. This is done through a variety of mechanisms, including ID and password combinations, IP address restrictions, and more sophisticated data security techniques like public/private key encryption.

11.2 Internet, Intranet, or Extranet: Which Do I Need?

The answer depends on your company's overall goals, not just your departmental objectives. The larger your company, the more you will need all three—an intranet, an extranet, and the Internet. But to start, you should consider the simplest one, the Internet. Put up a Web page. This does not take a lot of time, effort, or money, and you can get your feet wet.

Setting up an intranet is the second easiest thing. Issues about security are not as complex because you only have company personnel looking at the material.

Not every company has an extranet. But they can be very powerful tools for the right business situation.

Your Company's Overall Goals

It is becoming very common for companies now to integrate their IT needs into the overall goals of the organization. IT is now a major force in many corporations, both from a personnel perspective and also from a revenue-generating perspective. The reason is simple: IT can now make the company serious money, and CEOs are listening.

Therefore, you need to work to integrate the capabilities of your department with the needs of your company. This can be a complex issue, and companies need to address it regardless of what industry you are in. The new "digital economy" is forcing every company to rethink its way of doing business and evaluate where IT should be in its plans. (A more complete discussion of e-commerce appears later in this chapter.)

Internet Sites

If you have any question as to whether or not you need an Internet site, the answer is probably "yes." If your company has a presence in the yellow pages, then chances are that you'll want a presence on the Internet. The content of an Internet Web site can be as simple as your company's name, address, and phone number. Or it can also contain your annual report, job openings, product listings and specifications, links for sending e-mail to customer service, prices, and the ability to order on-line. Virtually every type of company, whether a service provider or manufacturer, can benefit from providing access to the Internet, including hospitals, accounting firms, TV stations, electric utilities, mail-order catalogs, nonprofit and charitable organizations, retail outlets, newspapers, florists, bookstores, and car dealerships.

Intranet Sites

While the decision to have an Internet site might be a relatively easy one (it is almost always "yes"), the decision to use an intranet is not as straightforward. In general, there are two requirements that need to be satisfied in order to justify an intranet:

- The need to collect, distribute, or share information within your company
- Access to a network-connected PC for each person in your company

Of course, the first item covers virtually every company doing business. This is the determining factor and therefore is a little more subjective. You need to weigh the amount of information and the number of people against the cost and effort necessary to develop and maintain an intranet site that will serve the intended purposes.

An intranet for the corner grocery store probably does not make sense. It does make sense for a large company with offices in every state. And it might make sense for a small real estate brokerage of even only a few people as a convenient way to keep track of clients, properties, and so on.

Extranet Sites

As we said before, an extranet Web site is really just an Internet Web site, except that the extranet site is for a certain subset of the public. And the distinction between an Internet site and an extranet site can be hard to see—especially if you have a portion of your Internet site intended to function as an extranet.

Extranets primarily serve to allow companies and their customers and partners to trade data. Depending on the data being shared, they may have very high levels of security. Companies with computer-sophisticated employees and customers use extranets more frequently than others, although that distinction is fading.

The three major U.S. automakers have announced plans to form what may amount to the world's largest extranet. Jointly, they are developing a network to be used for the procurement of parts from all their various suppliers.

11.3 Content Issues: What Should I Put on My Web Site?

You should decide this material based entirely on your company's overall goals. If they are planning a major e-commerce initiative, you will need to verse yourself not only on what your company's products are, but what your company's competition is offering.

The larger your company, the more likely that you will have (or need) all three, an Internet site, an intranet, and an extranet.

Overall Company Goals

What do you want to do with your site? There are four general activities that you can use your Web site for: informing, entertaining, selling products or services, and generating sales leads. Determine which of these—either one or a combination of several—you want or need to do on your Web site. (By "need to do," we are referring to the decisions companies have been forced to make lately about Web sites due directly to actions their competitors have performed.)

Informing

During the early history of the Web, providing information was the primary function of most Web pages. (The nickname "brochureware" was used to describe this idea. "Brochureware" is not a compliment.)

Information is an ideal use of Web pages: it is easy to set up, easy to maintain, and useful for your customers. Information on Web sites can range from simple material like your company hours and location to more sophisticated

What Is the Difference between the World Wide Web and the Internet?

The World Wide Web

The Web is a graphical component of the Internet. Web pages are a collection of files that can be viewed graphically on the Internet. But the Internet contains much more than just the World Wide Web. It contains millions of files, lots of data, that cannot be seen graphically but can still be accessed.

The Internet

The Internet is commonly called "the network of networks." It was developed to allow scientists to exchange files between their large mainframe computers. It began to be formalized in the mid- to late 1970s; the Web was a modification that was invented only in 1993.

   The Web is exciting, but the Internet is big. You may do business over the Web (especially if you have nontechnical customers), but a lot of work is done and a lot of information is exchanged over the Internet without the use of graphics of any kind.

   Your company can have a Web page on its Web site; these are on the Internet, but they are also on the World Wide Web. The Web is gaining popularity because it does not require a lot of technical knowledge to use. Getting around on a Web page is often a matter of clicking buttons as you are instructed.

   Papers detailing the history of the Internet are available at *www.isoc.org /internet/history.*

---

offerings like product specifications and on-line copies of manuals. Microsoft's Web site—*www.microsoft.com*—contains many different Web pages with many different uses.

Entertaining

If your goal is to entertain, the Web is rapidly providing you with plenty of methods of doing so. You can have audio and video on your Web site, as well as sophisticated graphics that are pleasing to the eye.

   Entertaining Web sites tend to be those that not only have valuable content, but that change that content frequently. Sophisticated graphics and audio components can be difficult to create, and it is more work to maintain a fresh site with this kind of material.

Generating Leads

If the purpose of your site is to generate leads for your sales team, you have to spend more time and money crafting your Web site. Selling and preselling over the Web have become a very sophisticated enterprise, and the days of throwing up a site in a day or two using shareware and a programmer in your garage are gone.

There are two key elements to designing a site that will generate sales leads:

1. Make it clear what your company does, and what products/services it offers. Have information on the Web site to help make this clear. This helps to ensure that the leads that are generated will more likely result in a sale.

2. Make clear what potential customers should do if they are interested. Do you want them to call you? Make your phone number (it should be an 800 number) obvious. Want them to fax you a complete form? Make the form easy to get to and your fax number available 24 hours a day. Better yet, make it an electronic form that they can submit on-line.

Once you have collected this information, it is up to you and your company to respond to these requests. Leads may be passed to different sales representatives, or generate mailings, and so on.

Sell Products or Services

This topic is the subject of entire books—it has become a complex and exciting area of the global marketplace. See Section 11.5 for a more complete discussion of selling goods and services on the Internet.

Ideas for Content: Static vs. Dynamic Web Sites

What you put on any Web site is generically called "content." If you simply have static content such as the company address and phone number on your Web site, it won't be very exciting and may not draw as many visitors (or "eyeballs" as the phrase goes these days).

Major sites like *www.yahoo.com* and *www.amazon.com* change a portion of their sites regularly to keep them fresh and to keep customers coming back to look at the new features.

At the other extreme, if the content is designed to be more dynamic (e.g., the constantly changing information at a newspaper's Web site), you have to deal with the burden of keeping the content updated. A static Web site may be created once and updated by a single person with some spare time a few times a year. A more dynamic site may require an entire department to continuously develop, post, and update the content, like *www.cnn.com.*

Of course, the decision about content is a reflection of the decision about what functionality you want your Web site to provide and who your intended audience is.

11.4 Setting Up: How Do I Design a Server for Internet, Intranet, or Extranet Uses?

Server size and bandwidth are key hardware considerations when implementing that choice. There are only two operating systems that have the bulk of the Web server market: Unix and Microsoft NT (although Linux is gaining rapidly in popularity; see Section 9.5). And there are two principal Web server software choices: Microsoft IIS and Apache.

Designing an effective Web site has become a complex affair. The key point, though, is to match your efforts and cost to the value you expect to get from the site; if you are not looking to build, or do not need, a complicated, interactive site, match your hardware and software purchasing decisions accordingly. There are several important Web page design tools, as well as issues regarding the Web server that you need to consider; this chapter discusses those tools in more detail.

As we said before, the only technical difference between an Internet, extranet, and intranet Web site is which side of the firewall they are connected to—the public side or the private side. (See the discussion of firewalls earlier in this chapter.) Other than that, all three are developed with the same tools and run on the same kind of server hardware and software. However, even though there are no technical differences among them, there are important technical issues you should consider when setting them up. The issues primarily revolve around performance and response time.

Issues When Planning a Web Site

The attention span of a Web surfer is notoriously short. If users have to wait too long (a time span usually measured in single-digit seconds), they may avoid your site, or may go there once, but never return. If you are depending on your site to draw new customers, or to offer you an advantage over your competitors, this is a serious consideration. As such, one of the most critical decisions in setting up a server is sizing it to ensure that it is fast enough.

However, the size of the box is only half the equation. The other consideration is to make sure that the network connection has enough bandwidth (also called "the pipe") to ensure that a bottleneck isn't created. The size of the server and the pipe are areas of detail that are beyond the scope of this book. However, there are many resources available to guide you on this subject.

Important resources for this kind of information include ISPs (Internet service providers, such as AOL, MSN, Earthlink, etc.), server hardware vendors (such as HP, Dell, Sun, Compaq, and IBM), and hosting services (such as PSINet, MCI, AT&T, and BBN Planet). In fact, many of these sources can set up a Web site for you on their hardware and software, and also do the care and feeding (another word for "site maintenance"). The rest of this section goes into some of the details about what's involved in terms of hardware and software for those of you who want to roll up your sleeves.

Hardware and Software Issues

The hardware for a Web site can be as small as a PC purchased at a retail store, or as large as a roomful of servers. If you expect your Web site to be highly complex, with a lot of activity, you probably want to invest in selecting the hardware and software that will provide the performance you need. On the other hand, if the Web site is not expected to draw a lot of activity, your hardware and software choice might be based on whatever equipment is readily available, or available at minimal cost.

Unix and Microsoft NT/2000

The computers that run a Web site generally run either Microsoft's NT/2000 operating system, or one of many versions of the Unix operating system. There are other platform choices, for example, Novell's Netware, but NT and Unix have proven to be the most popular.

Server Issues

There are many issues to attend to in order to ensure that people can get to your server.

- If the server is going to be functioning as an Internet or extranet site, you need to make sure that it is connected to the World Wide Web.

- If the server is in your own computer room, you want to make sure that the device is connected to the public side of the firewall. If some third party is hosting your server, they'll take care of this for you.

- If the server is going to be hosting your intranet site, it is almost certainly on your own premises and needs to be connected to your network on the private side of the firewall—just like any other file and print server, PC, or printer you might have.

- The final thing you need is to give the site a name so that people with their browser software can get to all the information you've posted. If you've set up an Internet or extranet site, you need to register the domain name (e.g., *www.mycompany.com*). Your ISP will probably do this for you, or help you do this at little or no charge. Or you can do it yourself by going to one of several services on the Web—this process is discussed in more detail later in the chapter. If all goes well, within 24 hours after registering, users will be able to type *www.mycompany.com* and discover the information you've posted for all the world to see.

- If you're developing the Web site to be an intranet, naming it is a little different. You don't need to tell the entire world about your domain name, only the people on your network. And, since your intranet server won't know of the world beyond the firewall, there is no point in telling the Internet administrative organizations about your server. To name your server, you need to have your network administrator enter its name into your DNS (domain name server). This DNS exists on your network and translates alphanumeric names to specific IP addresses. Since your intranet server is not on the Internet, the usual *www* and *.com* prefixes and suffixes are not necessary. So when users enter *companyhome* in the address window of their browser, they'll be able to see that the cafeteria is serving Yankee bean soup at lunch tomorrow.

Web Site Design

The complexity of the Web site is essentially its "design." The design refers to everything involved in a site, including colors, fonts, and placement of graphics. Anything that covers what the Web pages look like or a user's navigation through the Web pages is part of its design. The site's design is critical because it affects the site's ease of use, and may be as important (sometimes more important) than the site's content in determining if a user will return or how often. Fortunately, the World Wide Web offers us many examples of the best and worst of Web design. And, just like keeping content fresh, even the best designed Web sites are constantly being tweaked for improvements, or simply to keep them looking new. See Section 11.7 for a detailed discussion on Web site design.

Introduction to Tools

There are a variety of tools—and their number is growing rapidly—that allow you to create information and publish it on the Web.

Front Page and Page Mill

There are many software applications available (Microsoft's Front Page and Adobe's Page Mill are two of the most popular ones) that can help you design a Web site. Many come with several templates of different site designs so that you don't have to design the whole thing from scratch. With the design defined, the next step is to actually create the site's Web pages.

HTML

Web pages use a special language (HTML—HyperText Markup Language) that is understood by Web browsers (e.g., Netscape Navigator, Microsoft's Internet Explorer) to specify the placement of graphics, colors, size of text, and so on. Fortunately, you don't have to know a thing about these codes. By using tools like Front Page or Page Mill, you just point and click to develop your pages, and the tool will create all the necessary codes.

Tools: Java

More advanced Web site functionality can be created by coding in Java and by creating links to databases on other computers. (Java is a programming language, like C++ or Pascal, that is platform independent. That is, Java code can be written on a Windows machine but run on a Unix machine, for example. Sun Microsystems, which originated Java, uses the motto: "Write once, run anywhere." While the slogan sounds good, Sun is still trying to convince the marketplace.)

Although even word processors like Microsoft Word can create basic Web pages, you're probably better off using a tool designed specifically for the job. Not only will these packages help you develop pages easily and quickly, but they'll help with administrative functions like locating dead or broken links.

11.5 E-commerce: What Is It?

E-commerce is the act of conducting business electronically. While the term now refers specifically to conducting business over the Internet, e-commerce has been around for a long time. Nonetheless, since the late 1990s, the Internet has allowed the fire of e-commerce to blaze like never before.

Does your company sell auto parts? If so, you can do so on the Web, perhaps more efficiently, certainly with a greater exposure to more customers. Does your company manufacture widgets? Using e-commerce, you can expose and sell your products to potential customers all over the world.

E-commerce has two principal components: business-to-customer and business-to-business. Business-to-customer ("B2C") is, naturally, the portion of e-commerce that concerns itself with individuals. "B2B" is businesses selling directly to businesses. The rules for how to conduct each type of business are changing quickly. Both of these components are discussed in more detail below.

Rewards of Selling over the Internet

The business value is clear: business leaders look at the following statistics and are moved to action by the magnitude of the opportunity.

- Typical revenue enhancement of 10 to 20 percent
- Typical cost reduction of 20 to 45 percent
- Typical asset intensity reduction of 20 to 60 percent

Source: http://www.ebanx.net/Resources/Benefits/can-ecommerce-help.htm

Main Components of E-commerce

E-commerce has two main components:

- Business-to-consumer
- Business-to-business

While the former gets a lot of headlines, the latter is where the money is.

Business-to-Consumer

The principal advantage e-commerce offers business in their relationship with the consumer is the exponential increase in speed and convenience the Internet offers both parties. There are other benefits, but these two are the most important. You can search for the exact airline ticket you want, which airline, when you want to shop for it, and even specify how much you are willing to pay for it. An airline can change airfares and availability on a minute-by-minute basis (and they do!). Both parties gain a tremendous advantage over the old way of doing business.

In short, e-commerce allows consumers to purchase your company's goods and/or services directly via the World Wide Web. In its simplest form, e-commerce could be sending an e-mail message that says, "Please ship 2 boxes of widgets." More complex e-commerce transactions allow the consumer to fill out some sort of electronic order form at your Web site, perhaps by browsing through an on-line version of your catalog and clicking on the items they want, entering information for payment and shipping, and so on. When the consumer clicks OK, the order is sent directly to the warehouse or to regional distribution centers, and so on.

The customer gains in speed and efficiency: they ordered when they wanted to from the convenience of their computer. Your business gains by not only

The Value of Selling over the Internet

"E-commerce solutions come in every size and flavor. But that does not mean that e-commerce is just another marketing fad. E-commerce is here to stay. It is another vehicle—not the only one, but another one—that allows businesses to interact with their customers. Companies that have been using the Net for years (some have been regular users for over a decade) understand the power of personalization that selling on the Internet provides. No other medium provides the flexibility and the individualization."

—Nils Davis
Product Manager, NetIQ, San Jose, CA

shipping your products faster, but by having detailed customer data in digital form; you can use that data later for sales and marketing plans.

Business-to-Business

Although most people associate e-commerce with the Internet, in truth it has been around long before the World Wide Web reached its current popularity. Years ago, standards were set for EDI (electronic data interchange) to allow companies, vendors, manufacturers, suppliers, and customers to transmit purchase orders, invoices, and so on to each other electronically. Initially, EDI information was transmitted over standard telephone lines (dial-up, leased, etc.). With the connectivity of the Internet, the same EDI data and files can be transmitted among the same organizations over the WWW. The content and process is the same, only the transmission medium has changed.

E-commerce offers several distinct advantages in the business-to-business model. One of the critical ones is that a company can reduce, if not eliminate, the need to have "brick and mortar" stores, offices, and so on in all the areas it wants to serve. Instead, they can move most of their operations to warehouse facilities in parts of the country with reduced labor, real estate, and operating expenses. In addition, by having the order placed by the customer directly into your company's order fulfillment systems, you can greatly reduce the labor normally involved in taking and processing a customer's order.

Difficulties in Starting and Implementing E-commerce

While all those advantages make e-commerce sound like the greatest invention since pockets, there are some significant difficulties in implementing and executing a successful e-commerce plan.

- Your customers (be they companies or individuals) have to know your site is up and running.

- Your site has to be of a high quality. If customers are frustrated by slow response time, have difficulty figuring out how to place an order, encounter error messages, and so on, they may not trust your site enough to fork over their credit card number. And given the short attention span and low annoyance threshold for users on the Web, you may only have one chance to make that e-commerce sale to that customer. That's not so bad if they just decide to drive to the mall and visit your regular store instead, but perhaps they'll just visit your competitors' Web sites. If a customer encounters a rude clerk in your store, they still might come back. If a customer has a problem on your Web site, you may never see that e-customer again.

- You must be ready to handle the business, both from a computer traffic perspective (woe to the many dot com companies that ran Superbowl commercials and then crashed from the volume of traffic) as well as a product availability and shipment perspective.

- You must provide adequate security for the users of your site. Comfort is a large part of the selling process, and you need to provide your customers with the security that will protect their privacy. See Chapter 13 for a more complete discussion of security issues. Not only is security important to protect things like your customers' credit card numbers, but it is also important to make sure your site stays up and running. Hackers enjoy the challenge of affecting the operation of well-known sites. In 1998 and 1999 several Web sites (including at least one U.S. government site) were attacked when hackers changed the content of the home page. In 2000 several well-known sites (e.g., *cnn.com, yahoo.com,* and *zdnet.com* among others) were taken out of service for several hours when subject to a hacking technique called "denial of service."

The Web is ripe with disastrous e-commerce stories—everything from products that never shipped to incorrect shipments. In December 1999, Toys R Us gave some of its Web customers gift certificates to make up for the orders that wouldn't arrive in time for Christmas—even though they had been ordered weeks in advance. More fearful for the customers are Web sites that appeared to be legitimate but turned out to be sites simply set up to obtain credit card information for fraud. Another popular complaint from Web shoppers is being unable to contact a human (either by e-mail or phone) when they have a problem or question.

Is E-commerce Worth It?

Girding up for e-commerce isn't easy. On the front side, you need to make sure your customers and potential customers are aware of your Web site. On the back end, you need to be sure you have the inventory and other traditional mechanisms required for fulfilling the customer's request. But the excitement comes in the middle as your Web site connects these two sides and tries to do all the things that your sales representatives, store clerks, and phone operators normally do.

Although Seciton 11.7 on how to build a Web site makes the process sound pretty uncomplicated (and it certainly can be), the task of adding e-commerce functionality to your site is significantly more complicated.

The other side of that issue, however, is that the rewards for creating and executing a successful e-commerce initiative are astronomical. Entire new markets, new buyers and sellers, and new business models are emerging quickly in what has become known as the "digital economy." The rules of this new economy are evolving rapidly, but the rewards to be reaped are often orders of magnitude larger than the old one.

Some Important Technical Elements of an E-commerce Web Site

Some of the functions required of an e-commerce application are the following:

- **Shopping cart:** This is the function that allows users to browse your "store and "catalog" and keep track of each item that they select for purchase. Shopping cart software vendors include

  @Retail (*www.at.retail.com*)

  Cart32 (*www.cart32.com*)

  CartIt (*www.cartit.com*)

  Make A Store (*www.make-a-store.co*m)

  Sales Cart (*www.salescart.com*)

  Smart Cart (*www.smartcart.com*)

  Shoptron (*www.shoptron.com*)

  EasyCart (*www.easycart.com*)

  Intellivend (*www.intellivend.com*)

  Online Business (*www.olb.com*)

  Website Tool (*www.websitetool.com*)

  Bigstep (*www.bigstep.com*)

- **Payment processing:** Since most e-commerce is paid for via credit card, you need to be able to accept credit card numbers, validate them to be sure they aren't fraudulent or stolen, forward the payment information to the credit card company for collection, and so on.

- **Shipping and handling calculations:** Because most Web purchases are sent directly to the consumer, you need to calculate the cost of the shipment (often giving the customer several choices in regard to speed of delivery) and include it in the total cost of the order.

- **Security provisions:** This is the way of encrypting critical data (like credit card numbers) to minimize the chances of them being stolen while the information is sent over the World Wide Web, or from the database on your server.

- **Data exchange with other business applications:** Since the information is already in computer form after the customer enters the order, you'll want this data to feed into your business databases and applications. This might include accounts receivable, inventory, and shipping and receiving. In addition, you'll probably need to share this data with your business partners like credit card companies and various carriers.

Of course, you can't even begin to consider getting into e-commerce until you've developed your Web site and created "catalog pages" or "store aisles" that will allow your customer to locate and select what they want.

And, for some companies, e-commerce may be a complete change of business model. For example, it would be an enormous change for an appliance maker to get into e-business. If you think about it, appliance makers generally ship truckloads of their products to various appliance retail centers. The switch to e-commerce would require them to now ship units, one at a time, to individual consumer homes. This would have an enormous impact on their normal shipping procedures. They might have to dispense with their fleet of trucks and partner with some of the existing nationwide carriers. It would also impact their invoicing and receivables operations—since they'd now have a greater volume of transactions, each for a much smaller amount. In the end, it might generate more business and profits for the company, but it would be a significant change in business operations.

And as banks offer various services (loans, lines of credit, etc.) to help brick-and-mortar businesses, they are offering services for e-commerce sites as well. Bank of America, Wells Fargo, Key Corp, and Citibank offer resources for helping e-commerce vendors track inventory, arrange for billing, and carry out other on-line storefront activities.

11.6 Web Site: What Are Some Specific Examples of What the Web Can Do for My Company?

The ways that the Web can benefit your company are probably only limited by your imagination. However, some of the more successful efforts include the following:

- Increase product, brand, and company recognition. ESPN, for example, aggressively uses their Web site—*www.espn.com*—to market their magazine.

- Provide more product information (description, specifications, uses) or company data (financial, executive biographies, press releases) into the hands of your consumers. Most large corporations use their Web sites (e.g., *www.chrysler.com* and *www.kraftfoods.com*) for this reason, among others.

- Keep your "doors open" 24 hours a day. Airline sites, such as *www.ual.com* and *www.americanairlines.com,* for example, use the Web for this reason. Also, companies designed from the ground up to do e-commerce—like *www.amazon.com*—exploit this significant advantage they enjoy over their traditional brick-and-mortar competitors.

- Improve profits with direct sales by eliminating distributors and unnecessary layers of middlemen. (This process of eliminating the middleman is often referred to as *disintermediation.*) This strategy can backfire if it alienates your critical channel partners, so you need to address these concerns directly. For example, Merrill Lynch, one of the largest Wall Street stock brokerage houses, began offering the ability for consumers to buy stocks online, without consulting a Merrill Lynch broker (*www.ml.com*). The company is convinced that consumers who want to trade on-line will do so, while those who want the advice of a broker will continue to contact their broker. They made a painful decision to embrace the new business model of the Web, but without abandoning their long-established broker network.

- Alternatively, a Web site can bring together a buyer and seller that might not otherwise transact with each other (e.g., *www.ebay.com*). Assembling or reassembling components of the traditional supply chain like this is called *reintermediation.*

- Improve customer service via e-mail communications with customers. Many companies now provide e-mail feedback buttons, such as *www.schwab.com* and *www.etrade.com.* These sites are manned with technical staff that respond very quickly to e-mail feedback.

- Receive more precise and immediate market research by tracking customer activity on the Web, as well as Web-based surveys and direct marketing via e-mail. While this is a controversial and quickly changing aspect of the Web, the ability of the medium to provide much more targeted consumer information is undisputed. Issues of privacy arise quickly: Is it ethical to store a Web viewer's e-mail address if all they did was look at your site? Is it ethical to sell information you gathered about your customers to other businesses? The debate rages on, but the power is clearly there.

- Adjust to changing market conditions almost instantaneously with price adjustments, sales incentives, product placement, and so on. (See the above example about airfares.)

The potential advantages to virtually any company are essentially unlimited. But, as we've discussed in previous sections and will continue to discuss in the next section, to simply have a Web site is not enough. A Web site is just another business tool, and if a tool isn't used effectively, it doesn't matter how good a tool it is.

11.7 Web Site: How Do I Create One?

Creating a corporate Web site has become a complex endeavor. When the Web was new, in the mid-1990s, businesses could create their own Web sites and have them running—and used—in a day. Now, the abilities of the software are so great, the standards for design and functionality are so high, the expectations of the users are so large, that it is no longer possible to toss up an effective Web site in your spare time.

In particular, you and your company need to carefully focus the purpose of your Web site. Are you doing business-to-consumer? Business-to-business? Have you thought about who your users are, what they want, and how you want them to contact you?

As complex and daunting as its challenges are, though, so are its potential rewards. The soaring values of the Internet stocks point directly to their promise: there are millions of people now using the Internet, and thousands are joining daily. And those people are looking to be informed, entertained, and, most importantly to the corporate side of life, they are looking to buy.

There are four issues you need to consider when setting up a Web site (presented in the order in which you consider them):

1. Content
2. Design
3. Programming
4. Hosting

Section 11.4 talked about some of the mechanics and technical issues in putting together a Web server. However, just having software and hardware with a connection to the Internet doesn't mean you're "on-line." We also talked about design tools, and in Section 11.8 we will discuss getting your domain name(s) registered. Once you have these prerequisites, you can actually begin putting the pieces together to create your Web site. In this section, we'll discuss the process of creating your Web site from the perspective of the various phases of the project.

> ### Quicken.com: An Example of Innovative Content
>
> Quicken.com is a well-known financial software publisher. But Intuit, Quicken's parent, does a lot more than just sell software. At this site you can search for mortgages, check stock portfolios, get insurance, and find a host of other financial services. It is directly as a result of its content, its ability to deliver the information and goods you want, that it gets you to buy not only software, but many other things, too. Quicken could simply provide a searchable database of software products and allow you to click on them at will to place your order. However, the company allows users to go beyond that simple data gathering stage to actually order insurance, or to actually apply for a mortgage on-line. This site illustrates the power of e-commerce.

Content

The most important issue for you to consider is, what is the purpose of my Web site? If you are like most people, and most companies, you will have multiple purposes—and multiple pages on your Web site to accomplish these purposes. But overall, you should have one major driving force that is propelling you and your company to establish a Web site.

On the web, it is said that "content is king." The phrase simply means that no matter how snappy the design of your Web site is, no matter how fancy the graphics or how spectacular the audio is, if there is no "meat" to go with the "sizzle," your site will fail. It is not likely to attract eyeballs, or if it does, it will fail to keep those eyeballs returning.

Changeable Content

On the other hand, news-based sites (*www.nytimes.com, www.cnn.com, www.abcnews.com,* etc.) have content issues that have less to do with programming and design. For these sites, the content concern is to continually update their sites with breaking news that their "readers" want. While this may not sound too different from publishing a daily newspaper, in fact it is a radically different communication model. It is so different, in fact, that many organizations are setting up separate divisions to handle the different approaches.

Example: The Wall Street Journal

The *WSJ*'s Interactive version is one of the glowing successes of publishing on the Web. (They do so well that they charge a fee for a subscription to their site, one of the few content sites that has been able to do so successfully.) Their "Interactive" site contains not only material found in their daily newspaper, but also content specific to the up-to-the-minute medium of the Web.

Unchangeable Content

At the other extreme are sites where the content may never change. For example, an accounting firm may have a Web site that lists the office's address, phone number, services offered, and a message from the senior partner. Perhaps at tax time, the firm may post a few tax tips on their Web site. In a case like this, the site may get updated just a few times a year.

Design

The design of the Web site is discussed in detail in Section 11.4.

Programming

If the design of a Web site is similar to drawing the blueprints, then programming is akin to building the structure.

Off-the-Shelf Software

Depending on the design, the Web sites can be created, or "built," using Web development tools that have become "off-the-shelf" products. Microsoft's Front Page and Adobe's Page Mill are examples of this software.

Advanced Programming

More advanced needs may require you to use technologies like XML (Extensible Markup Language) and Java.

Web Pages and Databases

If the plans for the Web site call for queries, or updates, against your legacy databases (inventory, order processing, etc.), there may be needs for special tools and utilities to marry your state-of-the-art Java Web code with your been-around-the-block mainframe routines. There are tools that allow you to make this link. However, this is a growing and complex field, filled with companies that will help you write the custom software often required to make this typically complicated connection.

Like all types of computer programming, there is more to creating good code than simply meeting the specifications. Good programs are well documented, easy to maintain, and optimize performance. This last factor is of particular concern to Web sites, given the average Web users' intolerance for slow response times.

Hosting

Many companies do not want, or don't have the resources, to keep their own Web site up and running 24 hours a day, 7 days a week. They may not want to spend the money on the hardware, or they may lack the appropriate staffing levels or technical skills. For companies like this, an entirely separate industry has sprung up. There are numerous companies, from giants like AT&T, MCI, and PSINet to your local ISP, that are ready, willing, and anxious to run and manage your Web site for you. These hosting companies will rent you space on their own hardware, in their own facilities, and provide the skills and resources to make sure the site runs around the clock. In addition to these facilities, these providers can usually offer very high-speed Internet access.

Mirrored Sites

If your needs are justified, hosting companies can generally offer mirrored sites. Mirrored sites are generally for very active and very critical Web sites. In essence, a mirrored site is a copy of your Web site in another location. There are two primary reasons why you might need this service:

- First, a mirrored site ensures that your Web site continues to function even if there is some type of disaster (e.g., power failure) at the first site.

- In addition, by having multiple locations, response time is likely to be improved for end users, since special technology directs the user's request to the site that will provide the best response time. Often, due to the fewer number of "hops," the site that is physically closer to the user may offer the best response time. However, that is not *always* the case. A user's request may actually travel faster to a site that is further away because that route has lighter traffic—just like when you take side streets because of rush hour traffic on the highway.

FTP Sites

Many companies also have "ftp sites." These are sites on a company's computer, which is itself linked to the Internet; these sites are provided for customers to either get or place data. Outsiders can access the sites; sometimes companies password-protect these sites, and sometimes they don't. Using ftp sites requires some technical knowledge but can also be very useful to both the company and the customer. (If you have ever had to download a printer driver that did not come with your system, you probably used an ftp site.)

11.8 Domain Name: How Do I Register One on the Web?

The U.S. government has created a nonprofit organization, Internet Corporation for Assigned Names and Numbers (ICANN), to oversee Internet administration. In response to complaints from the public about Network Solutions, Inc. (NSI), the original administrator, and in an effort to improve the process and foster competition, ICANN has accredited many other companies to compete as registrars of the .com, .net, and .org domains. For more information about ICANN and registering domain names, see *www.icann.org.*

Getting a domain name on the Internet is relatively simple and cheap. Before we get to the procedure, however, keep in mind that you only need a domain name if your site is to be available to users via the Internet. If your site is completely private (it is an intranet that is only for users on your own network), you don't need to register a domain name.

Who Is in Charge of All This, Anyway?

At the time of this book's writing, ICANN oversees all domain registrars. ICANN is a nonprofit organization that has assumed responsibility from the U.S. government for coordinating certain Internet activities, such as the management of domain names. However, ICANN itself does not register the domain names; only those companies that ICANN has accredited can perform this function.

What You Need before You Start

The entire process for registering a domain is done on-line. All you need is a PC, a browser, a credit card, and access to the Internet. Before you register, you should have the following items:

- The domain name you want to register (e.g., *www.mycompany.com*). If your organization is nonprofit, you may choose to go with a ".org" domain as opposed to ".com." ".com" stands for "commercial," ".edu" for institutes of education, and .gov and .mil for U.S. government offices, agencies, and so on. If you try to register a domain name that is already taken, you'll find out almost immediately after you start the process.
- Your own e-mail address.

- Your organization's address information.

- Names, street and e-mail addresses, and phone numbers for administrative, technical, and billing contacts. These can be three separate individuals, or they can all be the same person.

- Host name and address for primary and secondary servers. You can also choose to provide the name and address for up to five additional secondary servers. Only the primary server and one secondary server, however, are required. Your ISP will usually provide you with this information. The servers listed here are domain name servers (DNS) and will have the information necessary to locate your server when someone on the Internet wants to access your Web site.

   When someone fires up their browser and wants to go to *www.mycompany .com,* for example, the Internet will direct them to one of these DNS servers; these will, in turn, provide the specific Internet address of your Web site.

While all this may seem confusing, the organization of domain names and DNS servers is designed to be hierarchical, to provide redundancy, and to balance the demand somewhat equally across all the Internet's resources.

Reserving a Domain Name

If you don't have some of the technical information because you haven't yet built your Web site, you can still register the domain name as a way of reserving it to be sure that no one else registers it before you.

Important Procedures to Follow

While we can't provide detailed step-by-step instructions on domain registration because the process varies from registrar to registrar, we can list the important procedures you should follow for the current process. The process is quite user friendly and straightforward. Once you have all the information, you simply point your Web browser at one of the registrars accredited by ICANN. You can find a list of the registrars at *www.icann.org*. Once you're at the Web site for an accredited registrar, you simply follow the instructions provided. Very often, the first step is making sure that no one has already registered the name that you're hoping to use.

   The fees for registration can vary from registrar to registrar, but less than $100 for the first two years is common. After that, the domain name is renewed annually. The renewal fees are paid to the registrar that you originally created the domain name with. However, you can move your domain name to another registrar if you want to for any reason (better service, cheaper fees, etc.). To move a domain name, contact the registrar that you want to move it to.

   When registering a domain name, it is vital that you enter accurate e-mail address information. Very often, changes to the domain name information can only be made from the e-mail addresses that the registrar has on record. If for some reason this isn't possible, the registrar will probably request some sort of proof that you are indeed the owner of the domain name.

The WHOIS Search

A handy tool provided by virtually all registrars is the WHOIS search. WHOIS allows you to look up the registration information for any domain that ends with .edu, .org, and .com. WHOIS provides the same type of information you're required to enter when registering (contact info, primary and secondary server, etc.). WHOIS is also a handy tool when you're trying to find out if a particular domain name is already registered.

11.9 ISPs: What Are They, and How Do I Pick One?

ISPs (Internet service providers) are companies that provide the connections to the Internet. There are three key issues that you need to consider when evaluating ISPs: speed, reliability, and cost. To best determine the importance of reliability to your company, carefully quantify how important an ISP is to your business.

ISPs Defined

ISPs provide the physical connection between you, your users, and your network to the Internet. Some ISPs service the home users (e.g., CompuServe, AOL, Earthlink), while others target the corporate environments (e.g., UUNET, PSInet), and still others service both (e.g., Bell Atlantic, AT&T). You can find ISPs in your area by searching *www.thelist.internet.com* and *www.thedirectory.com.*

In their simplest form, ISPs allow your users to connect to the Internet to surf the Web, and to send and receive e-mail messages. However, ISPs are anxious to extend their role beyond simply providing a pipe to your site. Many ISPs will provide firewall products to help protect your site from hackers. Numerous ISPs also provide Web-hosting services and will help you set up your Web server, including design and programming. They can provide these services to companies who have modest needs for a Web site, and to those that are high-volume and high-traffic e-commerce sites.

Evaluating ISPs

When looking for an ISP there are three factors that will drive your decision: speed, reliability, and cost.

Speed

When considering ISP speeds, it is tempting to focus only on the speed (or bandwidth) of the line between your company and the ISP. At the low end are lines at 56 Kbps, which are sufficient for smaller offices of up to 100 people or so. Larger offices may have pipes with more bandwidth—up to T-1 lines, which run at 1.54 Mbps. Some very large sites have T-3 lines at 45 Mbps. However, it is important to note that not all ISPs, nor all lines, are created equal. It is entirely possible that two different ISPs will provide different levels of response times, even if the line speeds to your site are identical. This is because of a variety of reasons, including the number of lines they have to all their customers, the speed and traffic volume of those lines, and the number of other users on that service.

It is important to remember that while lines connect you and your users to the ISP, there are additional lines that connect your ISP to a network access point (NAP), which is in essence the Internet itself (see Figure 11.4). NAPs, also called tier-1 providers, include AT&T, MCI Worldcom's UUNET, and Cable and Wireless, and can transfer data at speeds of 2.5 Gbps. An ISP has many customers and has to ensure that its own connection to the Internet can support the combined activity of its customers. So, while the Internet performance you experience is dependent on the speed of your line to the ISP, it is also dependent on the speed of the line from your ISP to the NAP, and your ISP's own internal network infrastructure. The last two items are important because your ISP has many customers, and while your company's traffic is the only data traveling on the line to the ISP, it then has to merge with the ISP's other customers' data and wait its turn to be moved along—just like multiple roads merging together to form a highway. In fact, it is possible for a large ISP to provide Internet services to several smaller ISPs, which in turn provide access to consumers and businesses.

Many factors affect Web response time: hardware, software, line speed, traffic, demand, Web site design, and so on. Accordingly each can be fine-tuned to optimize performance. There are various products available on the market to help you monitor and improve performance. Caching products, which store frequently accessed pages so that subsequent requests for the page can be retrieved much more quickly, can also boost performance.

Reliability: Define Your Tolerance for Risk

If your need for Internet access is primarily traditional surfing and e-mail, you may be easily able to tolerate an occasional few hours of downtime as a result of a line outage or problems at the ISP. On the other hand, if your business lives and dies by the Internet, and runs "mission-critical" applications with customers around the country or around the globe, an outage means a loss of significant business. You have much more significant concerns over reliability. Many companies now need "24 × 7"; that is, they need their sites up and running 24 hours a day, 7 days a week.

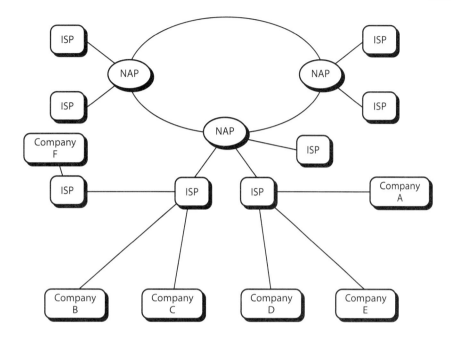

Figure 11.4 ISP Connections

You need to carefully define your tolerance for risk. You need to quantify, as carefully as possible, how important your ISP is. How long can you run your business without it? How long can you tolerate your Web site being inactive? Determine how much money it will cost your company when (not "if") your connection to the Internet is broken. If your Web site is down for a couple of hours, do you care? Some companies don't really mind—others go to enormous lengths to ensure that they have 100% connectivity. Once you have these numbers—once you have determined how much per hour and per day without connection to the Internet will cost your company—you can then decide how best to deal with the risk.

Multiple Lines

Some companies lessen their risk by having more than one line to their ISP, and some have each line from a different ISP. When choosing multiple ISPs, they may even choose providers that are geographically distant from each other. If a disaster (weather, power outage) strikes one area of the country, they increase their chances that at least one of the ISPs will continue to provide service. For companies that have multiple offices throughout the country, which are networked together, they may choose to have certain offices in different parts of the country with lines to local ISPs.

Hardware Issues

In general there are two components to consider in regard to ISP reliability. The first is the stability of the line from your site to the ISP. This line is provided by the phone company, not your ISP. Secondly, you have to consider the reliability of the services the ISP provides.

While phone line outages are rare, they are not unheard of. And the complexity that occurs when computers meet telephones is increasing, not decreasing. If the connection to your ISP suddenly goes down, whose fault is it? It could be your computer, it could be the phone line, or it could be the ISP itself.

Cost

Cost is always a factor in any business decision. Unfortunately, comparing costs between ISPs can be difficult. ISPs offer different levels of service, some with many variables of their own. For example, since the cost of the leased lines is based on speed and distance, you may find one ISP to be more expensive than another because of its distance to your company. If you ask an ISP for firewall services, you may be faced with choices about buying, leasing, or renting the appropriate technology at your site. If you don't have the expertise on site, you may have to pay the ISP for maintaining and supporting the firewall, often with pricing based on hours of coverage and response times. Costs for other site services (hosting, design, programming, etc.) can vary significantly with factors like complexity, size of the site, hardware required, and so on.

Some ISP fees have little room for negotiation (e.g., connectivity and hosting) since the ISP is simply passing on its fixed costs. Other services (design and programming) may be highly negotiable. Regardless, your leverage increases with the total projected revenue stream and by bundling multiple services together.

You can see what others think about ISPs that you're considering by checking out *www.worldwidewait.com* and *www.epinions.com/cmsw-isp*.

Changing ISPs

As a general rule, changing ISPs is relatively easy. If the only service your ISP provides is the pipe to the Internet, changing ISPs may be as simple as ordering a line to your new provider and giving the old one notice of termination. The only planning might be to make sure that you have the new service in place before terminating the old service. If your ISP provides hosting services, changing is a little more complicated, but not much. You can copy all the program logic and Web pages to servers at your new ISP; a simple notification to the domain name registrar is all it takes to have your domain name point to the new provider, and your users will probably never notice the change.

11.10
E-mail: What Are the Important Technical Issues to Consider When I Set Up E-mail Internet Connectivity?

Chances are that one of the main reasons you want to connect to the Internet is to send and receive e-mail. However, because of the many different types of e-mail packages available, it is not possible to provide specific directions here.

Still, you should know that virtually all e-mail packages (including the very popular Lotus Notes, Microsoft Outlook/Exchange, Netscape Communicator, and Novell GroupWise) allow for connectivity to the Internet to send and receive e-mail. For specific directions, you'll want to consult the manuals or on-line help for these packages.

SMTP

Keep in mind that among technical personnel, Internet mail is more commonly referred to as "SMTP messaging" (simple mail transfer protocol) or "SMTP mail." Between your e-mail vendor's support resources and your ISP's assistance, you should be able to provide connectivity between your in-house e-mail users and the rest of the cyber-messaging world.

Depending on your e-mail software and your network environment, you may want, or need, to set up a server specifically designed to handle the transfer of SMTP traffic between your in-house e-mail system and the Internet. The configuration and hardware specs of this device will be dependent on the volume of mail traffic. Typically, a low-end server should be able to handle thousands of messages per day with little effort.

MX Record

When setting up Internet e-mail, you're likely to hear about the "MX record." "MX" stands for mail exchange. This record tells mail servers all over the Internet where to send mail addressed to your company. For example, when someone sends e-mail to *theboss@mycompany.com*, it is the MX record that directs this message to the e-mail server in your computer room.

The MX record exists on the DNS server(s) for your domain name. This is the same server you had to provide the name and address for when you registered your domain name. Most likely, this server is at your ISP. The reason for the MX record is for those situations when the mail server and the Web server are not the same devices—which is quite often. For example, if you decided that you didn't have the time and resources to manage your own Web site, you may have outsourced it to some hosting service. It is entirely likely that the box that is your Web server is hundreds, if not thousands, of miles away from your corporate office.

Let's say you're in Virginia, but you have outsourced your Web site hosting to a company in Arizona. The DNS information, along with the MX record, ensures that *www.mycompany.com* takes surfers to the right box in Arizona, but mail addressed with *@mycompany.com* brings those messages right to your e-mail server in Virginia.

See Chapter 12 for a discussion of e-mail as an enterprise application.

11.11   Further References

Web Sites

- *www.epinions.com/cmsw-isp* (comments about ISPs)
- *www.icann.org.* (information about registering domain names)
- *www.isoc.org/internet/history* (brief history of the Internet)
- *www.thedirectory.com* (resource for ISPs in your area)
- *www.thelist.internet.com* (resource for ISPs in your area)
- *www.worldwidewait.com* (comments about ISPs)

Articles and Books

- Bayles, Deborah L., *Extranets: Building the Business-to-Business Web,* Prentice Hall, 1998.
- Bernard, Ryan, *The Corporate Intranet,* John Wiley and Sons, 1997.
- Copeland, Lee, "Big Three Automakers Join Forces Online," *Computerworld,* February 25, 2000.
- Hafner, Katie, and Matthew Lyon, *Where Wizards Stay Up Late: The Origins of the Internet,* Simon and Schuster, 1996.
- Haylock, Christina Ford, Len Muscarella, and Steve Case, *Net Success: 24 Leaders in Web Commerce Show You How to Put the Web to Work for Your Business,* Adams Media, 1999.
- Korper, Steffano, Juanita Ellis, and Jerry D. Gibson, *The E-Commerce Book: Building the E-Empire,* Academic Press, 1999.
- Minoli, Daniel, and Andrew Schmidt, *Internet Architectures,* John Wiley and Sons, 1999.
- Orenstein, David, "Toys R Us, Others, Face Online Woes," *Computerworld,* December 23, 1999.
- Pfaffenberger, Bryan, *Building a Strategic Extranet,* IDG Books, 1998.

- Rony, Ellen, and Peter R. Rony, *The Domain Name Handbook; High Stakes and Strategies in Cyberspace,* R&D Books, 1998.

- Seybold, Patricia, *Customers.com,* Random House/Times Books, 1998. A classic study of e-commerce.

- Siegel, David, *Creating Killer Web Sites,* Second Edition, Hayden, 1997.

Enterprise Applications

CHAPTER TWELVE

What You Will Learn

- What the value of an e-mail system is, what the different e-mail options are, and how to manage one
- What enterprise resource planning (ERP) is
- What groupware is and how to determine if you need it

Introduction

Simply put, an enterprise application is an application that is so widely used throughout the organization that it touches almost every aspect of the company's operation. E-mail is one example, and enterprise resource planning is another. Enterprise applications are very valuable but can be very complex pieces of software. For small companies, enterprise applications are very useful, easy to implement, and generally not particularly difficult to administer. For large companies, however, with hundreds and thousands of users, the value of connecting all these computers and their functions is enormous, but so are the tasks of implementing and administering the software. This chapter discusses the value of various enterprise applications and provides some management tips.

12.1 E-mail: What Is the Value of an E-mail System?

It is a measure of the speed of change of the business world in general, and the computer industry in particular, that not even 10 years ago, e-mail was considered an optional function. An e-mail address on a business card was viewed as understandable, perhaps, but not required. Now, every company has e-mail, and it is considered as required as a telephone.

We discuss the mechanics of managing an e-mail system later in this chapter. First, let's take a quick overview of the value of an e-mail system.

What Does E-mail Do for Me and My Company?

E-mail has several critical functions:

- It helps your employees to do their jobs.
- It helps your company's outside customers communicate more effectively with you and your organization.
- With simple e-mail as a foundation, you can add features and facilities to it to allow for more collaborative on-line work. For example, you may be able to use features of e-mail to allow for an on-line meeting (including chat, virtual whiteboard sessions, etc.). In addition, you may be able to use features of e-mail so that multiple people can work together to develop a document, spreadsheet, or presentation.

The Specific Values of E-mail in Your Company

Of course e-mail helps your company communicate better. But what does that mean? And how important is it? After all, there are still phones, fax machines, videoconferencing—what does e-mail bring to the table that all these options do not?

E-mail provides a unique method for both internal and external communication that is timely and enhances people's abilities to do their jobs.

That does not sound like all that radical a statement, but it could be a very useful sentence for you in the future. There are four key words in the above sentence: *unique, communication, timely,* and *enhances.*

Unique Features

E-mail is primarily a textual medium (although this is changing quickly). And in this information economy that we are operating in, exchanging text is what a lot of corporate workers do. They exchange information. They create information (a spreadsheet, a presentation, a document), and then they exchange it with their coworkers, their bosses, or their customers.

E-mail is often the fastest and most efficient method of making that exchange. Phone calls can be faster, but the information exchanged is (for the most part!) not recorded. Nor is it in a form that lends itself to re-evaluation. Nor are phone calls appropriate for all exchanges because of the length of the material. Also, voice-mail ("v-mail") does not lend itself to lengthy messages. E-mail, on the other hand, can be quite long and very detailed in its content, because the recipient can quickly scan the message for the pertinent items.

Faxes also are limited in their own way: length can be an issue (nobody likes getting or sending a 20-page fax, although it happens every day), not everyone has a fax machine, the machines can be busy, you cannot be sure about the quality at the other end, and so on.

The Quality of Communication

While the figures are hard to find, it is clear that the growth of e-mail has radically increased the communication both within the corporation and between the corporation and its customers. There is no question the quantity has increased; the issue commonly is "Has the quality of communication gotten any better?" In other words, we are all getting more e-mail, but is the content increasing? And in general, "Am I better off with e-mail, or is it just another task I need to do during the day?"

Overall, the answer is "Yes, you are better off using e-mail." Productivity studies of computer usage in the corporate environment generally state that companies receive a significant productivity gain by computerizing their workforce. E-mail is a large component of that process.

But e-mail is a tool, and tools can be used well or poorly. It is in your interests as an IT manager to monitor both the quantity and quality of the e-mail in your company. Keeping tabs on the amount of e-mail being sent is simple; there are tools built into the various programs that allow you to monitor usage. Keeping tabs on quality, however, is harder. But if you do so, it will radically affect the quantity of your company's e-mail.

How do you track the quality of your company's e-mail? You can't. But you can educate your users about the benefits of high-quality e-mail. Often, people only need to be told once and they will alter their behavior. Many people have never been taught how to effectively use e-mail, and they are ripe for a quick lesson or two.

Educate Your Users on the Key Principles of E-mail

You (or the training department, if you have one) can offer a formal class on the e-mail system you use and tips for effective communication. And you might have some success getting people to that class, especially if you have upper management buy-in. But the truth is, these programs are not that complex and the basic functions can be learned pretty easily. What you need to get across to all your users are some simple principles of using e-mail that are less software oriented and more usage oriented:

1. Keep it brief. If you don't like reading long e-mails, what makes you think others do? Keep it as brief as possible. E-mail is fast and efficient, but reading a lot of text on-line is not easy.

2. Make the subject line count. Be as clear in this line as possible. Do not say "Message about meeting." Say "Operations meeting rescheduled for Tuesday at 9 AM."

3. Reply to all e-mails that expect one. Not every e-mail sent needs a reply, but many do. If you send something to somebody, you expect a reply. Provide the same courtesy.

4. Use the "Reply All" button with extreme caution. This button is probably the largest contributor to e-mail waste. Everyone does not have to be copied on every e-mail. Sometimes, just replying to the sender suffices. Sometimes, a subset of the recipients needs to be informed. Much less frequently, all the recipients of the original e-mail need to be replied to; this occurs less often than people realize.

   If you can get your users to *think* before they use this button, the effect on your volume of e-mail will be dramatic. Many users do not know the damage they are causing by routinely using this button and will change their behavior when it is explained to them.

5. Spell-check every e-mail you send. All e-mail programs now have a function that allows e-mail to be automatically spell-checked. Even though proper spelling, grammar, and punctuation have been early casualties as the world has moved on-line, you should remember that you are still working in a busi-

ness environment. And, while the occasional typo or two may be forgiven, they should be avoided. Typos are at the very least annoying, but they can also be devastating and, in general, degrade the value of the message. Automatically spell-checking e-mail is an example of a very useful, everyday software function. Everyone should do it.

6. Delete old e-mails. We'll discuss the total volume of a company's e-mail in another place, but this is another example of when you tell people this, many will start doing it right away—they had no idea it was an option. (Others are hopeless pack rats, but that is another problem.)

7. Define policies and guidelines for saving e-mail. What do you want your users to do? How do you want them to save their e-mails? Provide your users with a specific plan. Do you want them to store up a month's worth on their hard drive? They need to save only the items that they will need quick access to. Your e-mail system probably has features to help you manage this. You may be able to automatically purge e-mail that reaches a certain age, or you may be able to limit the size of a message, as well as the size of a user's mailbox.

   Besides telling users that they can delete their old e-mail, you should tell them that their e-mail is being backed up daily. While the access to these backups can be difficult, it *is* being covered. So people do not need to save every little scrap.

12.2 E-mail: What Are the Different Options?

There are many different email programs to choose from, but fortunately, virtually all adhere to industry standards.

Industry Standards

There are many e-mail programs, and many methods of implementing those programs. One of the most important options when considering e-mail is the matter of *industry standards* to ensure that you can exchange messages with users who are not on your e-mail system. There are many, many products that adhere to industry standards (IMAP4, POP-3), and a few very popular products that are based on proprietary technology (e.g., Microsoft's Exchange, Lotus's Notes, and Novell's GroupWise)—although these products support the industry standards as well.

By adhering to industry standard protocols, you can mix and match server and client software products—and can very often find shareware or open source products to fit your needs (Netscape Navigator, MS Outlook Express, Eudora).

IMAP—Internet Message Access Protocol

IMAP (generally referred to as IMAP4 to denote its current incarnation) can be thought of as a client/server environment that allows you to view and manipulate mail while it is still on the server. The advantage to this is that users' mail files are accessible to them from any properly configured workstation. On the downside, it means that the mail server has to have a very large storage capacity.

POP-3 (Post Office Protocol 3)

POP-3 can be thought of as a store-and-forward environment. Your mail is held for you on the server until you connect; then it is downloaded to your workstation. So, if you then go to another workstation, you won't see your mail since it is now on the first workstation. POP-3 is supported by the major browsers (MS Internet Explorer, Netscape Navigator, etc.).

MIME (Multipurpose Internet Mail Extensions)

The MIME specification is for formatting nontext messages (e.g., graphics, audio, video) so that they can be sent over the Internet. A variation of MIME, called S/MIME, supports encrypted messages.

Proprietary Products

On the other hand, proprietary products (such as MS Exchange, Novell Group-Wise, Lotus Notes), which support the industry standards, will also offer many more additional features (group scheduling and calendaring, full-featured address books, collaborative discussions, bulletin boards, etc.) that make them very attractive as solutions for much more than e-mail.

Popular E-Mail Programs

The following are some of the most popular e-mail programs:

- Microsoft Exchange (which uses Microsoft's Outlook as the client)
- Lotus's cc:Mail and Notes
- Eudora
- Novell's GroupWise

Between them, they own the lion's share of the market for e-mail programs.

Why You Should Consider Using One of These Products

While the most popular software packages aren't often the best products, there are valid reasons for using those products that the market has embraced.

- The overall learning curve is not as sharp; because of their popularity, their use is widespread. New people joining your company more likely will have experience in one of these packages; they will not need training to get them going.
- As with any software, the more people that use it, the more support and third-party activity that will be available.
- Two of the vendors' products (Microsoft and Lotus) have become part of a bundled suite of software. The e-mail program's features are integrated tightly into the features of the other programs.
- It is easier to find IT staff who are skilled with the more popular packages.
- It could be more difficult, or even impossible, to integrate a less popular e-mail system with other software you have in your environment, such as antivirus software and your network operating system.

12.3 E-mail Programs: How Do I Choose One?

Choosing the e-mail program you will use in your organization is critical since e-mail is a key part of any company, and your decision will probably be with you for a long time. However, since you probably already have one, if the issue comes up for you to decide, it is probably because you are considering an upgrade or a replacement.

Environment's Infrastructure

First, look at the rest of your environment's infrastructure. If you rely on Novell's Netware product for your network operating system, you may want to give strong consideration to Novell's GroupWise product since it runs on Netware. Choosing another e-mail package might require you to bring in another NOS platform. Similarly, if you're a Microsoft-centric environment, you may want to consider looking at their Exchange product. Similarly, if your shop is based on the Unix platform, you may want to look at a less proprietary package, like Eudora.

What Do You Have Now for E-mail?

Carefully evaluate your current system. If you're using Lotus's original e-mail product, cc:Mail, the upgrade to Notes will probably be the least painful. Similarly, if you're using Microsoft's original MS Mail product, the upgrade to Exchange will be the path of least resistance. E-mail systems now are very similar in functionality. Changing e-mail systems may bring you small feature gains, but it will also bring along major implementation and migration headaches. Make sure all the work will be worth it.

Also consider what features you use beyond basic e-mail. For example, if you're making use of databases in Lotus Notes, you may have difficulty duplicating that functionality in another e-mail package.

Unified Messaging

Lastly, give some consideration to unified messaging. Unified messaging is the term applied to integrating your v-mail and e-mail systems. In short, you can use your e-mail system to access your v-mail (messages appear in your in-box as audio files), and use your v-mail to access your e-mail (a synthesized voice reads your e-mail messages to you). This technology is just beginning to gain acceptance and is still maturing. It is also important to note that there are several ways to attack the integration: (1) your v-mail vendor may sell a system that integrates to your e-mail environment, (2) your e-mail vendor may have an add-on to integrate with your v-mail, or (3) a third party may offer a product to tie the two messaging systems together.

Unified messaging can be complex and may be costly. Even if you are not planning to implement unified messaging immediately, however, you may want to consider it as an issue if you're evaluating new e-mail systems.

12.4 E-mail: How Do I Manage My E-mail System?

The short answer to that question is "aggressively." An e-mail system can quickly get out of control. Managing it can become a large part of your day or, if you have a large company, the entire responsibility of one or two of your people. Several other important aspects of e-mail are discussed in Chapter 13: external threats, viruses, and firewalls are all detailed in that chapter.

Junk Mail (Spam, Chain Letters, Jokes, etc.)

While e-mail can be a very valuable tool for circulating vital information very quickly, it can distribute junk just as quickly. If someone receives an e-mail of a joke or spiritual message that they happen to like, they can circulate it to one person, or thousands, with just a few clicks of the mouse. Although it may seem innocent at first, the growth can be exponential, and it results in massive storage requirements for e-mail servers. It can slow down the delivery of mail because your servers are backed up distributing hundreds or thousands of messages unrelated to work.

Many e-mail packages now let the user identify the sources of spammers or junk mail senders. With a feature like this, once a source of junk mail is identified, any future mail from the same source is immediately deleted.

Harassment

While e-mails with jokes and spiritual messages may seem innocent, they can easily cross the line—and some may be seen as offensive or harassment. Your organization should have a clear-cut policy (from senior management, not from IT) that indicates a zero tolerance for any material (including e-mail) that can be construed as offensive on grounds such as sexual harassment, racial discrimination, and so on. It is not uncommon for e-mail messages to be included as evidence in a variety of types of litigation. Work with your Legal and Human Resources departments regarding a policy.

See Table 12.1 on the next page for a list of vendors of content monitoring software.

Viruses

In the days of yore, computer viruses were most often spread via diskettes, and then through files shared on the LAN. Now, e-mail is the most effective method of spreading a virus. Virus creators, in addition to programming them with some sort of disruptive behavior, now also program them to go into your e-mail address book and to send themselves to your coworkers, friends, and family—down the hall, across the country, and around the globe. An effectively programmed virus can have an enormous global impact in just a matter of days. The Melissa virus of 1999, which was benign except for the relentless way it e-mailed itself ad infinitum, is an excellent example.

Although you should still warn your users about messages from unknown users, and to take other precautions, a more aggressive posture is called for. All your workstations and servers should run virus-checking software. In addition, you should have software specifically designed for your e-mail environment that scans messages and their attachments for viruses. Products from Intel, Network Associates, and Symantec, among others, are relatively inexpensive for the protection they provide. See Chapter 13 for more information regarding viruses and how to defend against them.

Table 12.1 E-mail content monitoring vendors and products.

Vendor (Web site)	Product name
Aspeon Software Inc. *www.aspeonsoftware.com*	Exchange Plus
Content Technologies Inc. *www.mimesweeper.com*	MailSweeper
Elron Software Inc. *www.elronsoftware.com*	Message Inspector
Marshal Software *www.marshalsoftware.com*	MailMarshal
SRA International Inc. *www.sra.com*	Assentor
Symantec Corp. *www.symantec.com*	MailGear
Trend Micro Inc. *www.antivirus.com*	ScanMail
TumbleWeed Communications Corp. *www.tumbleweed.com*	WorldSecure Mail

Data Size and Retention

Because e-mail is so often used to distribute games and jokes, the amount of storage required to keep it all on-line can be massive. As such, it not unusual to have a policy that sets limits on the size of messages, the size of mailboxes, and the age of messages. These limitations are available with the most popular e-mail packages. It is important that users be made aware of these policies, and that the limits be set after considering users' needs. Another way of addressing space concerns with e-mail is to archive older messages to tape storage.

Human Resources and/or your Legal department may want to get involved in setting these policies, particularly the one related to message retention.

Users should also be aware that limits may be in effect with the external users they send and receive mail with. As such, if you allow your users to send messages of a certain size, there is no guarantee that the message will get through since the recipient's mail environment could very well have a lower limit.

Personal Use

Just like with the use of the company phones, it is probably reasonable to expect that not every message that your users send will be work related. There will be an occasional personal message. Most organizations expect and tolerate this as long as they are not oversized and do not contain offensive e-mails. However, it is probably wise to have a formal policy (just like the one that probably exists for use of the company phones) saying that e-mail is for work-related material only. Similarly, most companies reserve the right to review e-mail messages that their employees send and receive, although usually the company will only invoke that right when some problem or policy violation is suspected.

12.5 ERP: What Is Enterprise Resource Planning?

This is a hot topic in corporate circles. For many companies, it is still a critical component of their activities—whether they are a provider of ERP software and solutions or a customer implementing an ERP solution. To avoid looking like the naive ITer in the popular TV commercial of 2000, keep in mind that ERP is pronounced "E-R-P," not "erp."

ERP is a term with a broad definition; it is used in a variety of ways to mean the set of activities that a company engages in to manage its resources across the entire enterprise. This can mean activities as diverse as product planning, sales programs, parts purchasing, maintaining inventories, and performing classically defined HR functions. Major software companies in the ERP space include SAP, Baan, Oracle, J. D. Edwards, and PeopleSoft.

Prior to ERP, companies would use different packages for various business functions: inventory, sales and distribution, financials, human resources, and so on. Different packages were used simply because no vendor had a product offering that could cross all these various disciplines. The various packages might be purchased or homegrown. To pass data among the various functions, a company would write numerous interface programs to extract data from one application's database for use in another application.

The Value of ERP Software

With the introduction of ERP, a company would essentially have a single application (or a single set of applications provided by a single vendor) and database for all its vital business functions. The value of this could be enormous. Since all the applications are integrated, a change in activity in one area of the company would ripple through the system to all affected departments so that they could react accordingly. A sudden spike in sales could notify the Purchasing department to increase orders of raw materials, as well as notify HR that more labor will be needed to fulfill the demands of the increased sales.

General ERP Implementation Issues

There are two elements of ERP to keep in mind when considering implementing an ERP system:

- ERP is not a trivial-sized activity. True ERP systems run across the entire enterprise—they literally affect every aspect of a company's business. Because the scope of an ERP implementation can be so far reaching, it almost acts as a magnifying glass. Problems are quickly seen throughout the organization.

- Implementation of an ERP system is a gut-wrenching experience for a corporation. Some companies thrive on the new system, embrace it as the salvation of their business, and explode forward. Others find the difficult medicine of ERP very hard to swallow, and eventually bail in midstream, leaving unhappy employees, customers, and vendors screaming in their wake—to say nothing of opening the gate of lawsuits. Trade journals are equally filled with success and failure stories of companies that have gone through ERP implementations.

Costs of Implementing ERP

In addition, the cost of implementing ERP will easily be in the hundreds of thousands of dollars, and could go to the tens of millions for larger and more complex environments. Usually, the biggest costs of an ERP implementation are the consultants that you will need to assist in the implementation. Because of the complexity of installing an ERP package, it is not uncommon for consulting costs to total two to three times the cost of the actual software package. Many very large consulting firms (e.g., PricewaterhouseCoopers, Anderson Consulting) have entire divisions dedicated to ERP implementations.

Major Changes Required

In many cases, the organization may find that it actually has to change the way it does business in order to implement an ERP package. While the traditional approach of implementing a package is to tailor it to your organization's needs, it is not uncommon to have to use the reverse approach when implementing an ERP package.

There are many core activities associated with ERP that are software related, although the thrust of the implementation is often not only software. It can include changing the way departments function, employees' roles, and a sea change in the way the company operates.

As the person responsible for a large part of the software and hardware health and well-being of the corporation, your job, your responsibilities, and your entire skill set are going to be radically affected by any ERP motions your company undertakes.

It Is Not Only IT's Decision

It is likely that you will not be the only one consulted before your company decides to implement an ERP system. More likely, you will be part of a group or committee making that decision. Or even more likely—because implementing an ERP system is almost always a multiyear adventure—you will join a company in midimplementation. Your decisions will not be so much "Should my company do this?" as "How can I help my company do this in the most efficient manner possible?"

ERP may be the single largest IT project your company has ever undertaken. Its success or failure may lead to the success or failure of many executives and departments. Stories abound of ERP implementations that led to cost overruns, 20-hour days, 7-day weeks, loss of key team members, and more.

If you're involved in an ERP implementation, chances are you will be making more use of some of the topics in this book (project management, budgeting, etc.) than with any other project you'll ever be involved in.

You, as well as everyone else involved, should look at an ERP implementation as the single greatest opportunity to re-engineer the way your organization works, and to have a huge beneficial impact that will probably live on for many, many years.

12.6 Groupware: What Is It and How Do I Know I Need It?

"Groupware" refers to software that allows employees at different locations to work together collaboratively on a single project. Like ERP, "groupware" is a broad term that can refer to a wide range of products. Groupware facilitates bring together, in the virtual world, the knowledge, individuals, and processes of an organization, so that the organization can work effectively and productively.

Lotus Notes, Microsoft Exchange, and Novell's GroupWise are examples of three of the most popular groupware products. Other definitions of groupware include your company's intranet. Users of these products can do more than just send each other e-mail. They can create discussion groups that allow only certain members to post to, they can create common data locations where one user can deposit files that other users can pick up at a different time, and they can chat over networks in real time.

Reasons Why an Organization Might Want Groupware

Groupware provides the technology for bridging time and space gaps. There are a wide variety of reasons why users want the capabilities that groupware technology provides. Among those reasons are the following:

- It enhances collaboration between different members of an organization who might not otherwise be able to work together.
- It enables communication between users in different places and different time zones.
- It reduces travel.
- It enables telecommuting.

There have traditionally been two players in the groupware space: Lotus Notes and Novell GroupWise. However, GroupWise has been losing popularity since it requires Novell's Netware network operating system (and since many companies are standardizing on Microsoft Windows for their NOS, they are reluctant to have multiple platforms in their environment). On the other hand, Microsoft's Exchange, originally used solely as an e-mail platform, has been gaining ground in the groupware space as it has added more functionality.

Typical Groupware Features

Though the definition of groupware can vary, it generally includes these features:

- E-mail (allowing for communication of information)
- Calendaring (group and individual, for tracking scheduling)
- Routing of information (so that the right people are informed)
- Document management
- Work flow, also known as "process management" (defining the processes so that steps aren't omitted, duplicated, followed incorrectly, etc.), which will usually include features for escalation or alerts when called for
- Knowledge management (to facilitate the easy access, storage, and sharing of individuals' expertise)

■ Collaborative work (to allow people in different locations to use on-line facilities to work together in real time)

Depending on need, each organization will use varying amounts of each of these features as they adopt groupware as a resource.

12.7 Further References

Web Sites

■ *www.antivirus.com* (virus software vendor)

■ *www.baan.com* (ERP software vendor)

■ *www.eudora.com* (groupware vendor)

■ *www.intel.com* (virus software vendor)

■ *www.jdedwards.com* (ERP software vendor)

■ *www.lotus.com/home.nsf/welcome/notes* (ERP software vendor)

■ *www.microsoft.com/exchange/* (groupware vendor)

■ *www.nai.com* (virus software vendor)

■ *www.novell.com/groupwise/* (groupware vendor)

■ *www.oracle.com* (ERP software vendor)

■ *www.peoplesoft.com* (ERP software vendor)

■ *www.sap.com* (ERP software vendor)

■ *www.symantec* (virus software vendor)

Articles and Books

■ Chaffey, Dave, *Groupware, Workflow and Intranets: Reengineering the Enterprise with Collaborative Software,* Digital Press, 1998.

■ Clewett, Annette, Dana Franklin (Contributor), and Ann McCown (Contributor), *Network Resource Planning for SAP R/3, BAAN IV, and PEOPLESOFT: A Guide to Planning Enterprise Applications,* McGraw-Hill, 1998.

■ Hughes, Lawrence E., *Internet E-mail: Protocols, Standards, and Implementation,* Artech House Telecommunications Library, 1998.

■ Langenwalter, Gary A., *Enterprise Resources Planning and Beyond: Integrating Your Entire Organization,* CRC Press/St. Lucie Press, 1999.

- Lindquist, Christopher, "You've Got (Dirty) Mail," *Computerworld*, March 13, 2000.

- Lozinsky, Sergio, and Paul Wahl (Foreword), *Enterprise-Wide Software Solutions: Integration Strategies and Practices*, Addison-Wesley, 1998.

- Overly, Michael R., *E-Policy: How to Develop Computer, E-Policy, and Internet Guidelines to Protect Your Company and Its Assets*, Amacom, 1998.

Security

CHAPTER THIRTEEN

Introduction

There's a ton of reasons for wanting to break into a computer system: the challenge of it, a shot at notoriety, revenge, and money are some of the most popular reasons. And of course, some do it just for kicks. Regardless of the reason, there's no disputing the fact that there are lots of attempts against computer security. Unlike football, where the best defense is a good offense, in computers a strong and vigilant defense is the only defense.

13.1 External Threats: How Do I Protect My Company from Them?

There is a simple but important distinction to make between the two different types of threats your company will face: internal and external. This section discusses the external threats; the next section discusses internal ones.

Internal vs. External Threats

In the war of computer security, we generally think that the people who are employees of the company are "on our side" and the real threat comes from "outsiders." Often, however, reports are that the greatest security threats come from within. Of course, with the prevalence of remote access, the World Wide Web, intranets, and extranets, too often the difference between external and internal threats is more of a logical one than a physical one. The point is, your data, your networks, your infrastructure, and your company are all at risk, and it is a key element of your responsibility as an IT manager to manage that risk. You will never eliminate all security risks, but you can certainly be aggressive about trying to minimize them.

To protect yourself from external threats there are two fronts you must address:

- Your company's connection to the Internet
- Your remote dial-in capabilities

Connections to the Internet

The first, the connection to the Internet, is the easiest to deal with. In general, a company has so few physical connections to the Internet—most often only one—that it easy to focus on. If your connection to the Internet isn't protected by a firewall, it's like going away for vacation and leaving the door unlocked—there

> **The Realities of Security**
>
> "Because computer systems work relatively well on a daily basis, it is easy to become lax about the dangers of not protecting your system. But both on my personal and my corporate systems, I spend a lot of time and effort making them as secure as I can. Networks and access are almost universal now, and that means unauthorized access to my data, to my documents, to my files, is possible. I make it very, very hard for them to do."
>
> —Jon Ganz
> *Documentation Manager, Informix Software, Menlo Park, CA*

may not be any visible indication that you're vulnerable, but the first person who comes knocking on the door is going to find out.

Firewalls

Firewalls are hardware and software combinations that guard the border between your private network and the public Internet.

For example, firewalls can control who, if anyone, can surf the Web, download files, listen to music via Real Audio, and so on. Firewalls can also hide your network's identity from the rest of the world on the Internet. For example, when your users surf the Web, the IP address that goes with them is the one associated with the firewall's connection to the Internet—your internal IP addresses are never used. In this capacity, your firewall is functioning as what's called a "proxy server." A more detailed discussion of firewalls appears later in this chapter.

Remote Dial-In Capabilities

The other front you have to defend against external threats is your remote dial-in capabilities. While each company generally only has one or two connections to the Internet that it has to keep an eye on, there might be hundreds of dial-in threats—most of which might be unknown to the security administrator. Any user in the company with a phone line and a modem attached to his PC is an exposure for external access.

Keep several issues in mind when evaluating remote dial-in capabilities: remote access, RAS, SecurID, and what the weak points of your environment are.

Remote Access

Years ago, users had modems connected to their PCs to allow them to connect to external resources such as vendor bulletin boards. Now most of these resources are available on the Web. Still, users frequently have modems for accessing services like AOL, or to use for sending faxes from their PCs. To reduce the threat of all these "open doors," there are several steps you can take. First, you might be able to eliminate the use of these stand-alone modems by creating a modem pool on the LAN, which is administered and monitored by IT. While there still might be exposure, the exposure is at least known and localized, and there is centralized control. In addition, if sending and receiving faxes is important, there are a variety of fax server solutions that can be implemented. Modems that only need to dial out can be configured to not answer incoming calls.

Still, you'll probably need to provide some type of remote dial-in access for users who travel or work from home and need access to e-mail, company data and applications, and so on. With a remote dial-in connection, a user across the country can function like they are on your network down the hall. And, while you may have faith in the security precautions you use internally, it is a good idea to add an extra level of protection for remote dial-in facilities where it could be virtually anyone knocking on your door to see if it's unlocked.

Remote access is discussed in further detail in Chapter 10.

RAS: Remote Access Servers

Fortunately, vendors of remote access servers, commonly called RAS, are aware of this need and offer a variety of options. One option is for the RAS server to prompt the user for a remote access password, which must be supplied before the user has to enter their regular password. In a stricter scenario, a RAS server can be configured for "dial-back." With dial-back, once the user connects to the RAS server, she enters a predefined ID. At that point, the RAS server hangs up the phone and calls the user back at a number that is associated with that ID. In this way, remote access connections can only be established to certain, predefined phone numbers.

While there is some possibility that some unknown hostile person may dial into your RAS server, it is unlikely that this person will be doing so from the home of one of your authorized users. Of course, this dial-back ability has some limitations, particularly if you have users who travel a lot and don't know in advance what number they'll be calling from, or if there is not direct dial to reach them and the call has to go through a switchboard.

SecurID

One of the most secure techniques for remote users is a technology called SecurID from Security Dynamics, Inc. To the user, SecurID is a credit-card-size device that is carried with him. When it's time to login, the user must use his regular ID and password, as well as a sequence of numbers provided by the SecurID. The user then has 60 seconds to enter this number sequence in order to login to his network. As a result of the password being valid for only 60 seconds, the user must have the device with him whenever he wants to login. This ties the security to a physical device, which can be deactivated if it is ever lost or stolen. Of course, users generally hate having to keep another piece of hardware with them, and those who are slow typists can be frustrated by the 60-second limitation.

Where Are Your Weak Points?

Just like in protecting your home, there are many products, solutions, and technologies available to protect your environment against external threats. However, if you don't know where all the doors and windows are, you can't be sure they're locked when you go to bed. If you need help in identifying the weak points, there are many security consultants available who can help you identify them. If you're confident that all your doors and windows have been locked tight, there are consultants who will try to infiltrate your network to see if you are right.

13.2 Internal Threats: How Do I Protect My Company from Them?

Often the greatest security exposures are internal. There are various techniques for increasing the security in your computer network from internal users. Formal security policies that are carefully followed are your best protection. These policies should address the following:

- Passwords
- User terminations
- Special privilege IDs
- Access reviews
- Authorization levels
- User information
- Routine maintenance
- Software updates
- Virus checking
- Physical considerations

Internal Security Helps External Security, Too

It is important to realize that once an external user gets access to your network, he is, for all intents and purposes, now an internal user. So, whatever you do to protect yourself against internal threats will very likely be a defense to external threats as well.

The strongest protection you can have is a set of effective security policies that are strictly adhered to. There are entire tomes written about computer security and the related technical issues. Here we'll simply list some basic security policies that any self-respecting IT shop should have.

Formal Security Policy Components

Having and following a formal security policy can go a long way in protecting your environment.

Passwords

Passwords should be at least five characters in length, should expire regularly (but not so often that a user has to write down her current password on a Post-it note attached to the monitor), and should not be the same as the user's ID, nor be a common word. When it's time to change passwords, users should not be able to reuse the same one. At the very least, they should have to go through three password change cycles before being able to use the first again.

Some software has the ability to disable an ID if too many failed attempts are made within a specified period of time. This convenient feature can considerably slow down an automated attempt to guess a password by rapidly trying every combination.

User Terminations

Too often when an employee leaves the company, the IT security administrator is the last to hear of it. It could be weeks before that employee's ID is terminated. HR should notify IT immediately of any employment terminations so that IDs can be disabled and deleted. When an employee does leave the company, there should be a procedure for moving her files, e-mail box, and so on to another employee's ID, so that there is no need for maintaining the terminated employee's ID.

When it comes to temps, interns, and contractors, HR may not even know when these individuals start and end their assignments. IDs for these users could be configured to be automatically disabled after a certain period of time, or they might be set up with a special naming convention so that security administrators can spot them easily and monitor their activity quickly.

Special Privilege IDs

Network and system managers usually have special IDs and passwords that provide carte blanche access to the system(s). These are often called root, supervisor, or administrator IDs/passwords. Because of their special access, only a handful of people might know these passwords. System administrators tend to ignore their own security rules and often set these passwords to never expire. It is important that these passwords be changed regularly, and changed immediately when someone who knows them leaves the company.

Access Reviews

Large environments might have thousands of users, and hundreds of thousands, if not millions, of files on their computer networks. Usually groups of files are set up that can only be accessed by certain groups of users—and vice versa. It is important that some type of user administrator review these access privileges every now and then (perhaps twice a year) to ensure that unauthorized users haven't mistakenly been given access to the wrong files.

Authorization Levels

Security administrators who process the requests to grant and revoke privileges, change access, and create IDs need to know who is authorized to make these requests. For example, the payroll manager may be authorized to determine who has access to the payroll files, and the VP of sales may be authorized to determine who has access to sales figures. It is up to the IT manager and the security administrator to make sure it is clear who has authority over what, and that requests are made in writing—usually via e-mail. HR should alert IT of new employees in advance of their start date so that IDs with basic privileges (e-mail, etc.) can be created.

Inform Users

Your users need to be made aware of security issues. For example, users should be aware of the security issues associated with storing a file on the LAN versus on their local hard drive. They should be aware of being able to put passwords on files that have sensitive information, and they should be aware of the risks of printing certain information to a network printer. Users should be in the habit of logging off at night or when they'll be away from their desk for an extended period of time.

Routine Maintenance

In addition to access reviews, as mentioned above, there are activities that should be performed regularly by security administrators in order to identify and minimize risks. IDs that haven't been used in a predefined period of time (say, two or three months) should be disabled. Many systems can report when unsuccessful login attempts have been made; these logs should be reviewed and investigated. Public areas of the LAN (places where all users have read and write access) should be regularly purged of files that have not been accessed in a while (not only does this free up space, but it might also remove files with confidential information that users placed there by mistake).

Software Patches and Updates

Security administrators should regularly check with their software vendors to obtain, and apply, any updates or patches that close security holes.

Virus Checking

All file servers and workstations should be regularly monitored for viruses. Not only must antivirus software be installed, but the "pattern files" must be updated regularly so that new viruses can be trapped and removed. With e-mail becoming the prevalent form for propagating viruses, it is important that the antivirus software be installed on mail servers to scan message attachments. See Section 13.4 for a more detailed discussion of viruses.

Physical Considerations

In addition to obvious building security (door locks, access cards), the physical access to the IT areas should be controlled. Access to the computer room or data center should be limited to those individuals that require it. Other IT areas (e.g., wiring closets) should be locked. Because of the concerns of confidential content, printed report distribution should be controlled, and an industrial-strength shredder should be available to dispose of output that is no longer needed.

13.3 Firewalls: What Are They?

A *firewall*, as the name implies, is a barrier. A firewall is a combination of hardware and software. From a hardware perspective, a firewall is sized like a small to medium-size server. It generally requires only a minimum amount of disk space since very little data is actually stored on the firewall and most of that data is very transient in nature. Depending on need and traffic activity, the horsepower of the firewall might be beefed up with additional memory or a faster processor. A key distinguishing feature of a firewall's configuration is that it must have two network cards. More about that topic below. (See also Section 11.1 for a brief introduction to firewalls.)

Firewall Software

The software that runs on the firewall device must be software that is specifically designed to operate and function as a firewall—for example, Microsoft's

Proxy Server, Novell's BorderManager, Gauntlet from Trusted Information Systems (now part of Network Associates, Inc.), or Firewall-1 from Checkpoint Software Technologies, Ltd. The software, operating system, and hardware all have to be compatible. (For a general discussion of intranets, extranets, and the Internet, see Chapter 11.)

The Two Sides of a Firewall

Since a firewall controls the flow of information between two networks, it is considered to have two sides: *the private side* (the one that connects to your network) and *the public side* (the one connected to the Internet). It is because of the dual connection that a firewall must have two network interface cards (NICs).

Without a firewall, your network is fully exposed to all the risks, perils, maliciousness, and unknowns of the Internet. With a firewall, you not only can control outsiders' access to your network and its resources, but you also control what kind of access your users on your network have to the public Internet.

Configuring a Firewall

In general, most firewalls are configured to allow very few types of data streams into your network. Typically, e-mail is allowed in so that your users can receive Internet mail. And, depending on users' needs, file transfers may be allowed.

On the other hand, the firewall may be configured *not* to allow other traffic types. For example, because of fears that it will clog up your network, you may not want to allow Real Audio data into your network. Similarly, you may be able to configure your network so that only certain users are allowed to surf the Web. Or you might want to configure it so that certain Web sites (such as porn sites) are unavailable to your users. You might configure the firewall to log user activity so that abuse can be monitored. The ability to configure the firewall to meet your needs is entirely the function of the firewall software, not the hardware. And, just as functionality can differ, so can ease of use. Some firewalls may require the use of complex command syntax to configure, while others may be configurable with a graphical user interface that you can point and click your way through.

You may be able to rent or lease a firewall from your ISP (Internet service provider), or they may have the resources and staff to implement one at your site and maintain it.

Proxy Services

A firewall usually provides proxy services. As the term proxy implies, this means that the firewall essentially stands in for your users when they want to access the Internet. When a user wants to access the Internet, the user's request is handed to the firewall, which then executes it. The advantage to this is that the proxy server appears—to the rest of the Internet—as the only source of requests from your network. So, for example, only the proxy server's IP address is seen by the Internet, as opposed to the IP addresses of your entire network. With a proxy server, it is virtually impossible to tell if there is a giant corporation behind the firewall, or a mom-and-pop operation.

13.4 Viruses: How Do I Protect My Systems from Them?

There are many types of viruses, including those known as "Trojan horses" and "worms." Viruses are any type of programming code that intentionally causes a system disruption. The disruption might be benign, or even amusing—like displaying the message "May the force be with you!" on your screen; or it might be terribly hostile and destructive—like erasing files or entire hard drives without notice.

Major Viruses in the News

While viruses had been one of those occupational annoyances for IT managers, during the late 1990s several high-visibility incidents proved to be a reminder of how much havoc they can wreak. Four examples of major viruses include "Melissa," "Chernobyl" (a.k.a. "CIH"), "ExplorerZip.Worm," and "I Love You." These viruses caused severe disruptions, system shutdowns, and loss of data for IT environments that lacked appropriate virus protections. All four of these viruses made the headlines and the evening new reports. If nothing else, they reminded IT managers of the very real threat of viruses and served as a wake-up call to review and revise virus protection programs, policies, and procedures.

Antivirus Software

Most antivirus products run on a variety of operating system platforms. The most important thing to remember about antivirus software is that it must be used properly to be effective. Also, antivirus software cannot be used on an ad hoc basis—it needs to be a constant part of any IT environment's operations. Every workstation and server in your environment where files can be stored needs to be regularly scanned for viruses. Fortunately, the software offerings make it almost effortless for these products to run continuously with virtually no user intervention.

There are numerous products available (e.g., Symantec's Norton AntiVirus, Network Associates' Total Virus Defense Product Suite, and Intel's LANDesk, etc.) to scan files and systems and to detect and remove viruses. Since hackers around the world are constantly programming and releasing new viruses "into the wild," vendors of antivirus software must continuously update their products to scan for all the latest viruses. To do this, vendors regularly update the "pattern file" that their software uses. The pattern file contains all the information that the actual antivirus program uses to look for viruses. Pattern files are sometimes called signature files since each virus has its own telltale mark, or signature.

Updating Software

One of the often-neglected areas in managing virus prevention in an environment is the regular update of the pattern files. It is important to remember that if these data files are not updated regularly, you are leaving your environment fully exposed (as if you had no protection) to newly created viruses that are released into the wild.

Some software (e.g., Network Associates' McAfee product) have eased the burden of pattern updates by allowing you to schedule regular and unattended downloads of the latest pattern file from the Internet. Other alternatives might be to regularly download the most current pattern file to a central server, and then have it copied (via electronic distribution software, or perhaps via the network's login script) to the individual workstations.

Protect Your E-mail Server

When considering antivirus strategies, it is important not to overlook your e-mail server. However, since e-mail messages are stored in special databases and files, standard antivirus software may not detect viruses that are in e-mail attachments. Many vendors offer special flavors of their antivirus software that scan through your e-mail messages as they flash through your network, and scan the message attachments for viruses. Popular packages include Groupshield from McAfee, and Norton AntiVirus from Symantec.

Spam (junk mail) can be a nuisance as it can clog networks and chew up valuable mail server resources. Usually, mail servers and/or firewalls can be configured to ignore or discard messages from certain domains that are known to be spam sources.

Protect Your Workstations and Servers

On workstations, the virus software will usually display a message to the user when a virus is found. The software will first alert the user that a virus has been detected, and then prompt the user for what kind of action to take (clean the virus, delete the file, ignore, etc.). However, on a file server, there is often no user per se for the antivirus software to take direction from. So, for file servers, the software is often configured at the time of installation for what action to take. Typically, the virus software will automatically remove the virus, if it can.

Or it might move the file to a special area on the server where the network administrator can review it and decide what to do.

With antivirus software for e-mail messages, the software might allow the original message, but without the infected file attachment, to reach the addressee. Or it might clean the virus from the software, but send a message to the user about the action taken.

In a large environment, standard virus defenses might automatically remove hundreds of viruses from files and message attachments in a single day. It is important that your virus software be configured to log all activity so that you can periodically review it to see the amount of virus activity in your environment, and assure yourself that your defenses are working properly.

Many antivirus software vendors have offerings for multiple platforms (e.g., Netware, Windows, Unix) and different functions (end user workstation, file server, firewall, e-mail server).

Hoaxes and Chain Letters

Not quite the security threat of viruses or hacker attacks, hoaxes are often an enormous burden for IT security. A hoax is generally an e-mail that warns that user of a nonexistent virus. The e-mail tells the user to forward the warning to all friends, relatives, and coworkers. As a result, the e-mail network becomes saturated as each user receives the e-mail and forwards it to tens or hundreds of their associates. The growth can be exponential.

Other hoaxes have been messages to warn people about nonexistent legislation that might increase taxes, or invade their rights to privacy, and so on. There have also been e-mail chain letters that claim a user will get money, or good fortune, if they forward the message to others.

Some of the more famous hoaxes include Good Times (warning of a nonexistent virus), Bill 602P (warning of nonexistent legislation to tax e-mail), and Gap giveaway (information about a nonexistent promotion by the Gap to give away merchandise to those who forwarded the e-mail).

In dealing with hoaxes and chain letters, the security administrator should keep users informed and educated. Users should be told that if they receive any virus warnings or chain letters that they should be forwarded first to the IT security administrator who can search various Web-based resources to determine if it is indeed a hoax.

13.5 Suspicious Activity: How Do I Monitor It?

With all the concern about security for information technology, it is reasonable to ask the question: "Just how far can I go in protecting my environment?" Many tools are available to monitor activity within an environment. However, just because the tools are available doesn't mean it is proper, fair, moral, or legal to use them as you might like to. Of particular concern in this area is the fear of violation of an individual's right to privacy.

Disclosing Your Activities

Statutes, precedents, legislation, and case law lags behind the advances in technology. And, while many issues are still vague and cloudy, there is one guideline that seems to serve as a firm foundation for IT managers: "full disclosure." If you are going to monitor activity within your environment, it is important to let your users know.

Many corporations now include such statements in their employee handbook or policy book. Typically, a company might say that virtually all employee activity may be monitored. This might include video surveillance, monitoring phone conversations, and monitoring computer usage—including the content of e-mail and files. Computer monitoring is on the rise, with 27% of U.S. corporations reporting that they store and review e-mail messages, and 21% that they store and review computer files. (Source: *Computerworld*, 6/28/99, p. 14, reporting on a 1/99 survey by American Management Association).

Intrusion Detection

Many of your network resources can track, log, and inform you of suspicious activity on the network. Firewall logs can report attempts to breach security and give you information (like IP addresses) that may help you track down the source. Your network operating system (NOS) and application software may be able to tell you when there have been too many attempts to login using an incorrect password. Viewing logs for "normal" activity at unusual times may also help you identify intrusions.

You should scan these logs for patterns of activity. Perhaps one type of security attack is being used far more than others. Or perhaps there is a common source address for the attacks. Your tools can only report data about the attacks to you. You'll need to put on your detective hat to interpret the data and investigate.

Using network-monitoring protocols (discussed in Chapter 10), you may be able to configure your network resources to send alerts (via e-mail or beepers, for example) when a certain type of security intrusion is detected.

Monitoring Employee Activity on the Web

The issue of employee monitoring by companies has become critical. It is important for IT managers to consult with their company's Legal and Human Resources departments, as well as coordinate directly with the executive team, to determine exactly what the company's monitoring policies and activities should be. Accountability is key here: when the legal aspects of technical decisions become this big, don't try to go it alone because the consequences can be too large. Make sure you have help from other parts of the company and that the overall decisions are those that key players in the organization agree with.

With the recent explosion of Internet surfing activity, many companies now announce that they will monitor employees' activity on the Web, including time spent on the Web, sites visited, and files downloaded. However, many companies are also loath to appear too Big Brotherish or to create a distrusting atmosphere by frequently snooping. (The legality of these activities is still not completely decided either.)

Frequently, just announcing that activity will be monitored can deter inappropriate usage. Other subtle reminders to employees that their activities might not go unnoticed can also be effective. For example, many companies have set up their firewalls to require an ID and password, so that individual surfing can be tracked. Each time the user enters their ID when they want to surf the Web, it serves as a reminder that their activity is being noted.

Other companies have configured their firewalls to prevent employees from surfing to sites that contain patently offensive material. If your firewall can generate usage reports, you can contact the most active users and say you were concerned that their high usage is due to problems they are experiencing. This benign inquiry can be a subtle reminder that their high usage has not gone unnoticed.

There is still a large amount of debate if the problem of employees wasting time on the Internet is an IT problem or a supervisory problem. IT departments frequently argue that if an employee is prone to wasting time, they'll find another way to do it if Web access is blocked, and that the employee's supervisor needs to do a better job of making sure that employee is working. Sometimes, an analogy is drawn between an employee using the Web for personal activity and using the phone for personal calls. Both can be abused.

Additional hardware and software tools allow IT to view the traffic crossing the network, as well as to have a "virtual" view of a user's PC. This functionality, called "remote control," allows a privileged IT user to see on her monitor exactly what appears (as well as what is being typed) at another user's PC. In fact, the IT user could literally use her own mouse and keyboard to take control of the user's workstation. Most often, this type of remote control functionality is used by Help Desk staffs as an effective way of helping users without having to go to the user's desk. Along these lines, many technologies that allow users to dial into the office for remote access also provide the administrator with a way of monitoring the remote users' activities, including keystrokes and screen views.

Suggested Guidelines

The courts will be deciding what is appropriate monitoring in the cyber-world for years to come. However, corporate environments can best protect themselves by making several policies and guidelines clear to employees:

- Computer usage, including contents of e-mail, Internet activity, file contents, and so on, can and will be monitored.

- All hardware and software belongs to the company and should only be used for appropriate business activity.

- Inappropriate use of company property can lead to disciplinary action, up to and including termination of employment.

It is important to remember that preventing employees from visiting XXX sites and using e-mail to distribute chain letters and jokes is also of serious concern to your Human Resources and Legal departments. Employers should know that the contents of computer files will be used as incriminating evidence in lawsuits—not only lawsuits about monopolistic business practices, but also ones regarding sexual harassment, racial discrimination, and misuse of company resources.

13.6 Security Breach: How Do I Handle One?

When there is a security breach, it is important to react quickly. Most likely, you'll find that a breach in security is not physical—that is, no one has broken into your computer room. Instead, most security breaches are virtual, such as a stolen password.

First, you need to consider why you suspect that there is a security breach. There might be some telltale signs like altered files, changed passwords, or logs that show activity that can't be confirmed by authorized users. Or the breach might be more hostile, like an unauthorized change to your Web pages or crashing your server. Often, a security breach might be a result of user carelessness—like leaving their PC unattended but logged into the network, which is tantamount to leaving their password on a Post-it note attached to their monitor. Alternatively, some thought has to be given to the possibility of "hostile threats," where someone is intentionally trying to do some type of damage to the environment.

Steps to Take after a Breach

When there is a breach in security, there are several steps you can take:

- Change passwords
- Shut down the environment and restart it
- Contact key vendors
- Contact authorities
- Keep your eyes open
- Stay alert

Change Passwords

At the very least you want to change the passwords for all privileged users. Although this can be an arduous process, it is something that should be done regularly, even when there is no fear of a breach. And depending on the severity of the breach, it may be worthwhile to change the passwords for all user IDs as well. Depending on your software, each user can be forced to change their own password if the administrator simply resets the password expiration dates.

Shut Down the Environment and Restart It

If the "outsider" is already logged into your network while you're changing passwords, it is equivalent to changing your door locks while the burglar is in the house—you need to kick him out first so that the new lock (password) will be between you and him. While this is a relatively simple procedure, it can be quite disruptive to the environment. However, if there is reason to believe that the security breach was "localized" (i.e., perhaps only one server or one technology type), then the disruption of restarting the environment can be limited.

Contact Key Vendors

You should contact the vendors of key technologies that are responsible for securing your environment (network operating system, firewalls, Web servers, etc.) and make sure that you have the latest versions, patches, and security fixes for their products installed in your environment. While security on the Web is improving, it seems that the IT trade press is regularly reporting on hackers discovering new security flaws (which are usually fixed by vendors within hours or days, but only if you download and install the fix).

Contact Authorities

As computers have become an integral part of our society, various organizations (including state and federal authorities) have become increasingly involved in identifying security threats, preventive measures, and prosecution of perpetrators. The "Further References" section at the end of this chapter includes several organizations you can notify if you suspect your environment has been attacked.

Keep Your Eyes Open

After the breach, you want to gather as much information as possible to try to pinpoint the time and method of the breach. It is entirely likely you may not be able to do this, but you may be able to rule out certain areas as suspects and become more watchful of others. To do this, you might want to review hardware and software logs for errors, warnings, or specific events. You should also alert the entire IT staff to the breach, so that they can be on the alert and report any unusual system occurrences. Very often, once a breach is discovered, and the staff is notified, they will remember some unexplainable oddities and anomalies that occurred. It is entirely possible that one of these may help you narrow down the time or location of the breach.

When investigating a breach, it is important to try to create a chronology of events. Discussions with users, log files, date and time stamps, and so on will help you do this. This chronology should be as detailed as possible. It may help serve as a useful comparison if there are other breaches, or it could prove to be a useful document if you feel the need to bring in security experts.

Although it is like closing the barn door after the horse got out, a security breach is an excellent time to review security procedures and policies, and to remind all users about the importance of computer security. Just as the Melissa virus in 1999 and the well-publicized denial of service attacks in 2000 resensitized the world to the importance of rigorous virus protocols, a security breach can be just the justification you need, as an IT manager, to invest in security resources.

Stay Alert

The world of computer security is constantly changing. It is vital to stay aware of what's going on. To help you do so, you should be aware of several organizations dedicated to tracking computer-security related events:

- CERT (*www.cert.org*)
- National Security Agency (*www.nsa.gov*)
- Center for Education and Research in Information Assurance and Security (*www.cerias.purdue.edu/*)
- Federal Computer Incident Response Capability (*www.fedcirc.gov/*)
- National Infrastructure Protection Center (*www.fbi.gov/nipc/welcome.htm*)

13.7 Further References

Web Pages

Firewalls

- *www.checkpoint.com/*
- *www.microsoft.com/proxy/default.asp*
- *www.novell.com/bordermanager/*
- *www.pgp.com/asp_set/products/tns/gauntlet.asp*

Viruses and Hoaxes

- *www.mcafeeb2b.com*
- *www.cert.org/other_sources/viruses.html*
- *www.intel.com/network/products/landesk/index.htm*
- *www.symantec.com/nav/indexB.html*

Security Resources

- *www.cerias.purdue.edu/*
- *www.cert.org*
- *www.fbi.gov/nipc/welcome.htm*
- *www.fedcirc.gov/*
- *www.nsa.gov*

Articles and Books

- *Computerworld,* June 28, 1999, page 14, reporting on January 1999 survey by American Management Association.
- Amoroso, Edward G., *Intrusion Detection: An Introduction to Internet Surveillance, Correlation, Trace Back, Traps, and Response,* Intrusion.net Books, 1999.
- Bace, Rebecca Gurley, *Intrusion Detection,* MacMillan, 1999.
- Brenton, Chris, *Mastering Network Security,* Mass Market, 1998.
- Goncalves, Marcus (Editor), *Firewalls: A Complete Guide,* McGraw-Hill, 1999.
- Kovacich, Gerald, *The Information Systems Security Officer's Guide: Establishing and Managing an Information Protection Program,* Butterworth-Heinemann, 1998.
- Krause, Micki, and Harold F. Tipton (Editors), *Information Security Management Handbook, Fourth Edition,* CRC-Auerbach, 1999.
- Ludwig, Mark A., *The Giant Black Book of Computer Viruses,* American Eagle Publications, 1998.
- McClure, Stuart, Joel Scambray, and George Kurtz, *Hacking Exposed: Network Security Secrets and Solutions,* McGraw-Hill, 1999.
- Northcult, Stephen, *Network Intrusion Detection: An Analyst's Handbook,* New Riders, 1999.

Disaster Recovery

CHAPTER FOURTEEN

What You Will Learn

- Why you need a disaster recovery plan, what components should be in it, specific contact information, and documentation you will require

- The various levels of disasters

- How to determine where everyone will go when disaster strikes

- How to plan for retrieval of off-site backups

- Some key hardware availability issues

- Why a disaster planning/recovery committee should include companywide membership

- How to keep your disaster plan current

- Why regional and catastrophic outages are different

Introduction

Disaster recovery is like buying insurance; you're planning for the worst, but all the time hoping that it doesn't happen. IT disasters come in all shapes and sizes—from easy-to-repair hardware failures, to blizzards that cause power outages, to terrorist attacks. You can't plan for every possible scenario, but you can still plan.

14.1 Disaster Recovery: Why Do I Need It?

IT environments are replete with ways and technologies to deal with outages and failures: redundant servers, transaction logs, dial-up lines in case of leased line failures, tape backups, RAID disk drives, and on and on. The problem with these is that each can only handle the failure of a specific component. This leaves IT managers with the issue of what to do if the entire environment fails.

Be it fire, flood, earthquake, terrorism, weather, or the proverbial plane falling on the building, there is the remote chance that your organization could be completely inoperative for a significant length of time. As an IT manager, you need to plan on how you would restore services.

Two Key Items You Need to Know before Planning

The extent to which you have to, or can, plan for a disaster is primarily dependent on two items:

- How much your organization depends on IT for its day-to-day operations
- How much money your organization is willing to invest in a disaster recovery plan

Because the above items can vary so widely, there is no boilerplate disaster recovery template to use. And once you start thinking about all the things that could go wrong, it becomes an insurmountable task to try to plan for every possibility. However, we'll discuss some of the major factors that go into planning for disaster recovery.

14.2 Levels of Disaster: What Are They?

Not all disasters are created equally. Different types of disasters have different impacts.

Levels

You should think about planning for different levels of disaster. For example:

- A blizzard may prevent your employees from getting to work for several days.
- Because of a major crime at or near your facilities, police do not allow access for an extended period of time.
- An earthquake or flood causes extensive damage to your organization's offices, perhaps resulting in its virtual destruction.

Responses

Each of the above would have different responses.

- In the first scenario, loss of access for a few days may be entirely tolerable, or the use of remote dial-in facilities for your users could be sufficient.
- In the second scenario, it might be necessary for the organization's key personnel to find temporary office space for a few weeks.
- And, in the third scenario, the organization would have to virtually rebuild itself it at a new location.

14.3 Disaster Recovery Plan: What Components Should Be in It?

If you expect to have any hope for any level of success in the event of a disaster, there are several key items you must have and should include in your disaster recovery plan:

- **Contact information:** Ways to contact key personnel, customers, vendors, and so on (home phones, beepers, and cell phones).
- **Documentation:** Of the existing environment, procedures for declaring a disaster, procedures for re-establishing services in a disaster recovery mode, procedures for contacting key resources, and identification of disaster recovery resources.
- **Real estate:** Where people will meet, and where a temporary data center will be established if the organization's offices are suddenly out of commission.

- **Off-site storage of backups:** If your facility is destroyed, or inaccessible, you'll want to be sure you have an up-to-date set of backup tapes at an off-site facility that you can retrieve.

- **Hardware availability:** You want to make sure that you can get replacement hardware if yours is destroyed. This list includes servers, workstations, routers, hubs, and so on.

- **Disaster recovery committee:** Identified members from key parts of the organization that can make decisions in the event of an emergency, and communicate activities and plans to the rest of the organization.

- **Regular updating and testing:** Your environment changes regularly (technology, people, needs, etc.). You need to regularly test and update your disaster recovery plan to make sure that it retains its value.

Each of these items is discussed in more detail in the following sections.

14.4 Contact Information: Who Do I Need to Contact?

In the event of a disaster, there are two key groups of contacts you will need:

- Those within your company
- Those outside the company

Within the Company

You need a way of contacting key people in the organization; at the very least this should include home phone numbers, but it can also include cell phones, beeper numbers, and personal e-mail addresses. Ideally, some sort of phone tree should be established as a way of quickly disseminating information throughout the organization. The contact information should also indicate those that will be the key decision makers in the event of a disaster—for example, the people who will decide that the plan needs to be invoked.

Develop a company-specific list of individuals you will need should an emergency arise. This list is certainly not limited to IT. It probably includes executives, managers, and directors from every department.

Outside the Company

You will also need a list of contacts for people and companies outside your organization. Figure 14.1 on the next page has a suggested chart for this type of information.

Item	Data
Keep a list of key IT vendors, suppliers, providers, and partners	
• Phone numbers and e-mail addresses	
• Tech support numbers	
• Account representative contact information	
• Identifying information (your account number, customer ID, etc.)	
Location, map, and directions to any facilities to be used during a disaster recovery • If you're contracting with a disaster recovery company to provide space, the document should include the procedures necessary for notifying the company that you have declared an emergency.	
Information for recalling backup tapes from off-site storage	
• Name and phone number for storage facility	
• Directions for identifying most recent backup tapes	
• Identifying information (customer ID, authorization codes, etc.)	
Information regarding any providers of emergency equipment • If you're contracting with a disaster recovery company to provide equipment, be sure to include procedures for notifying the company that you have declared an emergency, and for requesting equipment be made available to you.	
Lists of nearby hotels • In case it is inconvenient, or impossible, for personnel to return home during the recovery effort.	

Figure 14.1 Suggested Contact List

14.5 Documentation: What Do I Need?

Thorough and up-to-date disaster recovery documentation is often the hallmark of an effective disaster recovery plan. Although the document can be distributed in electronic form (Web based, word processing document), it must also be distributed on hardcopy. After all, in the event of a disaster, there is no certainty that the electronic version will be available. Every key member of the team should have two copies of the disaster recovery documentation—one copy at their office and one in their home—since there is no guarantee that a disaster will happen between 9 and 5 on a business day. Lastly, keep a copy with your off-site backup tapes.

The disaster recovery plan document will become an indispensable resource. Memories fail, particularly in crisis situations. In fact, aside from your backup tapes, your documentation may be the only resource from your facility that is available to you during a disaster. As such, it is in your best interest to make it as useful as possible by including as much information as possible in this document. This should include documentation about the existing environment and procedures (e.g., LAN schematics, procedures for doing a restore from backup, data center inventory).

14.6 Real Estate Issues: Where Will Everyone Go When Disaster Strikes?

One of the first questions that has to be considered in regard to disaster recovery planning is "Where?" If you are unable to use your organization's facilities, where will everyone go when disaster strikes? If your organization is very small, you might be able get away with operating for a small time out of someone's residence. A slightly larger organization might be able to use a meeting or banquet room at a nearby hotel—assuming that the same disaster hasn't wiped out these facilities. Other alternatives might include a nearby branch office of your organization, or perhaps the office of a sister, subsidiary, or parent company.

However, if your IT organization is of any size, you are probably going to need specialized facilities to rebuild—facilities with sufficient space, air-conditioning, electricity, telecommunications resources, and so on. This may be the case even if you are only supporting a portion of your normal operation, even for just an interim period.

There are many companies that offer disaster recovery facilities. They can generally tailor their offerings to your needs, perhaps just providing space, or at the other extreme, also providing specified computer hardware, telecommunications, perhaps even some staffing in case disaster strikes. There are several disaster recovery service providers listed in the "Further References" section of this chapter.

Of course, the ultimate in disaster recovery facilities is for an organization to maintain its own standby site with redundant hardware. In the most critical situation, the standby site is always live, with a mirrored copy of the database, applications, and so on.

Specific Issues

When looking at companies that provide disaster recovery facilities, you have to consider several issues:

- Proximity to your location
- Costs
- Number of clients
- Services that can be provided

Each of these items is discussed in more detail below.

Proximity to Your Location

You want a nearby location, but not so close that the facility is likely to be hit by the same disaster that affects yours. You may need to consider a facility that is reachable by mass transit if you're in a large metropolitan area where not everyone has their own car.

Costs

The more services and facilities you want to be ready for your needs, the more it will cost. Contracts for disaster recovery usually last at least two years and are billed monthly. However, there are several aspects to disaster recovery fees:

- Standby fees: the monthly fees you pay to have contracted facilities available for your use
- Activation fee: a fee you pay when you decide that you have a disaster that warrants use of the facilities
- Use fee: the rate (weekly, monthly) that you pay while you are using the facilities during a disaster
- Test fee: a fee that is paid when you want to make use of the facilities while testing your disaster recovery plans

Number of Clients

You want to make sure that the provider you are working with hasn't contracted with more clients than it can provide services for. If there is a regional disaster, and all the provider's customers suddenly need to use the facilities, will there be enough to go around?

Other Required Services

Space, hardware, staff, telecommunications, air-conditioning, electricity? Don't forget basics like furniture, phones, and so on.

14.7 Retrieval of Off-Site Backups: How Do I Plan for That?

If you need to activate a disaster recovery plan, you want to make sure that you can get your company's data up and available. Most likely, you'll have to do some sort of restore from your backup tapes. If your regular facility is destroyed or inaccessible, you'll have to retrieve the backup tapes from your off-site storage vendor.

In order to be able to get those tapes, you'll need several items:

- Contact information for your off-site location
- A way of identifying which set of tapes you want retrieved
- A customer ID, account number, and possibly a password as a way of identifying yourself to the off-site location as someone authorized to request that the tapes be retrieved
- The address, and probably directions, of where the tapes should be delivered (you most likely won't want them delivered to your usual facility).

Getting the tapes is the first step. Then you have to begin the restore process. You'll need to make sure that you have access to compatible hardware and software that can read those tapes, and that you have procedures for doing the restore.

14.8 Hardware Availability: What Are Some Key Issues?

If your regular computer hardware is unusable for any reason (e.g., power outage or destruction of your facilities), you'll have to get your hands on some computer hardware before you can even begin rebuilding your environment.

Size of Your Environment

The smaller and more generic your environment is, the more solutions you'll have. For example, if your environment is based on Intel PCs and servers, you may be able to rely on local retailers or your regular reseller. Or you can contract with your disaster recovery facility to keep a quantity of these units on hand for you.

With larger or more complex environments, it will be more difficult (and more expensive) to make sure the equipment will be available. You may want to purchase some of this equipment yourself to have in an emergency, or your disaster recovery provider may do this and pass the cost on to you. Your manufacturer may also have options and provisions available to allow for you to receive emergency delivery of predetermined equipment in the event of a disaster.

Duplicating Your Entire Environment

In case of a disaster, you may not need to duplicate your entire environment. You probably just want to plan for bringing up the systems that are the most critical to the continued operation and survival of the organization. To make your recovery operation as smooth as possible, you'll want to ensure that you're using equipment as close as possible to your existing environment. The middle of a crisis is not the time to find out that the emergency tape drive you have is not compatible with the backup tapes you use, or that you don't have the proper drivers for the network interface cards you're using, or that your application software has to be recompiled before it will run on the hardware you have.

14.9 Disaster Planning/Recovery Committee: Companywide Membership

Although it relies heavily on IT, disaster planning and recovery is not the function of IT alone. It requires the involvement of virtually every department (finance, office services, manufacturing, human resources, etc.).

Specific Issues

- How would the warehouse or factory manufacture and ship products?
- How would the Accounting department make sure that the company suppliers are paid, and that receivables were collected?
- Could payroll continue to pay employees during the disaster?
- What would the Sales department do? Could/should they continue to try to sell products? How would they reassure customers?
- How would customers, suppliers, partners, and clients be kept abreast of the situation?

Because of questions like these, and many more, it is important that disaster recovery planning not be limited to IT alone.

The plan should be drafted, reviewed, and approved by a committee with members of departments throughout your company, and specific activities within the plan should include necessary activities with these various members. A subset of this committee can serve, in the event of a disaster, as a decision-making body—one that provides leadership and guidance to the rest of the organization for the duration of the disaster recovery effort.

14.10 Testing and Updating: Is My Disaster Plan Current?

A disaster recovery plan is something that needs to be regularly reviewed and updated. The items in Figure 14.2 on the next page identify items that should be routinely reviewed and updated.

14.11 Regional and Catastrophic Outages: Why Are These Different?

Regional Outages

Many disasters are often a result of the force of nature—earthquake, hurricane, snow, and so on. As such, if your organization suffers a disaster, it is entirely likely that many other organizations in your geographic area will also suffer, and they may also be scrambling for the recovery resources that you are planning to rely on:

- The local computer retailer may be rushed by other organizations trying to get their hands on some hardware.
- Hotel rooms may be sold out.
- Telephone companies will be working round-the-clock to get regular services restored—so your plans to install temporary dial-up services may not pan out.
- The very vendors and service providers you had planned on may not be functioning because of the same disaster you are suffering from.

A key issue to keep in mind in this regard when crafting your disaster recovery plan is to incorporate some nonlocal options for each category in the plan.

Is the emergency contact list current?

Check the list to verify it does not contain individuals who have left the company, work in other locations or departments, or are no longer relevant to the plan.

Are my own internal safety nets still working?

Often, IT may install redundant facilities to use in case of emergency (like dial-up lines to replace a failed leased line). However, when an emergency strikes the fallback facility can't do its job because it isn't working either, perhaps because it hasn't been used in so long it's fallen into disrepair, or, as in the case of the dial-up line, perhaps it was disconnected because someone stopped paying the bills. Regular testing of these facilities is important—a spare tire is of no use if there's no air in it.

Is the disaster recovery provider keeping stock of current hardware for us? What about the now-obsolete equipment that was contracted for three years ago?

You should be tracking the status of all your equipment anyway, and keeping your disaster plan current is an excellent cross-check mechanism.

Can our backup tapes be read by the emergency equipment we plan to use?

Do we have copies of the media and installation instructions for requisite software (operating system, backup software, etc.) that may have to be installed before we can even begin restoring from tapes?

Again, you should know this anyway, and verifying for disaster plan reasons gives you another reason for looking it up.

Are the dial-in numbers for our partners and suppliers still correct and working? Have area codes changed?

Area codes and phone numbers change faster than ever; periodic checks of this data can be very, very useful in an emergency.

Do we know the current critical passwords that will be needed?

Figure 14.2 Disaster Recovery Items for Regularly Reviewing and Updating

Catastrophic Disasters

As a final reminder that even the best of intentions and planning can go awry, it is important to remember that in the event of a truly catastrophic disaster, employees' priorities will quickly shift from trying to aid their employer to trying to aid their families.

14.12 Further References

Web Sites

- *www.capsbrs.com/* (CAPS Computer Alternative Processing Sites)
- *www.comdisco.com/products/business/* (Comdisco)
- *www.drj.com* (Disaster Recovery Journal)
- *www.drs.net* (DRS Disaster Recovery Services)
- *www.hp.com/ssg/recovery/index.html* (HP Business Recovery Services)
- *www.recovery.sungard.com/* (SunGard Recovery Services)
- *www.rentsys.com/* (Rentsys Recovery Services)
- *www.weyerhaeuser.com/disaster-recovery/* (Weyerhaeuser Recovery Systems)
- *www-1.ibm.com/services/continuity/recover1.nsf* (IBM Business Continuity and Recovery Services)

Articles and Books

- Butler, Janet G., and Poul Badura, *Contingency Planning and Disaster Recovery: Protecting Your Organization's Resources,* Computer Technology Research Corporation, 1997.
- Jaffe, Brian D., "Wishing You All a Successful Recovery," *PC Week,* September 28, 1998.
- Jaffe, Brian D., "Double Your Pleasure and Halve Your Stress," *PC Week,* August 16, 1999. *http://www.zdnet.com/pcweek/stories/columns /0,4351,2312049,00.html.*
- Marcus, Evan, *Blueprints for High Availability: Designing Resilient Distributed Systems,* Hal Stern, 2000.
- Schreider, Tari, *Encyclopedia of Disaster Recovery, Security & Risk Management,* Crucible Publishing Works, 1998.
- Toigo, Jon William, and Margaret Romano Toigo (Illustrator), *Disaster Recovery Planning: Strategies for Protecting Critical Information Assets,* Prentice Hall, 1999.

Bibliography

Web Sites

- *www.antivirus.com* (virus software vendor)
- *www.baan.com* (ERP software vendor)
- *www.bsa.org* (software licensing and piracy)
- *www.caldera.com* (Linux distribution)
- *www.capsbrs.com/* (CAPS Computer Alternative Processing Sites)
- *www.cerias.purdue.edu/*
- *www.cert.org*
- *www.cert.org/other_sources/viruses.html*
- *www.checkpoint.com/*
- *www.cnet.com* (online publisher)
- *www.comdisco.com/products/business/* (Comdisco)
- *www.computerworld.com/home/features.nsf/all/980914tcolinks* (This link has a great number of asset management and TCO links.)
- *www.digidata.com* (RAID controllers)
- *www.drj.com* (Disaster Recovery Journal)
- *www.drs.net* (DRS Disaster Recovery Services)
- *www.ebanex.net/resources/benefits/can-ecommerce-help.htm* (about e-commerce)
- *www.epinions.com/cmsw-isp* (comments about ISPs)
- *www.eudora.com* (groupware vendor)
- *www.fbi.gov/nipc/welcome.htm*
- *www.fedcirc.gov/*
- *www.gartner.com* (for Gartner's research analyst reports on TCO)
- *www.helpdeskinst.com* (Help Desk Institute)
- *www.hp.com/ssg/recovery/index.html* (HP Business Recovery Services)
- *www.ibm.com/services/continuity/recover1.nsf* (IBM Business Continuity and Recovery Services)

- *www.icann.org* (information about registering domain names)
- *www.idg.com* (online publisher)
- *www.imagecast.com* (disk cloning software)
- *www.intel.com* (virus software vendor)
- *www.intel.com/network/products/landesk/index.htm*
- *www.isoc.org/internet/history* (brief history of the Internet)
- *www.jdedwards.com* (ERP software vendor)
- *www.linux.org* (Linux resources)
- *www.linux.org/info/gnu.html* (GNU General Public License)
- *www.linuxresources.com* (Linux resources)
- *www.lotus.com/home.nsf/welcome/notes* (ERP software vendor)
- *www.mcafeeb2b.com*
- *www.metagroup.com* (for Meta's research analyst reports on TCO)
- *www.microsoft.com/exchange/* (groupware vendor)
- *www.microsoft.com/proxy/default.asp*
- *www.nai.com* (virus software vendor)
- *www.novell.com/bordermanager/*
- *www.novell.com/groupwise/* (groupware vendor)
- *www.nsa.gov*
- *www.oracle.com* (ERP software vendor)
- *www.oreilly.com* (online and print publisher)
- *www.peoplesoft.com* (ERP software vendor)
- *www.pgp.com/asp_set/products/tns/gauntlet.asp*
- *www.planetit.com* (online publisher)
- *www.pmi.org* (Project Management Institute)
- *www.powerquest.com* (disk cloning software)
- *www.recovery.sungard.com* (SunGard Recovery Services)
- *www.redhat.com* (Linux distribution)
- *www.rentsys.com* (Rentsys Recovery Services)
- *www.salary.com* (salary survey data)
- *www.sap.com* (ERP software vendor)
- *www.siia.net* (software licensing and piracy)
- *www.slackware.com* (Linux distribution)
- *www.symantec* (virus software vendor)

- *www.symantec.com* (disk cloning software)
- *www.symantec.com/nav/indexB.html*
- *www.tekcheck.com* (candidate skills testing)
- *www.thedirectory.com* (resource for ISPs in your area)
- *www.thelist.internet.com* (resource for ISPs in your area)
- *www.veritas.com* (software distribution tool)
- *www.wageweb.com* (salary survey data)
- *www.webopedia.com* (online encyclopedia)
- *www.weyerhaeuser.com/disaster-recovery/* (Weyerhaeuser Recovery Systems)
- *www.whatis.com* (online encyclopedia)
- *www.windowware.com* (batch automation software)
- *www.worldwidewait.com* (comments about ISPs)
- *www.zdnet.com* (online publisher)

Articles and Books

- Amoroso, Edward G., *Intrusion Detection: An Introduction to Internet Surveillance, Correlation, Trace Back, Traps, and Response,* Intrusion.net Books, 1999.
- Anderson, Christa, and Mark Minasi, *Mastering Local Area Networks,* Sybex, 1999.
- Bace, Rebecca Gurley, *Intrusion Detection,* MacMillan, 1999.
- Baker, Sunny, & Kim Baker, *OnTime/On Budget: A Step-by-Step Guide for Managing Any Project,* Prentice Hall, 1992.
- Bayles, Deborah L., *Extranets: Building the Business-to-Business Web,* Prentice Hall, 1998.
- Bender, Stephen A., *Managing Projects Well,* Butterworth-Heinemann, 1998.
- Bernard, Ryan, *The Corporate Intranet,* John Wiley and Sons, 1997.
- Brenton, Chris, *Mastering Network Security,* Mass Market, 1998.
- Broadwell, Martin M., and Carol Broadwell Dietrich, *The New Supervisor: How to Thrive in Your First Year as a Manager,* Perseus, 1998.
- Bruton, Noel, *How to Manage the I.T. Helpdesk, Digital Press, 1997.*
- Bultinck, Christina, *The Recruiter's Bible,* Infokey, 1998.
- Butler, Janet G., and Poul Badura, *Contingency Planning and Disaster Recovery: Protecting Your Organization's Resources,* Computer Technology Research Corporation, 1997.

- Bysinger, Bill, and Ken Knight (Contributor), *Investing in Information Technology: A Decision-Making Guide for Business and Technology Managers,* John Wiley and Sons, 1996.

- Chaffey, Dave, *Groupware, Workflow and Intranets: Reengineering the Enterprise with Collaborative Software,* Digital Press, 1998.

- Clewett, Annette, Dana Franklin (Contributor), and Ann McCown (Contributor), *Network Resource Planning for SAP R/3, BAAN IV, and PEOPLESOFT: A Guide to Planning Enterprise Applications,* McGraw-Hill, 1998.

- Copeland, Lee, "Big Three Automakers Join Forces Online," *Computerworld,* February 25, 2000.

- Cortada, James W., *Best Practices in Information Technology: How Corporations Get the Most Value from Exploiting Their Digital Investments,* Prentice Hall, 1997.

- Czegel, Barbara, *Help Desk Practitioner's Handbook*, Wiley, 1999.

- Czegel, Barbara, *Running an Effective Help Desk,* 2nd edition, Wiley, 1998.

- Dawson, Charlie K., *The Complete Guide to Technical Recruiting,* Management Advantage, 1999.

- Doyle, Michael, *Making Meetings Work,* Berkeley Publishing Group, 1993.

- Droms, William G., *Finance and Accounting for Nonfinancial Managers: All the Basics You Need to Know,* Perseus, 1998.

- Evans, Philip, and Thomas S. Wurster, *Blown to Bits: How the New Economics of Information Transforms Strategy,* Harvard Business School Press, 1999.

- Fein, Richard, *101 Hiring Mistakes Employers Make . . . and How to Avoid Them,* Impact Publishers, 2000.

- Fowler, Dennis, *Virtual Private Networks,* Morgan Kaufmann Publishers, 1999.

- Finney, Robert G., *Office Finances Made Easy: A Get-Started Guide to Budgets, Purchasing, and Financial Statements,* Amacom, 1999.

- Fournies, Ferdinand F., *Why Employees Don't Do What They're Supposed to Do and What to Do about It,* McGraw-Hill, 1999.

- Fowler, Dennis, *Virtual Private Networks,* Morgan Kaufmann, 1999.

- Freed, Les, Frank J., Jr. Derfler, *How Networks Work,* Que, 1998.

- Galliers, Robert D., et al. (Editors), *Information Technology and Organizational Transformation: Innovation for the 21st Century Organization (John Wiley Series in Information Systems),* John Wiley and Sons, 1998.

- Gates, Bill, *Business @ the Speed of Thought*, Warner Books, 1999.

- Goncalves, Marcus (Editor), *Firewalls: A Complete Guide,* McGraw-Hill, 1999.

- Hafner, Katie, and Matthew Lyon, *Where Wizards Stay Up Late: The Origins of the Internet,* Simon and Schuster, 1996.

- Hallows, Jolyon E., *Information Systems Project Management: How to Deliver Function and Value in Information Technology Projects,* Amacom, 1997.

- Haylock, Christina Ford, Len Muscarella, and Steve Case, *Net Success: 24 Leaders in Web Commerce Show You How to Put the Web to Work for Your Business,* Adams Media, 1999.

- Hughes, Lawrence E., *Internet E-mail: Protocols, Standards, and Implementation,* Artech House Telecommunications Library, 1998.

- Jaffe, Brian D., "Maturity Is a Help Desk Prerequisite," *PC Week*, February 7, 2000.

- Jaffe, Brian D., "Double Your Pleasure and Halve Your Stress," *PC Week*, August 16, 1999.

- Jaffe, Brian D., "Be a Signpost for Employee Career Paths," *PC Week*, June 21, 1999.

- Jaffe, Brian D., "Wishing You All a Successful Recovery," *PC Week*, September 28, 1998.

- Jaffe, Brian D., "Taking the Measure of Customer Service," *PC Week*, June 5, 1998.

- Jaffe, Brian D., "Following a Few Simple Rules Can Ease the Pain of Employee Reviews," *InfoWorld*, January 26, 1998.

- Jaffe, Brian D., "One Manager's Look at TCO," *Computerworld*, November 17, 1997.

- Jaffe, Brian D., "Checking Up," *Computerworld*, June 9, 1997.

- Jesse, Chris, *A Journey through Oz: The Business Leader's Road Map to Tracking Information Technology Assets,* Kendall/Hunt, 1999.

- Kerzner, Harold, *Project Management: A Systems Approach to Planning, Scheduling, and Controlling,* 6th ed., Wiley, 1997.

- Korper, Steffano, Juanita Ellis, and Jerry D. Gibson, *The E-Commerce Book: Building the E-Empire,* Academic Press, 1999.

- Kovacich, Gerald, *The Information Systems Security Officer's Guide: Establishing and Managing an Information Protection Program,* Butterworth-Heinemann, 1998.

- Krause, Micki, and Harold F. Tipton (Editors), *Information Security Management Handbook, Fourth Edition,* CRC-Auerbach, 1999.

- Langenwalter, Gary A., *Enterprise Resources Planning and Beyond: Integrating Your Entire Organization,* CRC Press/St. Lucie Press, 1999.

- Laub, Lori and Navtej Khandpur, *Delivering World-Class Technical Support*, Wiley, 1996.

- Laudon, Kenneth C., and Jane Price Laudon, *Management Information Systems: Organization and Technology in the Networked Enterprise,* Prentice Hall, 1999.

- Lewis, Bob, *Bob Lewis's IS Survival Guide,* Sams, 1999.

- Lewis, James P., *The Project Manager's Desk Reference: A Comprehensive Guide to Project Planning, Scheduling, Evaluation, and Systems,* McGraw-Hill, 1999.

- Lewis, James P., *Team-Based Project Management,* Amacom, 1997.

- Lewis, James P., *Fundamentals of Project Management: The Worksmart Method AMACON, 1995.*

- Lewis, Robert, "The Winding Road to TCO Includes Calculations That Are Both Tricky and Useless," *InfoWorld,* November 3, 1997.

- Lindquist, Christopher, "You've Got (Dirty) Mail," *Computerworld,* March 13, 2000.

- Lozinsky, Sergio, and Paul Wahl (Foreword), *Enterprise-Wide Software Solutions: Integration Strategies and Practices,* Addison-Wesley, 1998.

- Lucas, Henry C., Jr., *Information Technology and the Productivity Paradox: The Search for Value,* Oxford University Press, 1999.

- Ludwig, Mark A., *The Giant Black Book of Computer Viruses,* American Eagle Publications, 1998.

- Marcus, Evan, *Blueprints for High Availability: Designing Resilient Distributed Systems,* Hal Stern, 2000.

- Marcus, J. Scott, *Designing Wide Area Networks and Internetworks: A Practical Guide,* Addison-Wesley, 1999.

- Marks, Kristin (Editor), *Handbook of Server Management and Administration 1999,* CRC Press–Auerbach, 1998.

- Maslach, Christina, and Michael P. Leiter (Contributor), *The Truth about Burnout: How Organizations Cause Personal Stress and What to Do about It, Jossey-Bass Publishers, 1997.*

- McClure, Stuart, Joel Scambray, and George Kurtz, *Hacking Exposed: Network Security Secrets and Solutions,* McGraw-Hill, 1999.

- Minoli, Daniel, and Andrew Schmidt, *Internet Architectures,* John Wiley and Sons, 1999.

- Northcult, Stephen, *Network Intrusion Detection: An Analyst's Handbook,* New Riders, 1999.

- Orenstein, David, "Toys R Us, Others, Face Online Woes," *Computerworld,* December 23, 1999.

- Overly, Michael R., *E-Policy: How to Develop Computer, E-Policy, and Internet Guidelines to Protect Your Company and Its Assets,* Amacom, 1998.

- Palmer, Michael J., and Robert Bruce Sinclair, *A Guide to Designing and Implementing Local and Wide Area Networks,* Course Technology, 1999.

- Pennypacker, James S. (Editor), *The Principles of Project Management*, John R. Adams (Introduction), Project Management Institute Publishers, 1997.

- Pfaffenberger, Bryan, *Linux: Clearly Explained*, Morgan Kaufmann, 1999.

- Pfaffenberger, Bryan, *Building a Strategic Extranet*, IDG Books, 1998.

- Plotnick, Neil, *The IT Professional's Guide to Managing Systems, Vendors & End Users*, Aviation Archives, 1999.

- Potter, Beverly, et al., *Overcoming Job Burnout: How to Renew Enthusiasm for Work*, Ronin Publishing, 1998.

- Reed, Archie, *Implementing Directory Services (Enterprise Computing)* McGraw-Hill, 2000.

- Remenyi, Dan, Michael Sherwood-Smith, and Terry White, *Achieving Maximum Value From Information Systems: A Process Approach*, John Wiley and Sons, 1997.

- Rizzo, John, *Macintosh Window Integration*, Morgan Kaufmann, 1999. This is an excellent book, almost 600 pages long and including a CD, that discusses everything you would ever want to know about this topic.

- Robichaux, Paul E., *Remote Access 24Seven*, Sybex, 1999.

- Rony, Ellen, and Peter R. Rony, *The Domain Name Handbook; High Stakes and Strategies in Cyberspace*, R&D Books, 1998.

- Schreider, Tari, *Encyclopedia of Disaster Recovery, Security & Risk Management*, Crucible Publishing Works, 1998.

- Schreyer, Ray, and John Lewis McCarter, Jr., *The Employer's Guide to Recruiting on the Internet*, Impact Publishers, 1998.

- Seybold, Patricia, *Customers.com*, Random House/Times Books, 1998. A classic study of e-commerce.

- Sheresh, Doug, and Beth Sheresh, *Understanding Directory Services*, New Riders Publishing, 1999.

- Siegel, David, *Creating Killer Web Sites*, Second Edition, Hayden, 1997.

- Sinclair, Joseph T. and Mark Merkow, *Thin Clients Clearly Explained*, Morgan Kaufmann, 1999.

- Stephenson, Neal, *In the Beginning . . . Was the Command Line*, Avon Books, 1999.

- Strassman, Paul A., "GAAP Helps Whom?," *Computerworld*, December 6, 1999.

- Strassmann, Paul A., *The Squandered Computer: Evaluating the Business Alignment of Information Technologies*, Information Economic Press, 1997.

- Straub, Joseph T., *The Rookie Manager: A Guide to Surviving Your First Year in Management*, Amacom, 1999.

- Taylor, James, *A Survival Guide for Project Managers*, Amacom, 1998.

- Thibodeau, Patrick, "Gov't IT Execs Seek Software Accountability," *Computerworld,* October 18, 1999.

- Thorp, John, *The Information Paradox: Realizing the Business Benefits of Information Technology,* DMR Consulting Group, McGraw-Hill, 1999.

- Toigo, Jon William, and Margaret Romano Toigo (Illustrator), *Disaster Recovery Planning: Strategies for Protecting Critical Information Assets,* Prentice Hall, 1999.

- Tourniaire, Francoise, and Richard Farrell, *The Art of Software Support: Design and Operation of Support Centers and Help Desks,* Prentice Hall, 1996.

- Trulove, James, *LAN Wiring: An Illustrated Guide to Network Cabling,* McGraw-Hill, 1997.

- Ulfelder, Steve, "So, When Do I Start?" *Computerworld*, January 10, 2000.

- Vaas, Lisa, Anne Chen, and Matt Hicks, "Web Recruiting Takes Off," *PC Week*, January 17, 2000.

- Vacca, John R., *The Cabling Handbook,* Prentice Hall, 1998.

- Young, Robert, and Wendy Goldman Rohm, *Under the Radar: How Red Hat Changed the Software Business and Took Microsoft by Surprise,* The Coriolis Group, 1999.

- Zachary, G. Pascal, *Show-Stopper,* Free Press, 1994. An excellent book on Microsoft's building of NT.

Glossary

Term Definition

ACD Automatic call distribution (ACD) can route calls to technicians based on menu prompts and can provide you with detailed reports about activity.

ANSI/EIA American National Standards Institute/Electronic Industries Association.

AppleTalk Network communication protocols generally used for Mac environments.

Asset management If TCO (total cost of ownership) is the costs associated with computers, then asset management refers to what you do to keep those costs down.

ATM Asynchronous Transfer Mode.

Automatic call distribution Automatic call distribution (ACD) can route calls to technicians based on menu prompts and can provide you with detailed reports about activity.

B2B Business-to-Business e-commerce marketing direction.

B2C Business-to-Customer e-commerce marketing direction.

Backbone The backbone of a network is a high-capacity portion of the network that carries/transfers data collected from lower-speed portions of the network that interconnect with it.

C Programming language that was very popular (it was used to write many of the Unix operating systems) but has now been supplanted in many areas by C + + and Java.

C++ Programming language that gained popularity with the advent of object-oriented programming. It is a subset of the C programming language and still widely used.

Call tracking A software category designed specifically for managing large volumes of calls at call centers.

Capital expenditure A capital expenditure is for an item that will have a useful life of several years—like a piece of hardware. Some companies consider software to be a capital expenditure.

CAT-5 wiring CAT is short for "category," and currently there are five of these categories for twisted pair wiring specified by ANSI/EIA (American National Standards Institute/Electronic Industries Association).

CBT Computer-based training generally refers to a software application that trains the user in a particular product set.

Certified Netware Engineer Certification for Novell's Netware product.

Chassis devices In networking, a chassis device is an architecture that refers to the hardware design of some sort of hub device in a wiring closet or data center.

CNE Novell's Certified Netware Engineer.

Collision In Ethernet, if two devices on the same network try to transmit simultaneously, there will be a data collision. When this occurs, each device picks a random time to wait, and then retries.

Collision domain Consists of all workstations/servers, nodes, and repeaters interconnected without a bridge, switch, or router. In other words, a device only has to worry about data collisions with other devices in that same collision domain.

Computer-based training (CBT) CBT generally refers to a software application that trains the user in a particular product set.

Database management system (DBMS) Sophisticated software system that controls the databases.

Direct reports Employees who work directly for one individual. If you manage five people in your department, they are all considered your direct reports.

Directory services In networking, a directory refers to the means of keeping track of resources (printers, users, servers, etc.).

DNS Domain Name Servers: translates alphanumeric names to IP addresses.

Driver (software) Software that allows one device to interact with another; a printer driver is software that allows a computer to work with a particular brand of printer.

DSL Digital subscriber link is a way of bringing high-speed connectivity to homes and small businesses over standard copper phone lines.

EB (Exabyte) 1,000,000,000,000,000,000 bytes.

E-commerce A term to describe the many activities involved in buying and selling over the Internet.

ERP Enterprise resource planning.

ESD Electronic software distribution.

Ethernet 10, 100 (a.k.a. fast Ethernet), 1,000 (a.k.a. gigabit) is the most popular LAN topology.

Exabyte (EB) 1,000,000,000,000,000,000 bytes.

Expense item An expense item is something whose value is gone in a shorter period of time. In general, accounting departments give IT equipment an estimated life of 3–5 years. On the other hand, the equipment used on an assembly line in a factory might have a life of 10–20 years.

Extranet An extranet site is similar to an Internet site except that it is specifically designed for use by the company's partners (suppliers, customers, etc.).

FDDI Fiber Distributed Data Interface is the protocol for transmitting data on fiber optic cable.

Firewall A firewall, as the name implies, is a device that prevents the rest of the world from getting into your network and controls your internal users' access to the Internet.

FireWire Apple's new IEEE standard for connecting devices.

Fiscal year Budgeting is the process of assigning specific amounts of money to specific departments within a company for a single fiscal year. Frequently, the fiscal year that a budget tracks is not the January–December calendar year. The year that the budget tracks can be any 12-month period, although it generally begins on January 1, April 1, July 1, or October 1.

Fractional T-1 A fractional T-1 refers to using one, or more, of the channels available in a T-1 circuit. While this reduces bandwidth, there is also a cost savings.

Frame relay A cost-effective method of connecting distant points in a WAN using packet switching technology with packets of variable sizes.

FTP File transfer protocol: an application protocol that transfers files from the source where they were created to a server that makes them accessible to users on the Internet.

Gigabyte (GB) 1,000,000,000 bytes.

Groupware Software that allows employees at different locations to work together collaboratively on a single project.

Hot swappable Being able to remove a component or module from a device without having to first shut down the device.

HTTP HyperText Transfer Protocol: transfers displayable Web pages.

Hub/concentrator A generic term for a device that interconnects several nodes on a network.

ICANN   Internet Corporation for Assigned Names and Numbers is a nonprofit organization that has assumed responsibility from the U.S. government for co-ordinating certain Internet activities, such as the management of domain names.

IEEE   Institute of Electrical and Electronics Engineers. A key standards setting body. They are a worldwide organization with journals and conventions, but the reason most IT people know them is because of their standard-setting activities.

IKE   Internet Key Exchange.

IMAP   Internet Message Access Protocol: an e-mail standard.

Intranet   An intranet site is a private site available only to those with the company or organization.

IPsec   Internet Protocol Security.

ISDN   Integrated Service Digital Network is a way of transmitting digital signals over standard telephone company copper lines.

ISP   Internet service provider.

Java   One of—if not the most—popular programming languages for developing software. Java was used to create many of the applications that run the Internet. Originally created by Sun, there are now other (nonlicensed) versions of the language being used. Java programming skills are in great demand.

Kernel   The core components of an operating system.

Kilobyte (KB)   1,000 bytes.

LAN   Local Area Network.

Leased line   A leased line (a.k.a. private line, point-to-point-circuit) is a circuit provided by the telephone company that connects two points—anywhere from across town to across the country.

MAN   A metropolitan area network is a network that covers locations in a single metropolitan area.

Megabyte (MB)   1,000,000 bytes.

Milestone   A point in a project that represents the completion of an important sequence of key tasks and activities.

MIME   Multipurpose Internet Mail Extensions: an Internet e-mail standard.

MX record   Mail-eXchange record. This record tells mail servers all over the Internet where to send mail addressed to your company.

NAP   Network Access Point.

Network Computers (NCs) NCs are PCs configured only with essential equipment (no CD-ROMs, floppy drives, or expansion slots, for example) and maintained from a single central location.

Networking Two relevant meanings to IT: (1) the hardware and software that makes it possible for individual computers to talk to each other, and (2) the process of proactively making contacts with other people.

NIC Network Interface Card connects a hardware device to the local area network.

Object-oriented programming (OOP) A methodology or a method that defines how you write a software program in a very specific way; rather than have a series of commands that specify certain actions, OOP (as it is known) suggests that the program writer have objects interact with each other. C + + is a object-oriented programming language; C is not.

OC-X Optical carrier. Refers to SONET connection speeds.

Outsource Contracting with a third party to perform a particular task. Whether to outsource a specific job or not is the subject of much debate and should be based on a number of factors, including your budget, how much time you have to get the job done, if you and your team have the skills to do it yourself, and if it is your core competency.

Passive/active hubs A passive hub (a.k.a. dumb) is a hub device that does nothing more than pass all the data and signals it receives to all the devices connected to it. It is an inexpensive device for interconnecting network nodes. An active hub (a.k.a. intelligent) adds value to its general function of interconnecting network nodes.

PB (petabyte) 1,000,000,000,000,000 bytes.

PCMCIA standard cards Personal Computer Memory Card International Association standard for expansion cards used in laptops.

Perl Programming language that uses primarily scripts. Perl programming has certain very specific strengths, and Perl programmers tend to be very devoted to their language.

Petabyte (PB) 1,000,000,000,000,000 bytes.

POP-3 Post Office Protocol 3: an Internet e-mail standard.

Port replicator A device for easily connecting external peripherals (keyboard, monitor, printer, etc.) to a laptop.

Position description A relatively detailed description of a specific job function. Your human resources department may ask you to do this so that they can post it internally within the company, or they may use it to relay the pertinent details to agencies and recruiters.

POTS line   A plain old telephone system (POTS) line is a single line analog jack usually found in homes and is typically used for fax machines, modems, etc.

PPTP   Point-to-Point Tunneling Protocol.

Private side   A reference to your local area network when it is connected to a firewall.

Production environment   The regular, working system, as opposed to a test or production test environment.

Production test environment (PTE)   A test environment is a distinct system, apart from the regular, working system, which is called the production environment.

Project room   This room provides team members a place to work on the project that is separate from their work area.

Public side   A reference to the Internet when connected to your firewall.

RADIUS   Remote Authentication Dial-In User Service.

RAID storage   Redundant Array of Independent Disks: method of storing the same data on multiple disks.

RAS   Remote Access Servers.

RMON   Remote Monitoring. RMON (two standards RMON-1 and RMON-2) is an extension of the SNMP protocol.

Router   A router is a device that connects two networks. A router's function can be hardware or software based, although the term is usually used in reference to a hardware device.

SAP   SAP is the world's fourth largest software company; based in Germany, they create and sell enterprise resource planning (ERP) applications that are used by corporations—generally large ones—throughout the world.

Segment   A network segment is the same as a collision domain.

Service level agreements (SLAs)   Service level agreements (SLAs) represent a declaration to the user community of what type of service your Help Desk can provide, and how quickly it hopes to provide it.

Shared   In conventional Ethernet, all nodes attached to the hub "share" the available bandwidth (usually 10 Mbps or 100 Mbps). As a result, as more devices are added, the traffic and number of collisions increase, and the available bandwidth per node falls. See also Switched.

SID   Security ID. A unique identifier for each installation of Windows NT.

SLAs   Service level agreements (SLAs) represent a declaration to the user community of what type of service your Help Desk can provide, and how quickly it hopes to provide it.

SMP (symmetric multiprocessing) Processing of programs by multiple processors that share a common operating system and memory.

SNMP Simple Network Management Protocol is a standard for monitoring networks.

SONET Synchronous Optical Network is the technology for providing very high-speed connections (from 51.84 Mbps to 2.4 Gbps) for geographically distant connections (hundreds and thousands of miles).

SQL Programming language for creating and maintaining databases.

Stackable devices Stackable devices are an alternative solution for the chassis architecture. Stackable devices (so named because they can be easily stacked on top of each other and are often rack-mountable) don't require the upfront investment of a chassis.

Subnet A subnet refers to a specific portion of an organization's network. It is a logical grouping of devices that can be identified based on their network number. It can refer to all the devices at a single geographic location, or on the same LAN.

Success metrics Methods of defining achievement. Sales people have long had success metrics: sales quotas.

Switched In a switched environment, each node connected to the switch can use the full amount of bandwidth available (unlike in a shared environment, where the available bandwidth is shared).

Symmetric multiprocessing (SMP) Processing of programs by multiple processors that share a common operating system and memory.

T&M (Time-and-Material) contracts Time and material arrangements: when you place a service call for a piece of hardware, the vendor will bill you for the technician's time, and the parts that are needed—similar to a repair on your car.

T-1 A T-1 line is a leased line that provides data transmission speeds of 1.544 Mbps. A T-1 line consists of 24 channels, each of which can support 64 kpbs transmissions.

T-3 A T-3 line is a leased line that provides data transmission speeds of 44.736 Mpbs. A T-3 line consists of 672 circuits, each of which can support 64 kpbs transmissions.

TCO (total cost of ownership) Total cost of ownership refers to the fact that there is a lot more related to the cost of the personal computer besides the price of the hardware and the software (e.g., training, support, etc.).

Terabyte (TB) 1,000,000,000,000 bytes.

Time-and-Material (T&M) contracts Under these arrangements, when you place a service call for a piece of hardware, the vendor will bill you for the technician's time, and the parts that are needed—similar to a repair on your car.

Token-Ring A star topology networking environment that was popularized by IBM in the 1980s, with speeds of 4 Mbps and 16 Mbps. However, Ethernet is far more popular and is available with higher speeds.

Topologies A network topology refers to the architecture of how network nodes are connected.

Total cost of ownership (TCO) Total cost of ownership refers to the fact that there is a lot more related to the cost of the personal computer besides the price of the hardware and the software (e.g., training, support, etc.).

Twisted pair A somewhat generic term for the copper cabling that connects devices to the network.

UPS Uninterruptable power supplies.

V-mail Voice-mail.

VPDN A way of using public (e.g., the Internet) telecommunication facilities for the transmission of data, but ensures privacy with the use of various security and tunneling facilities.

VPN Virtual Private Network.

WAN Wide-Area Network.

War room This room provides team members a place to work on the project that is separate from their work area.

Yottabyte (YB) 1,000,000,000,000,000,000,000,000 bytes.

Zettabyte (ZB) 1,000,000,000,000,000,000,000 bytes.

There are excellent online resources for helping you keep abreast of technical terms and acronyms:

www.whatis.com
www.webopedia.com

Index